Cambridge
IGCSE®
and O Level

Economics

Paul Hoang and
Margaret Ducie

HODDER
EDUCATION
AN HACHETTE UK COMPANY

® IGCSE is the registered trademark of Cambridge International Examinations

The questions, example answers, marks awarded and/or comments that appear in this book and CD were written by the authors, and are not the responsibility of Cambridge International Examinations

Although every effort has been made to ensure that website addresses are correct at time of going to press, Hodder Education cannot be held responsible for the content of any website mentioned in this book. It is sometimes possible to find a relocated web page by typing in the address of the home page for a website in the URL window of your browser.

Hachette UK's policy is to use papers that are natural, renewable and recyclable products and made from wood grown in sustainable forests. The logging and manufacturing processes are expected to conform to the environmental regulations of the country of origin.

Orders: please contact Bookpoint Ltd, 130 Milton Park, Abingdon, Oxon OX14 4SB. Telephone: (44) 01235 827720. Fax: (44) 01235 400454. Lines are open 9.00-5.00, Monday to Saturday, with a 24-hour message answering service. Visit our website at www.hoddereducation.com.

© Paul Hoang and Margaret Ducie 2013

First published in 2013 by
Hodder Education
An Hachette UK Company
Carmelite House, 50 Victoria Embankment
London EC4Y 0DZ

Impression number   5 4
Year   2016

Cover photo © Oleksandr Dibrova – Fotolia
Illustrations by Aptara, Inc.
Typeset in ITC Galliard by Aptara, Inc.
Printed in Dubai

A catalogue record for this title is available from the British Library

ISBN: 978-1-4441-9641-2

Contents

Introduction

Economics can help to explain real-world events, issues and problems, such as why:

- the most expensive can of Coca-Cola, made for astronauts, is $1250 per can!
- the world's fastest car, the Bugatti Veyron, is priced at a cool €1.95 million ($2.57m)
- the price of a bus fare is relatively low
- the average doctor, lawyer, pilot or dentist has high earnings
- private-sector firms do not supply street lighting and public roads
- Zimbabwe has no official currency
- diamonds (a non-essential product) are expensive whereas water (a vital good) is not
- farm workers (who harvest products essential for life) are paid low wages whereas bankers (who produce nothing of real substance) are paid high salaries.

Economics helps to explain everyday issues that occur in a constantly changing global environment. It is a 'live' subject and you are encouraged to watch the news and read newspapers to refresh the case studies you learn in class. Up-to-date, real-life examples greatly enhance your answers in examinations.

How this book can help you

This book has been written with the international student in mind.

- It explains economic theory using real-life examples and **case studies** from around the world.
- The suggested **activities** encourage you to investigate real-life applications of economics as a dynamic subject in your local environment as well as globally. They enable you to extend your learning of the subject, both within and beyond the classroom environment.
- The '**Study tips**' encourage critical thinking and emphasise the need to be able to present and justify an opinion, underpinned by economic principles and theories.
- The '**Exam practice**' questions are designed for you to experience the types of question you are likely to get in an examination.
- The **end-of-chapter review questions**, which correspond with the chronological order of the text, are intended to encourage you to read, reflect and write your own answers. Therefore, there are no suggested answers for these comprehension-type questions.
- **Definitions** of key terms feature throughout the book and are collated at the end of each chapter as a glossary.

What's on the CD-ROM?

The CD-ROM contains:

- suggested answers to all the exam practice questions*
- weblinks for you to explore the topics and companies mentioned further
- a glossary of all key terms contained in the book, as a useful revision tool
- interactive activities to test the key terms of the syllabus
- exam techniques and further tips and advice for success.

Enjoy studying this course and using this coursebook!

Paul Hoang and Margaret Ducie

*The questions, example answers, marks awarded and/or comments that appear in this book and CD were written by the authors. In examination, the way marks would be awarded to answers like these may be different.

Acknowledgements

The authors would like to dedicate this book to their children:

Salvador, Gino and Isidora Boon
Jake and Luke Hoang

The authors would like to thank:

Their spouses, Derek Boon and Kin Hoang, for their patience, understanding and support.
So-Shan Au, their Commissioning Editor at Hodder Education, for her advice, support and dedication. This textbook would not have been possible without her guidance and hard work.

The publishers would like to thank the following for permission to reproduce copyright material:

Photos:
p.1 © pressmaster – Fotolia; **p.4** *tl* © lefebvre_jonathan – Fotolia, *tr* © lnzyx – Fotolia, *bl* © lnzyx – Fotolia, *br* © Kadmy – Fotolia; **p.11** © endostock – Fotolia; **p.12** © Paul Hoang; **p.17** © John Powell/Rex Features; **p.21** © Helix – Fotolia; **p.23** © So-Shan Au; **p.24** © FREDERIC J. BROWN/AFP/Getty Images; **p.34** *bl* © Reuters/Corbis, *br* © ckchiu – Fotolia; **p.35** © So-Shan Au; **p.36** © So-Shan Au; **p.39** © Imaginechina/Corbis; **p.41** © Koichi Kamoshida/Bloomberg via Getty Images; **p.52** © WILLIAM WEST/AFP/Getty Images; **p.54** © Gerald Herbert/AP/Press Association Images; **p.55** © Rodrigo Baleia/LatinContent/Getty Images; **p.56** © Paul Hoang; **p.59** © Scanrail – Fotolia; **p.60** *tr* © So-Shan Au, *br* © Photodisc/Getty Images; **p.61** © Lou-Foto/Alamy; **p.63** © Mary Evans Picture Library/Alamy; **p.66** © INDRANIL MUKHERJEE/AFP/Getty Images; **p.67** © Henny Ray Abrams/AP/Press Association Images; **p.69** © eillen1981 – Fotolia; **p.72** © Margaret Ducie; **p.75** © martin33 – Fotolia; **p.77** © ADEK BERRY/AFP/GettyImages; **p.83** © Imagestate Media (John Foxx); **p.86** © Joel Ryan/AP/Press Association Images; **p.92** © JEROME FAVRE/epa/Corbis; **p.96** © So-Shan Au; **p.100** © Chien-Min Chung/In Pictures/Corbis; **p.102** © Katia Torralba www.katiatorralba.com; **p.104** © Silkstock – Fotolia; **p.106** *c* © Vesna Cvorovic – Fotolia, *bl* © yellowj – Fotolia; **p.109** © Ben Chams – Fotolia; **p.110** © Paul Hoang; **p.112** *l* © OJO Images Ltd/Alamy, *r* © DragonImages – Fotolia; **p.113** *l* © LIU JIN/AFP/Getty Images, *r* © Chris Ratcliffe/Bloomberg via Getty Images; **p.114** *tl* © ADRIAN BRADSHAW/epa/Corbis, *tr* © Imaginechina/Rex Features, *c* © PETER MORGAN/Reuters/Corbis; **p.115** © Paul Hoang; **p.117** © Brent Lewin/Bloomberg via Getty Images; **p.119** © Melanie Stetson Freeman/The Christian Science Monitor via Getty Images; **p.121** © photomic; **p.127** © Kin Cheung/AP/Press Association Images; **p.128** *t* © Paul Hoang, *m* © JAVIER SORIANO/AFP/Getty Images; **p.129** © Monty Rakusen/cultura/Corbis; **p.132** © lightpoet – Fotolia; **p.138** © So-Shan Au; **p.139** © Business Wire via Getty Images; **p.142** © So-Shan Au; **p.145** © SEBASTIAN KAHNERT/DPA/Press Association Images; **p.148** © Ingrid Abery/Rex Features; **p.153** © Paul Sakuma/AP/Press Association Images; **p.154** *l* © PA Archive/Press Association Images, *r* © Chris Ratcliffe/Bloomberg via Getty Images; **p.155** *l* © branex – Fotolia, *r*

permission of Banks around the world, *www.relbanks.com*; **p.73** Table 7.2: Earnings by age, full-time workers (UK, 2010-2012), adapted, Office for National Statistics (ONS), http://goo.glCgoWo; Table 7.3: After-tax earnings by educational attainment (USA, 2011-2012), from *Consumer Expenditure Survey, U.S.* (March, 2013), published by the United States Department of Labor, Bureau of Labor Statistics; Table 7.4: Minimum wage rates per hour in Australia, 2013 in US$, from The Fair Work Commission, http://www.fwc.gov.au/, reproduced by permission of Fair Work Ombudsman; **p.78** Table 7.6: Labour Participant rates, selected countries, adapted, published by The World Bank, *http://goo.gl/ORrqc*; **p.79** Skills shortages, data from BBC News, Business, *http://goo.glYJjCK*; **p.81** Table 7.7: Earnings for selected occupations in the UK, April 2012, adapted, Office for National Statistics, *http://goo.gl/se7pm*; **p.82** Table 7.8: Difference in male and female working hours and earnings (UK, 2011-2012), adapted, Office for National Statistics, *http://goo.gl/JWMVs*; **p.84** Table 7.9: Difference in private and public sector earnings (UK, 2012), adapted, Office for National Statistics, *http://goo.gl/JWMVs*; **p.84** Table 7.10: Hourly earnings in selected industries (UK, 2012), adapted, Office for National Statistics, *http://goo.gl/JWMVs*; **p.91** 'Bharat bandh: Kerala remains paralysed as strike enters second day', adapted, NDTV (February 21, 2013); **p.93** Exam Practice: adapted from World Socialist Web, *http://goo.gl/BvY14*; **p.107** Exam Practice: Household debt to disposable income' ratio in South Korea, published by Reuters, *http://goo.gl/culSM*; **p.119** Cooperatives: data published by International Cooperative Aliiance, *http://goo.gl/oBJpA*; **p.94** Figure 8.2: Trade union membership in China and the UK (2000 to 2010), International Labour Organization, *http;//goo.gl/Jjmt5*; **p.98** Figure 9.1: from Kerry McQueeney, 'Revealed: How the poor, middle class and rich spend their money in America...and the 1% aren't so different after all', *Mail Online* (2 August, 2012); Figure 9.2: Real household disposable income in the USA, UK, Japan and the Eurozone, *OECD Factbook 2013*; **p.99** Figure 9.3: Consumer spending in the United States (2008-2013), published by Trading Economics, *http://bit.ly/YUOumP;* Figure 9.4: Consumer spending in the United Kingdom from (2008-2013), published by Trading Economics, *http://bit.ly/11UhPOF;* Figure 9.5: Consumer spending in Japan (2008-2013), published byTrading Economics, *http://bit.ly/11F4SuM;* **p.101** Figure 9.6: Consumer spending in Mauritius (2008-2013) from Trading Economics, *http://bit.ly/ZQUZ9i;* Figure 9.7: Inflation rates in Mauritius (2008-2013), published by Trading Economics, *http://bit.ly/XZmXDt;* **p.103** Figure 9.9: Office for National Statistics, from *Living Costs and Food Survey, December 2012, http://goo.gl/y961h;* **p.105** Figure 9.10: Household net savings rates, from *National Accounts at a Glance,* published by OECD, *http://goo.gl/1TMHq;* **p.128** Table 11.1: Top earners in football, *Forbes,* http://goo.gl/B6nDv; **p.152** Table 14.1: The The world's largest companies, *Forbes;* **p.171** Table 15.1: The world's richest people', from *Forbes magazine, www.forbes.com/billionaires;* Case Study: Cheung Chi-fai, from 'Government eyes extension of plastic bag levy', adapted, *South China Morning Post;* **p.191** Figure 18.2: US inflation rates (2000-2013), published by Trading Economics, *www.tradingeconomics.com;* **p.198** Table 18.3: The 5 wealthiest hip-hop artists, *Forbes Rich List 2013, http://goo.gl/EBXfq;* **p.199** Table 18.4: The world's most expensive cities, from *Worldwide Cost of Living Index 2013,* published by Economist Intelligence Unit, http://goo/gl/bnvry; Table 18.5: Inflation rate in Iran, *Reuters,* http://goo.gl/2yGLB; **p.200** Table 18.6: Deflation rates around the world, 2013, published by Trading Economics,*www.tradingeconomics.com*; **p.203** Figure 18.9: Japan Inflation Rate, published by Trading Economics, *www.tradingeconomics.com/ japan/inflation-cpi*; **p.205** Table 19.1: Output by sector (%), selected countries, *CIA World Factbook, http://goo.gl/DRrOh*; Figure 19.2: US unemployment (2000-2013), published by Trading Economics, *www.tradingeconomics.com/united-states/ unemployment-rate*; **p.208** Figure 19.2: Nigeria's unemployment rate, 2006-2013, published by Trading Economics, *www.tradingeconomics.com*; **p.222** Table 20.1: GDP per capita - selected countries, adapted, *CIA Factbook*; **p.227** Table 21.1: GDP for four countries, published by Trading Economics, *www.tradingeconomics.com*; Table 21.2 HDI classification of countries (selected countries), *HDI Report* 2013, United Nations Development Programme (UNDP); **p.222** Figure 20.3: China's GDP Growth, *http://www.economist.com.hk/blogs/graphicdetail/2012/12/daily-chart-18*; **p.229** Table 21.3: Internet users around the world, adapted, The World Bank, *http://data.worldbank.org*; **p.230** Table 21.4: Government debts around the world (2012), *CIA World Factbook*; Table 21.5: Output of the economy by sector, selected countries (2012), adapted, *CIA World Factbook*; **p.231** Figure 21.1: Selected economic development indicators: Congo, published by The World Bank,*http://data. worldbank.org*; **p.232** Table 21.6: Number of mobile phones in use, top 5 and bottom 5 countries, adapted, Wikipedia from *http://goo.gl/UFrWb*; **p.233** Case Study: The most livable cities in the world, from *Global Liveability Report, http://goo. gl/Zrj4*; **p.234** Table 21.7: The world's richest and poorest (2012), *CIA Factbook, http://goo.gl/u2Y2d*; **p.235** Case Study: Sierra Leone, adapted from *CIA World Factbook*; **p.241** Figure 22.1: The world's population 1973-2033 (predicted), adapted, from *www.ibiblio.org/lunarbin/worldpop*; **p.242** Tables 22.1 and 22.2: The world's least populous countries 2013, published by Trading Economics, *www. tradingeconomics.com*; **p.243** Figure 22.2:Ghana's age distribution (population pyramid), from *http://goo.gl/oHbHQ*; Figure 22.3: Japan's age distribution (population pyramid), from *http://goo.gl/Wd7IP*; **p.246** Table 22.3: Countries with highest and lowest population growth rates (%), adapted, *CIA World factbook, http:// goo.gl/EGUJy*; **p.247** Table 22.4: Comparison of employment by sector (for selected countries), adapted, *CIA World Factbook, www.cia.gov/index.html*; **p.249** Figure 22.5: Nigeria Population, published by Trading Economics, *www.tradingeconomics. com/nigeria/population*; Britain's ageing population: data adapted from Office for National Statistics,*www.ons.gov.uk/dcp171776_258607.pfd*; **p.253** Table 23.1: The world's three largest producers of selected products, *The Economist Pocket Book*; **p.259** Table 24.1: The current account balance, selected countries (top and bottom 5 ranks),*CIA Factbook 2012 (http://goo.gl/1Imxl)*; **p.261** Figure 24.1: Sri Lanka Balance of Trade, published by Trading Economics, *www.tradingeconomics.com/sri-lanka/ balance-of-trade*; **p.265** Figure 24.2: Kuwait Current Account, published by Trading Economics, *www.tradingeconomics.com/kuwait/current-account-to*-gdp.

Basic economic problem:
choice and the allocation of resources

Chapter

1   The basic economic problem

1 The basic economic problem

The nature of the economic problem

In every country, resources are limited in supply and decisions have to be made by governments, firms (businesses) and individuals about how to allocate scarce resources to satisfy unlimited needs and wants. This is the **basic economic problem** that exists in every economy: how to allocate scarce resources to satisfy unlimited needs and wants (see Figure 1.1).

Figure 1.1 The real cause of the economic problem

An **economic good** is one that is limited in supply, such as oil, wheat, cotton, housing and cars. **Free goods** are unlimited in supply, such as the air, sea, rain water, sunlight and public domain web pages.

> **Activity**
> Make a list of ten goods which are limited in supply (economic goods) and a second list of goods which are unlimited in supply (free goods). How many goods can you think of that are unlimited in supply?

Economics is the study of how resources are allocated to satisfy the unlimited needs and wants of individuals, governments and firms in an economy.

The three main **economic agents** or decision-makers in an economy are:

- individuals or households
- firms (businesses that operate in the private sector of the economy)
- the government.

The three **basic economic questions** addressed by economic agents are:
1 What to produce.
2 How to produce it.
3 For whom to produce it.
Firms and individuals produce goods and services in the **private sector** of the economy and the government produces goods and services in the **public sector**. Governments, firms and individuals both produce and consume goods and services. For example, the government might provide education and health care services for the general public.

Goods are physical items such as tables, clothing, toothpaste and pencils. **Services** are non-physical items such as haircuts, bus journeys, telephone calls and internet access.

Activity

1 Make a list of the goods and services provided by the public sector of your economy.
2 Identify the goods and services that are free to individuals and those for which you have to pay.
3 List which goods/services could be provided by a private firm as well as by the public (government) sector.
4 Compare and contrast the aims and objectives of a government-funded swimming pool and a private health and leisure club.

Needs are the essential goods and services required for human survival. These include nutritional food, clean water, shelter, protection, clothing and access to health care and education. All individuals have a right to have these needs met and this is stated in Articles 25 and 26 of the United Nations Universal Declaration of Human Rights, which was drafted in December 1948.

Article 25

Everyone has the right to a standard of living adequate for the health and well-being of himself and of his family, including food, clothing, housing and medical care and necessary social services, and the right to security in the event of unemployment, sickness, disability, widowhood, old age or other lack of livelihood in circumstances beyond his control.

Article 26

Everyone has the right to education. Education shall be free, at least in the elementary and fundamental stages. Elementary education shall be compulsory. Technical and professional education shall be made generally available and higher education shall be equally accessible to all on the basis of merit.

Wants are goods and services that are not necessary for survival. An individual's wants, or desires, tend to be unlimited as most people are rarely satisfied with what they have and are always striving for more. Wants are a matter of personal choice and human nature.

World Bank figures (2012) suggest that 3 billion of the world's inhabitants live on less than $2.50 per day and that their basic needs are not being met. In contrast, the richest 20 per cent of individuals receive 75 per cent of world income. The study of economics can help to explain why this happens and offer possible solutions to the basic economic problem.

Factors of production

Production of any good or service requires resources. These are divided into four categories, known as the **factors of production**:

1 **Land** refers to the natural resources required in the production process (such as oil, coal, water, wood, metal ores and agricultural products).
2 **Labour** refers to the human resources required in the production process (such as skilled and unskilled labour).
3 **Capital** refers to the manufactured resources required in the production process (such as machinery, tools, equipment and vehicles).
4 **Enterprise** refers to the skills a business person requires to combine and manage successfully the other three factors of production and the ability to undertake risk.

Factors of production: land, labour, enterprise and capital

The factors of production required in the production of a can of Coca-Cola are as follows:

- **Capital:** machinery, tools, a factory building and trucks to transport the drinks.
- **Enterprise:** the skills necessary to organise the production process successfully and to motivate workers so that they work to the best of their ability.
- **Labour:** people to work on the production line, perform administrative tasks and manage the company.
- **Land:** the natural resources required to make Coca-Cola (such as sugar, water and caffeine).

Study tips

The first letters of the four factors of production spell the word **CELL**. This is a useful way of remembering these four factors.

Production of all goods and services requires the four factors of production in varying proportions. For example, in a school, capital resources and labour are required in greater quantities than land (natural resources). By contrast, production of soft drinks, such as Coca-Cola, requires a large amount of machinery and therefore this process is **capital intensive** (see Chapter 11) as it requires more machinery (a capital resource) than labour.

An architectural practice designs buildings. It requires qualified architects to design the buildings and technicians, skilled in using computer-aided design software, to produce drawings. Computers, software, office space and enterprise are required to design high-quality creative buildings and to attract customers. It is **labour intensive** (see Chapter 11) because it requires a larger amount of human resources compared with technological resources and equipment.

Primary, secondary and tertiary sectors of industry

An economy is divided into three sectors of industry (see Figure 1.2):

- **Primary sector** – this contains firms that extract raw materials from the Earth (e.g. farming, fishing and mining).
- **Secondary sector** – this contains firms that:
  - manufacture goods and change raw materials into finished products
  - construct buildings, roads and bridges.
- **Tertiary sector** – this contains firms that provide services to the general public and other firms (such as retail shops, doctors, dentists, schools, hairdressers, advertising agencies, lawyers, financial advisers, insurance companies and banks).

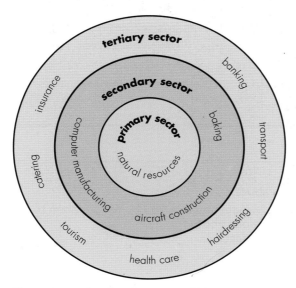

Figure 1.2 The three sectors of industry

The primary, secondary and tertiary sectors of an economy are **interdependent** (they are dependent upon each other), as a firm cannot operate without using goods and services from all three sectors of industry to make its goods or services and to sell them to the final customer. The three sectors of industry are linked together in what is known as a **chain of production**.

Consider the textbook that you are currently using. What is the chain of production of a book and which of the sectors does each stage of the process use? The raw material for the book comes from forests and trees. The growing and cutting down of the trees is a primary industry. The wood is formed into pulp and turned into paper in a paper mill, which is a secondary sector industry. The paper is then used when the book is printed, which is another secondary sector industry. The book is transported to shops where it is sold, both processes being tertiary sector industries (see Figure 1.3).

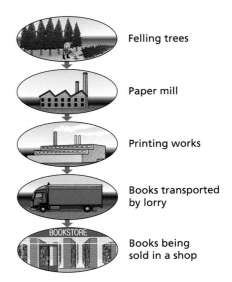

Felling trees

Paper mill

Printing works

Books transported by lorry

Books being sold in a shop

Figure 1.3 The chain of production of a book

Case Study: Yellow Moon

Yellow Moon is an independent jewellery shop that is located in Pondicherry, India. The business owners design and make the jewellery in their workshop and it is sold to customers from its store and via the internet through the firm's website.

The following table shows examples of goods and services from the primary, secondary and tertiary sectors that are necessary for Yellow Moon to operate successfully. The firms in each sector represent links in the chain of production.

Activity/Sector	Examples of goods/services required
Primary	Silver, gold and semi-precious stones
Secondary	Designers and jewellery makers to create the jewellery products
Tertiary	Advertising, insurance, banking and finance, transport of finished goods, website designers and a shop to sell the jewellery

---

Activity

Refer to the case study above.

1 Identify the factors of production required by Yellow Moon to operate its business.
2 Produce a table like the one above for:
   a) a mobile phone manufacturer
   b) a fast food restaurant chain
   c) a shop selling kitchen equipment.

Opportunity cost

Opportunity cost is a very important concept in economics. Opportunity cost is the cost measured in terms of the next best choice given up when making a decision. Every choice made has an opportunity cost because in most cases there is an alternative. Some examples of opportunity cost are as follows:

- The opportunity cost of taking IGCSE Economics is the other subject you could be studying instead.
- The opportunity cost of visiting the cinema on Saturday night is the sum of money you could have earned from babysitting for your neighbour instead of going to the cinema.
- The opportunity cost of building an additional airport terminal is the public housing for low-income families that the same government funds could have been used for.
- The opportunity cost of a school purchasing 100 laptops for use in the classroom might be the science equipment that cannot be bought as a result.

Case Study: Government spending in Hong Kong

In the 2013 Hong Kong Budget, the government announced the following:
- 17 per cent of the budget would be spent on infrastructure
- 17 per cent on education
- 14 per cent on social welfare
- 12 per cent on health care.

The government raises a finite amount of taxation revenue and must decide how much of the budget to allocate to each area of public spending. There is an opportunity cost attached to the decisions made, as increased spending in one area may lead to decreased spending in another.

Opportunity cost can be represented on a diagram known as a **production possibility curve** (PPC). The PPC represents the maximum amount of goods and services which can be produced in an economy, if all resources are used efficiently. It represents the **productive capacity** (maximum output) of an economy.

Assume a country called Tullassa can only produce two types of good: wooden furniture and olive oil. Tullassa has a limited amount of land, labour and capital. In Figure 1.4, if producers wish to increase production of olive oil from O_1 to O_2 then the amount of wooden furniture manufactured will have to decrease from W_1 to W_2. The opportunity cost of producing an extra $O_1 - O_2$ litres of olive oil is therefore $W_1 - W_2$ tonnes of wooden furniture. The production possibility curve is usually drawn concave as, in order to produce more litres of olive oil, it is necessary to give up an increasing amount of wooden furniture, thus reflecting the increasing opportunity cost.

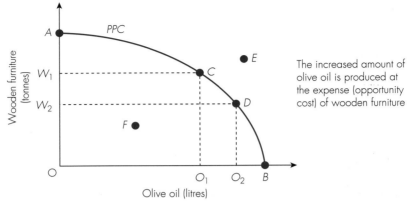

Key:
A – All resources dedicated to the production of wooden furniture
B – All resources dedicated to the production of olive oil
C – W_1 tonnes of wooden furniture are produced alongside O_1 litres of olive oil
D – W_2 tonnes of wooden furniture and O_2 litres of olive oil are produced
E – This point is beyond the production possibility curve and lies outside the productive capacity of the economy, so it is unattainable
F – This point is within the productive capacity of the economy and production of both olive oil and wooden furniture can increase without any opportunity cost as some factors of production are not being used

Figure 1.4 The production possibility curve (PPC) of Tullassa

Increases in the productive capacity of a country

There has been advancement in technology in Tullassa, which means that yields of olive oil and the productivity of furniture makers have increased. In Figure 1.5, the PPC shifts outwards, from PPC_1 and PPC_2, and represents an increase in the productive capacity of Tullassa. With the same amount of factors of production, more can be produced.

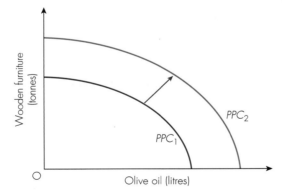

Figure 1.5 An outward shift of the PPC

Decrease in productive capacity of a country

A powerful storm hits Tullassa and destroys a large percentage of the factories and buildings. Much of the olive crop is destroyed and transport links are interrupted. In Figure 1.6, the PPC shifts inwards from PPC_1 to PPC_2 and represents a decrease in the productive capacity of Tullassa.

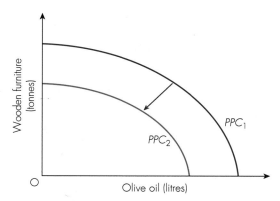

Figure 1.6 An inward shift of the PPC

Exam practice

Low-lying areas of Bangladesh are prone to flooding each year. Crops are lost and thousands of people lose their homes. During times of severe flooding, roads and railways are damaged and farmers find it impossible to get their dwindled crops to market.

1 Draw a PPC diagram to show the impact of flooding on the productive capacity of Bangladesh. [4]

2 On the diagram, draw a point where some of the factors of production will be idle. [1]

3 On the diagram, draw and label a point that is unattainable. [1]

Figure 1.7 summarises the basic economic problem.

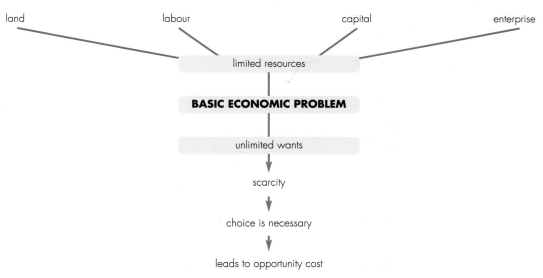

Figure 1.7 Summary: the basic economic problem

Chapter review questions

1 What is the difference between a need and a want?
2 What is meant by the basic economic problem?
3 How is the term 'opportunity cost' defined?
4 What factors of production are required to construct a road?
5 How would a firm producing running shoes answer the three basic economic questions?
6 What are the three sectors of industry?
7 What is meant by productive capacity?
8 What is a production possibility curve used to show?

Key terms

The **basic economic problem** is how to allocate scarce resources to satisfy unlimited needs and wants.

The **chain of production** describes how businesses from the primary, secondary and tertiary sectors work interdependently to make a product and sell it to the final customer.

Economic agents are households (private individuals in society), firms that operate in the private sector of an economy and the government (the public sector of an economy).

Economic goods are those which are limited in supply.

Free goods are goods which are unlimited in supply, such as air or sea water.

Goods are physical items such as tables, cars, toothpaste and pencils.

Interdependence means that the three sectors of industry are dependent upon each other and cannot operate independently to produce goods and services.

Needs are goods that are essential for survival.

Opportunity cost is the cost of the next best opportunity foregone when making a decision.

The **production possibility curve** (PPC) represents the maximum amount of goods and services which can be produced in an economy, i.e. the productive capacity of the economy.

Services are non-physical items such as haircuts, bus journeys, telephone calls, and internet access.

Wants are goods and services that are not necessary for survival but are demanded by economic agents.

② Economic systems

By the end of this chapter, you should be able to:
- describe the allocation of resources in **market and mixed economic systems**
- evaluate the merits of the market system.

Taken from Cambridge International Examinations Syllabus (IGCSE 0455/O Level 2281)
© Cambridge International Examinations

Economic systems

An economic system describes the way in which an economy is organised and run, including alternative views of how resources are best allocated. A key question in economics is the extent to which a government should intervene in the economy or leave economic agents (households and firms) to operate freely.

There are three main categories of economic system (see Figure 2.1).

Market	Mixed	Planned

Figure 2.1 Economic systems

1 **Market economy** – This economic system relies on the market forces of demand and supply to allocate resources, with minimal government intervention.

Hong Kong is widely accepted as the world's freest market economy

2 **Planned economy** – This economic system relies on the government allocating resources. It is often associated with a communist political system that strives for social equality. Examples include North Korea, Laos and Cuba.
3 **Mixed economy** – As its name suggests, this economic system is a combination of the planned and market economic system, with some resources being owned and controlled by private individuals and firms whilst others are owned and controlled by the government in the public sector. Examples include the UK, Germany and Canada.

Whichever economic system is used, all countries must address three fundamental economic questions:

1 **What** production should take place? This question is about deciding which goods and services should be provided in the economy.

For example, is it better for the economy to have more roads and airports or to have more schools and hospitals? As resources are limited in supply, decision-makers realise there is an opportunity cost (see Chapter 1) in answering this question.

2 **How** should production take place? This question is about the methods and processes used to produce the desired goods and services.

For example, decision-makers have to decide which combination of factors of production should be used in the production process.

3 **For whom** should production take place? This question is about which economic agents receive goods and services.

For example, should any goods and services be provided free to everyone in the economy, irrespective of their willingness and ability to pay for these? Or should goods and services only be produced for those who can pay?

Planned economic system

The planned economic system is sometimes referred to as the socialist or command system. In the past, China and the former USSR were often used as the best examples of planned economies, with over 95 per cent of economic activities state controlled. The main features of such an economic system are:

- Production decisions (what, how and for whom production should take place) are decided by the government.
- Hence, resources are controlled by the government on behalf of its citizens.
- Production schedules are devised on a long-term basis, such as 5-year plans.
- Wage differentials are minimal (i.e. labour is paid almost equally due to the belief in equality).
- There is minimal engagement in international trade (i.e. the government prefers the economy to be self-sufficient).

Advantages of the planned system

The planned system has a number of advantages:

- **Economies of scale** – Large state monopolies can achieve huge cost savings known as economies of scale (see Chapter 14). This is achieved by operating on a very large scale, such as a national supplier of electricity or postal services.
- **Prevent wastage** – Economists believe that competition can be wasteful in some instances and so should be eliminated (for example, that national defence should be placed under government control). The state will only provide the goods and services deemed necessary, so there is less wastage of scarce resources.

For example, some economists argue that excessive advertising is wasteful; ultimately it is the customer who pays for the marketing costs of a business (see the Super Bowl case study below). A lack of competition also avoids the drawbacks of bankruptcies (the collapse of businesses).

- **Social equality** – A planned economic system enables basic needs to be met for everyone in society. For example, everyone in society has access to education, health care and employment. By contrast, in capitalist (free-market) economies, production is geared disproportionately towards those with high incomes and wealth.

Prices do not need to be excessively high either, as private firms do not exist to maximise profits (see Chapter 12). Hence, in command economies, there is far less inequality in income and wealth distribution.

- **Social protection** – In a planned economic system, government rules and regulations are used to protect consumers and producers. For example, there may be strict laws that constrain economic growth in order to protect the environment by conserving non-renewable resources, or to minimise the impact of negative externalities such as pollution (see Chapter 5) caused by economic activity.
- **Employment of resources** – Careful state control and planning can ensure that factors of production (see Chapter 1) are fully utilised. Thus, full employment of resources can be maintained and economic growth can be planned.

For example, the People's Bank of China controls the country's money supply (see Chapter 6) by limiting the amount of money that individuals can transfer each day (currently capped at 20 000 yuan – or approximately $3180) per individual customer per day.

> **Case Study: The Super Bowl**
>
> The saying that 'time is money' really does apply in the world of advertising. The 2013 Super Bowl – America's biggest sporting bonanza – demanded a record $4 million for companies to air their 30-second commercial!

> **Activity**
>
> Refer to the case study above. Discuss how decision-makers could possibly justify spending $4 million on a 30-second advertising commercial.

Disadvantages of the planned system

The planned system suffers from a number of disadvantages:

- **Lack of economic freedom** – As the state plans all production decisions, individuals do not have economic freedom to choose from competing goods and services. They also lack career choices, as the government allocates jobs based on production schedules and long-term plans for the economy. As the government prefers to be self-sufficient by having strict controls on imports, this causes retaliation from other countries, which restrict exports from the command economy.
- **Lack of incentives** – As resources, jobs, goods and services are determined (planned) by the government, there is a lack of incentive to be innovative. For example, the lack of competition or the absence of a profit motive for firms means there is less of an incentive to produce more goods and services or to produce these at a higher quality. Much of economics assumes that economic agents react to incentives. The lack of incentives can therefore limit the standard of living (see Chapter 21) for people in command economies.
- **Bureaucracy** – For a planned economy to work effectively, many officials are needed to administer and operate the system. Bureaucrats (official government administrators) are responsible for decisions, but they do not take entrepreneurial risks – unlike private owners of businesses in market economies. Hence, production

decisions can be very inefficient when price does not determine the allocation of resources (see Chapter 3), leading to shortages in some industries and surpluses in others.

Case Study: Top-paid jobs

Some jobs are paid more than others – see Table 2.1 for data from the USA. Due to the vast complexities of the job, the world's highest-paid profession in 2013 was surgeons, with the average surgeon at the top end of the pay scale in the USA earning $181 850.

Table 2.1 Top five highest-paid jobs in the USA, 2013

Rank	Profession	Annual salary (top end)	Training time (years)
1	Surgeon	$181 850	10–15
2	Chief executive officer	$140 890	Variable
3	Engineering manager	$140 210	6–7
4	Airline pilot	$134 090	5–10
5	Dentist	$132 702	8

Source: **www.top10facts.com**

Activity

Refer to the case study above. Discuss the incentives for people wanting to become dentists, pilots and surgeons.

Market system

This economic system relies on the market forces of demand and supply to allocate resources. The private sector decides on the fundamental questions of what, how and for whom production should take place. The market economic system is also known as the **free market system** or the capitalist economy. Features of the market system include the following:

- No government interference in economic activities – resources are owned by private economic agents who are free to allocate them without interference from the government.
- Resources are allocated on the basis of price – a high price encourages more supply whereas a low price encourages consumer spending. Resources are sold to those who have the willingness and ability to pay.
- Financial incentives allocate scarce resources – for example, agricultural land is used for harvesting crops with the greatest financial return, whilst unprofitable products are no longer produced.
- Competition creates choice and opportunities for firms and private individuals. Consumers can thus benefit from a variety of innovative products, at competitive prices and of high quality.

The market economy is central to **supply-side economics** (see Chapter 16) and the associated gains from free international trade (see Chapter 26).

The Heritage Foundation compiles an annual economic freedom index for all countries. Hong Kong has topped the league table as the world's freest economy since records began in 1995, with Singapore being ranked second during the same time period (see Figures 2.2a and 2.2b).

Source: The Heritage Foundation, 2013

Figure 2.2a The five 'freest' economies, 2013

Source: The Heritage Foundation, 2013

Figure 2.2b Regional leaders, 2013

According to the Heritage Foundation, there is a high correlation between a country's level of economic freedom and its standard of living (see Chapter 20). Its research data suggest that market economies substantially outperform others in terms of economic growth, health care, education, protection of the environment and the reduction of poverty.

Advantages of the market system

The market system has the following benefits:

- **Efficiency** – Competition helps to ensure that private individuals and firms pay attention to what customers want. This helps to stimulate innovation, thereby making market economies more responsive and dynamic.
- **Freedom of choice** – Individuals can choose which goods and services to purchase and which career to pursue, without being restricted by government regulations.
- **Incentives** – The profit motive for firms and the possibility for individuals to earn unlimited wealth creates incentives to work hard. This helps to boost economic growth and living standards in the country.

Disadvantages of the market system

The market system also has a number of disadvantages:

- **Environmental issues** – There are negative consequences of economic prosperity under the market system, such as resource depletion, pollution and climate change.
- **Income and wealth inequalities** – In a market system, the rich have far more choice and economic freedom. Production is geared to meet the needs and wants of those with plenty of money, thus basic services for the poorer members of society may be neglected.
- **Social hardship** – The absence of government control means the provision of **public goods** (see Chapter 15) such as streetlighting, public roads and national defence may not be provided. Relief of poverty in society might only be done through voluntary charities.

- **Wasteful competition** – Competitive pressures can mean that firms use up unnecessary resources to gain competitive advantages over their rivals, such as excess packaging and advertising clutter. Consumers might be exploited by marketing tactics such as pester power (see the activity below). The lack of government involvement could also mean that products are less safe for consumers.

Activity

Pester power is the marketing term used to describe the ability that children have to persuade their parents to make certain purchasing decisions, perhaps by constant nagging or annoyance.

Use the internet to find examples of pester power and be prepared to share your findings with the class.

Mixed system

The USA is often given as an example of a modern capitalist society. However, the State and Federal governments do get involved in providing some basic services. In reality, the USA is a mixed economy but with a much larger private sector proportionally than most nations.

The mixed economic system is a combination of both the planned economy and the market economy. The degree of public and private sector involvement in economic activity is determined by the government. Essential services are provided by the public sector, such as state education, health care and postal services. The government exists to redistribute income by providing unemployment benefits and state pensions, for example. In the private sector, profit acts as the motive for firms to provide the goods and services demanded by consumers.

In the UK, the public sector accounts for around 45 per cent of gross domestic product (GDP) whereas in France this figure is around 43 per cent, so both are good examples of mixed economies. Other examples are Australia, Japan, Iceland, Sweden and Italy.

The mixed economic system obtains the best of both the planned and market systems. For example, necessary services are provided for everyone whilst most other goods are competitively marketed. Producers and workers have incentives to work hard, to invest and to save. There is large degree of economic freedom with plenty of choice for private individuals and firms.

The disadvantages of the extreme economic systems also apply to the mixed economy. For example, consumers still pay higher prices due to the profit motive of private sector businesses. Public sector activities must also be funded by taxes and other government fees and charges.

Activity

Use the internet to find relevant economic data for two different countries (such as North Korea and Hong Kong) to distinguish between the two main types of economic system. You might also find it useful to look at newspaper articles on current topics related to economic systems.

Case Study: Education systems

The Economist Intelligence Unit rankings of the world's top education systems, which combine international test results and data such as graduation rates, showed that two contrasting economies topped the league table for 2006–10: Finland and South Korea. The report concluded that, while the amount of spending on education is important, it is less influential than an economy having a culture that is supportive of learning.

Education in Finland is 100 per cent state funded and is rather unorthodox given that students do not start schooling until the age of seven and rarely have tests or homework until their teenage years. In South Korea, education is crucial for success so huge pressures are placed on students, who start school aged three. Testing is regular and rigorous, making after-school private tuition classes extremely popular.

According to the report, the top ten countries were ranked as follows:

1 Finland
2 South Korea
3 Hong Kong
4 Japan
5 Singapore
6 UK
7 Netherlands
8 New Zealand
9 Switzerland
10 Canada

Source: adapted from **www.bbc.co.uk/news/education-20498356**

Exam practice

1 Describe how scarce resources are allocated in a mixed economy. [3]
2 Discuss whether education should be funded by the government. [7]

Chapter review questions

1 What is meant by an economic system?
2 What are the three fundamental economic questions that any economic system seeks to answer?
3 How are resources allocated in a market economic system?
4 How are resources allocated in a planned economic system?
5 What are the merits of the market system?

Key terms

An economic system is the way in which an economy is organised and run, including how best to allocate society's scarce resources.

The fundamental economic questions are the key questions that all economic systems strive to answer: what, how and for whom production should take place.

A market economy is a type of economic system that relies on the market forces of demand and supply to allocate resources with minimal government intervention.

A mixed economy is a type of economic system that combines elements of both the planned and market economic systems, with some resources being owned and controlled by private individuals and firms while others are owned and controlled by the government.

A planned economy is a type of economic system that relies on the government allocating scarce resources. It is often associated with a communist political system that strives for social equality.

③ Demand and supply

By the end of this chapter, you should be able to:
- demonstrate the principle of equilibrium price and analyse simple market situations with changes in demand and supply
- describe the causes of changes in demand and supply conditions and analyse such changes to show effects in the market.

Taken from Cambridge International Examinations Syllabus (IGCSE 0455/O Level 2281)
© Cambridge International Examinations

The meaning of demand

Demand refers to both the *willingness* and the *ability* of customers to pay a given price to buy a good or service. This is sometimes referred to as **effective demand** to distinguish genuine demand from a want or a desire to buy something. The amount of a good or service demanded at each price level is called the **quantity demanded**.

In general, the quantity demanded falls as price rises, whilst the quantity demanded rises at lower prices. Therefore, there is an inverse relationship between the price of a good or service and the demand. This rule is known as the **law of demand**. There are two reasons for this relationship:

- As the price of a good or service falls, the customer's 'real' income rises (i.e. with the same amount of income, the customer is able to buy more products at lower prices).
- As the price of a good or service falls, more customers are able to pay, so they are more likely to buy the product.

Demand curves

Diagrammatically, the demand curve is shown as a downward-sloping curve to show the inverse relationship between price and quantity demanded (see Figure 3.1).

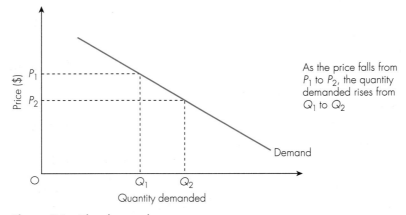

As the price falls from P_1 to P_2, the quantity demanded rises from Q_1 to Q_2

Figure 3.1   The demand curve

The **market demand** curve refers to the sum of all individual demand for a product. It is found by adding up all individual demand at each price level (see Figure 3.2). For instance, suppose that a cinema charges $10 for its movie tickets and the demand from male customers totals 500 per week while 400 females purchase tickets at that price per week. The market demand for cinema tickets at $10 per ticket is therefore 900 tickets per week.

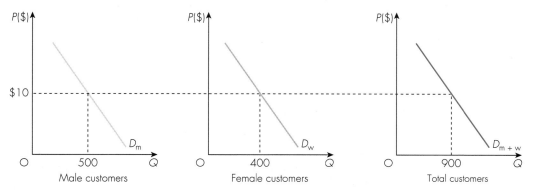

Figure 3.2 The market demand curve

> **Activity**
> Choose an item that you can buy in your country.
> 1 What are the factors that affect the demand for this product?
> 2 Which factor is the most important? Why?
>   Produce your findings in an A3 poster format for displaying in the classroom.

Determinants of demand

Although, price is regarded as the key determinant of the level of demand for a good or service, it is not the only factor that affects the quantity demanded. Other factors that affect a person's level of demand for goods and services are listed below:

Fashionable products lead to an increase in demand

> **Study tips**
> Some of the non-price determinants of demand can be remembered by the acronym **MISC**: **m**arketing, **i**ncome, **s**ubstitutes and **c**omplements.

● **Habits, fashion and tastes** – Changes in habits, fashion and taste can affect the demand for all types of goods and services. Products that become fashionable (such as smartphones) enjoy an increase in demand, whereas those that become unfashionable (such as last season's clothes) experience a fall in the level of demand. Luxury fashion brands from France are highly popular amongst women in China (see Table 3.1).

Table 3.1 Top ten fashion brands for Chinese females

Rank	Brand
1	Chanel (France)
2	Louis Vuitton (France)
3	Cartier (France)
4	Tiffany & Co. (USA)
5	Apple (USA)
6	Montblanc (Germany)
7	Gucci (Italy)
8	Prada (Italy)
9	Dior (France)
10	Burberry (UK)

Source: Hurun Chinese Luxury Consumer Survey, 2013

- **Income** – Higher levels of income mean that customers are able and willing to buy more goods and services. For example, the average person in America has a higher level of demand for goods and services than the average person in Vietnam or Turkey.
- **Substitutes** and **complements** – Substitutes are goods or services that can be used instead of each other, such as Coca-Cola or Pepsi and tea or coffee. If the price of a product falls, then it is likely the demand for the substitute will also fall.

  Complements are products that are jointly demanded, such as tennis balls and tennis racquets or cinema movies and popcorn. If the price of a product increases, then the demand for its complement is likely to fall.
- **Advertising** – Marketing messages are used to inform, remind and persuade customers to buy a firm's products. Companies such as Coca-Cola, McDonald's, Apple and Samsung spend hundreds of millions of dollars each year on their advertising budgets to increase the demand for their products.
- **Government policies** – Rules and regulations such as the imposition of taxes on tobacco and alcohol will affect the demand for certain products. Sales taxes cause prices to increase, thereby reducing the level of demand. By contrast, government subsidies for educational establishments and energy-efficient car-makers encourage more demand for education and environmentally friendly cars due to the relatively lower prices.
- **Economy** – The state of the economy (whether it is in an economic boom or a recession) also has a huge impact on the spending patterns of the population.
  - The global financial crisis of 2008, for example, caused the demand for most goods and services around the world to decline because households and businesses lacked confidence in the economy.
  - By 2013, the financial crisis had caused unemployment to exceed 26 per cent in both Greece and Spain – the highest unemployment figures ever experienced in the European Union. This undoubtedly reduced the level of demand for goods and services in these countries.

There are many other factors that can influence the level of demand for a particular good or service.

- For example, the weather can affect the demand for ice cream, beach resort holidays, winter jackets and umbrellas.

- The size and the demographics (such as age, gender, ethnicity or religious beliefs) of the population can also have an effect on the level of demand for goods and services. For example, males and females can have very different buying habits.

> **Activity**
>
> Visit your nearest shopping mall.
>
> 1 Investigate the number of stores which cater specifically (or primarily) for women and compare this with the number of stores which cater only (or mainly) for men.
> 2 Using demand theory, explain why there is such a difference.

The demographics of a population can have an effect on the level of demand for goods and services

Movements and shifts in demand

A change in price

A change in the price of a good or service causes a **movement along** the demand curve. A price rise will cause a decrease (**contraction**) in the quantity demanded of the product, whereas a reduction in price will cause an increase (**expansion**) in the quantity demanded, as shown in Figure 3.3.

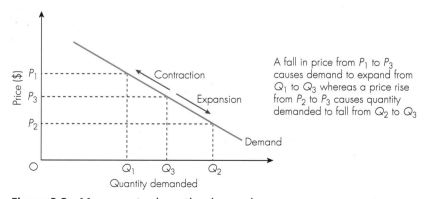

A fall in price from P_1 to P_3 causes demand to expand from Q_1 to Q_3 whereas a price rise from P_2 to P_3 causes quantity demanded to fall from Q_2 to Q_3

Figure 3.3 Movements along the demand curve

An increase in demand

A movement along the demand curve is caused by price changes only. A change in all other (non-price) factors that affect demand, such as income levels, will cause a **shift in demand**.

An **increase in demand** (rather than an increase in the quantity demanded) is represented by a rightward shift of the demand curve from D_1 to D_3 in Figure 3.4.

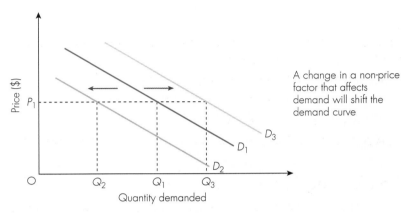

A change in a non-price factor that affects demand will shift the demand curve

Figure 3.4 Shifts in the demand curve

For example, BMW experienced record profits in 2012 when an increase in demand from China and other emerging markets boosted its car sales. Hence demand for BMW cars became higher at all price levels. At P_1 the quantity of cars demanded was previously Q_1 but has now increased to Q_3.

By contrast, a **decrease in demand** (rather than a fall in the quantity demanded) is shown by shifting the demand curve to the left, from D_1 to D_2, resulting in less quantity being demanded at all price levels. For example, at a price of P_1, demand was previously Q_1, but has now fallen to Q_2. Financial problems and rising unemployment across Europe led to a 16.5 per cent decline in the demand for Peugeot Citroën cars in 2012.

BMW saw record profits when increasing demand in China and other emerging markets boosted its car sales

> **Activity**
>
> France is the most visited tourist country in the world, with over 80 million visitors each year; the USA is second with 63 million visitors.
>
> 1 Investigate the most popular tourist cities in Europe.
>
> 2 Using demand theory, explain the factors that make these cities so popular.

Exam practice

Using an appropriate demand diagram, explain the impact on the demand for Apple smartphones in the following cases:

1 An increase in the price of Apple smartphones. [4]

2 An increase in the price of Samsung smartphones. [4]

3 An increase in consumer incomes. [4]

4 A successful advertising campaign promoting Samsung's latest smartphones. [4]

The meaning of supply

Supply is the *ability* and *willingness* of firms to provide goods and services at given price levels. Firms will have more incentives to supply their products at higher prices – the higher the price, the greater supply tends to be (see Figure 3.5). There are two reasons for this relationship:

- Existing firms can earn higher profits if they supply more.
- New firms are able to join the market if the higher price allows them to cover their production costs.

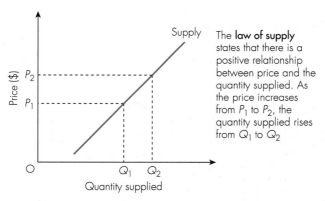

The **law of supply** states that there is a positive relationship between price and the quantity supplied. As the price increases from P_1 to P_2, the quantity supplied rises from Q_1 to Q_2

Figure 3.5 The supply curve

The **market supply** curve is the sum of all supply at each price level, as shown in Figure 3.6. Suppose that at a price of $300 000 Airbus is willing and able to supply 300 aircraft per time period while its rival Boeing supplies 320 aircraft. At this price, the total market supply is 620 aircraft per time period.

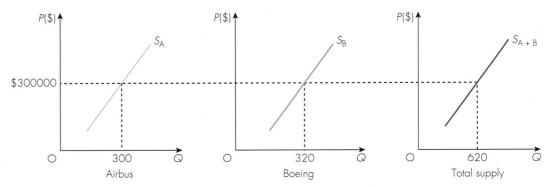

Figure 3.6 The market supply curve

> **Activity**
>
> 1 Investigate the factors that affect the supply of one of the following products:
>   a) coffee
>   b) chocolate
>   c) tea
>   d) sugar
>   e) oil
> 2 Organise your findings as a PowerPoint document and be prepared to present it to the class.

Determinants of supply

Although price is regarded as the key determinant of the level of supply of a good or service, it is not the only factor that affects the quantity supplied. Non-price factors that affect the level of supply of a product include the following:

● **Costs of production** – If the price of raw materials and the cost of other factors of production fall, then the supply curve will shift to the right, assuming all other things remain unchanged. There is an increase in supply at each price level as the costs of production fall and vice versa.
● **Taxes** – Taxes imposed on the supplier of a product add to the costs of production. Therefore the imposition of taxes on a product reduces its supply, shifting the supply curve to the left.
● **Subsidies** – Subsidies are a form of financial assistance from the government to help encourage output by reducing the costs of production. Subsidies are usually given to reduce the costs of supplying goods and services that are beneficial to society as a whole, such as education, training and health care.

● **Technological progress** – Technological advances such as automation, computers and wireless internet mean that there can be greater levels of output at every price level. Hence, technological progress will tend to shift the supply curve to the right.

● **Price and profitability of other products** – Price acts as a signal to producers to move their resources to the provision of goods and services with greater levels of profit. For example, if the market price of corn falls while the price of rapeseed increases, then farmers are likely to reduce their supply of corn and raise their supply of rapeseed.

● **Time** – The shorter the time period in question, the less time suppliers have to increase their output, so the lower the supply tends to be. Over time, output can be increased. For example, it is not possible for a farmer to increase the supply of agricultural products in a short time period.

● **Weather** – The supply of certain goods and services can also depend on the weather. Agricultural output will clearly depend on whether suppliers have favourable or unfavourable weather conditions. Similarly, some service providers may also limit or close their operations during adverse weather conditions, thereby shifting the supply curve to the left.

Movements and shifts in supply

Movements in supply

A change in the price of a good or service causes a **movement along** the supply curve. A price rise will cause an increase (**expansion**) in the quantity supplied of a product, while a price fall will cause a decrease (**contraction**) in the quantity supplied (see Figure 3.7).

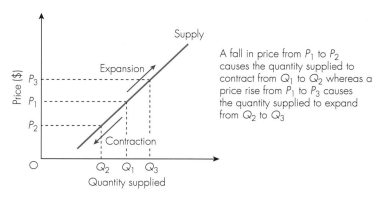

Figure 3.7 Movements along the supply curve

Shifts in supply

By contrast, a change in all non-price factors that affect the supply of a good or service will lead to a **shift** in the supply curve. In Figure 3.8, a rightward shift of the supply curve from S_1 to S_2 is described as an **increase in supply** (rather than an increase in the quantity supplied) whereas a leftward shift of the supply curve from S_1 to S_3 results in a **decrease in supply** (rather than a fall in the quantity supplied).

For example, Japan's tsunami in March 2011, the country's worst natural disaster, reduced the supply of major manufacturers such as Sony, Panasonic, Toyota and Honda (see the case study below).

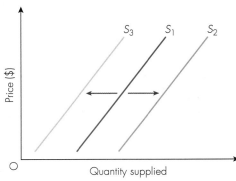

An increase in supply is shown by a rightward shift of the supply curve from S_1 to S_2. Similarly, a fall in supply is represented by a leftward shift of the supply curve from S_1 to S_3

Figure 3.8 Shifts in the supply curve

Study tips

- A *shift* in supply is caused by changes in non-price factors that affect supply, such as taxes and adverse weather.
- A *movement* in supply is caused only by changes in prices.

Case Study: Effect of Japanese earthquake and tsunami, 2011

In March 2011, a 9.03 magnitude undersea earthquake hit Tōhoku, Japan – the most powerful on record. This triggered a tsunami with waves reaching 40.5 metres (133 feet).

Manufacturers such as Toyota, Honda, Panasonic and Sony had factories completely wiped out, halting production.

Toyota loss the top spot in global car sales in 2011, but reclaimed the title from General Motors in 2012 when it met global demand for its cars by getting its supply back on track.

The World Bank estimated the economic damage at $235 billion, making this the world's most costly natural disaster.

Activity

Discuss as a class how supply theory can be used to explain the way natural disasters, such as the tsunami in Japan, affect the output of manufactured goods such as Toyota cars.

Exam practice

1 Using an appropriate supply diagram, explain the impact on the supply of educational computer games in the following cases:

   a) The government provides subsidies for the purchase of educational computer games. [4]

   b) There is an increase in the rate of commission paid to creators and the fee paid to distributors of educational computer games. [4]

   c) The government introduces a 15 per cent sales tax on all computer games. [4]

   d) There are technological advances in the production of educational computer games. [4]

2 Using an appropriate diagram, explain how the following changes affect the supply or the quantity supplied in each scenario:

   a) Beijing raises the minimum wage for factory workers by 20 per cent. [4]

   b) Drought causes vegetable prices to soar in France. [4]

   c) New technology boosts productivity at Tata Motors, India's largest car-maker. [4]

   d) The US government subsidises the output of hybrid cars. [4]

   e) South Korea's Samsung launches new tablet computers to rival Apple's iPad. [4]

Market equilibrium

The equilibrium price (also known as the **market-clearing price**) is determined where the demand for a product is equal to the supply of the product. This means that there is neither excess quantity demanded nor excess quantity supplied at the equilibrium price (see Figure 3.9).

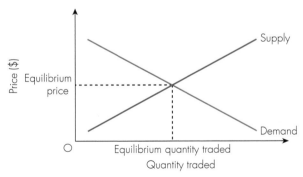

Figure 3.9 Equilibrium price

Changes in a non-price factor that affects demand or supply will tend to cause a change in the equilibrium price and therefore quantity traded. For example, in Figure 3.10, a government sales tax imposed on tobacco will shift the supply curve for cigarettes to the left. This raises the market-clearing price from P_1 to P_2 and reduces the equilibrium quantity traded from Q_1 to Q_2.

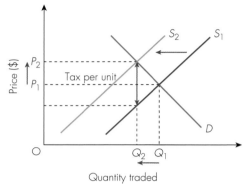

Figure 3.10   Imposition of a sales tax

In contrast, favourable weather conditions will shift the supply of agricultural output outwards to the right (see Figure 3.11). The increase in supply reduces the equilibrium price of agricultural output from P_1 to P_2 but increases the quantity traded from Q_1 to Q_2.

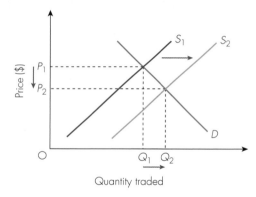

Figure 3.11   Favourable weather conditions

Activity
Investigate house prices in a city of your choice.
1 Do you think that the phrase 'what goes up must come down' applies to house prices?
2 Use demand and supply diagrams to justify your answer.

If price is set too high (above the market-clearing price), then supply will exceed demand, as shown in Figure 3.12. This results in surplus production known as **excess supply**. In order for firms to get rid of their excess supply (shown by the distance between Q_s and Q_d), they will need to reduce price (from P_1 to P_e). This is a key reason why leftover stocks of Christmas cards are reduced in price after 25 December and why unsold summer clothes go on sale during the autumn.

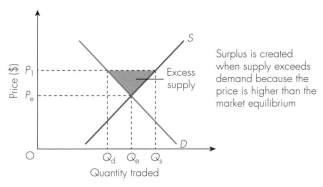

Surplus is created when supply exceeds demand because the price is higher than the market equilibrium

Figure 3.12 Excess supply (surplus)

By contrast, if the selling price of a product is set too low (i.e. below the equilibrium price), the demand will exceed the supply. This creates a shortage in the market, caused by the **excess demand** (see Figure 3.13). At a price of P_1, the demand is Q_d while supply is only Q_s so demand exceeds supply. The excess demand causes prices to rise back to the equilibrium price of P_e.

When Apple launched its iPhone 5 in Hong Kong in late 2012, demand outstripped supply so much that the price of the smartphone increased from HK\$5588 to almost HK\$8000 – an increase of 43 per cent!

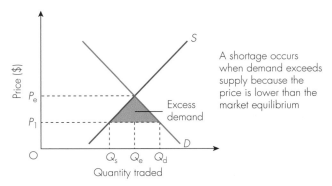

A shortage occurs when demand exceeds supply because the price is lower than the market equilibrium

Figure 3.13 Excess demand (shortage)

Exam practice

1   Using an appropriate demand and supply diagram, explain the impact on the market price and quantity traded in each of the following cases:

    a) The market for air travel following the imposition of higher fuel taxes. [5]

    b) The market for Pepsi Cola following a fall in the price of Coca-Cola. [5]

    c) The market for sushi following a successful marketing campaign promoting the health benefits from eating rice and raw fish. [5]

    d) The market for Samsung digital cameras following new technologies that improve productivity in its factories. [5]

2   In 2012, Danish toymaker LEGO launched LEGO Friends to appeal primarily to girls. The products include mini-doll figures, pink and purple toy sets and pets.

    Founded in 1949, LEGO's popular toy construction bricks were targeted mainly at boys with popular LEGO theme sets such as LEGO Racers, LEGO Star Wars, LEGO Batman and LEGO Ninjago.

    In early 2013, the *San Francisco Chronicle* reported that LEGO had sold twice as many of the LEGO Friends toys as was expected. The company said that demand from children and their families was overwhelmingly positive. *Business Week* reported that LEGO had spent $40 million in its global marketing of LEGO Friends.

    a) Define the term 'demand'. [2]

    b) Explain two possible reasons for the higher than expected demand for the LEGO Friends toy construction bricks. [6]

3   Below is a demand and supply schedule for carrots in a country.

Price per kg ($)	Quantity demanded per month (kg)	Quantity supplied per month (kg)
9	10 000	40 000
8	15 000	35 000
7	20 000	30 000
6	25 000	25 000
5	30 000	20 000
4	35 000	14 000
3	40 000	8 000

    a) Plot and label the demand and supply curves on a suitable graph. Establish the equilibrium price and quantity traded. [6]

    b) Using your graph, determine the excess demand at a price of $5 per kilo. [2]

    c) Using your graph, determine the excess supply at a price of $8 per kilo. [2]

Chapter review questions

1 What is meant by 'demand'?
2 What is meant by 'supply'?
3 Outline the factors that affect the level of demand for a product.
4 Outline the factors that affect the level of supply for a product.
5 How is equilibrium price and quantity traded determined?
6 What is the difference between excess demand and excess supply?
7 What is the difference between a shift and a movement in demand and supply analysis?

Key terms

Complements are products that are demanded (for their use) together with other products. For example, tea and milk or the cinema and popcorn are jointly demanded.

Demand refers to the willingness *and* the ability of customers to pay a given price to buy a good or service. The higher the price of a product, the lower its demand tends to be.

Equilibrium occurs when the quantity demanded for a product is equal to the quantity supplied of the product (i.e. there are no shortages or surpluses).

Excess demand occurs when the demand for a product exceeds the supply of the product at certain price levels. This happens when the price is set below the equilibrium price, resulting in shortages.

Excess supply occurs when the supply of a product exceeds the demand at certain price levels. This results in a surplus because the price is too high (i.e. above the market equilibrium price).

Substitutes are products that are in competitive demand as they can be used in place of each other. For example, tea and coffee or McDonald's and Burger King meals are substitute products.

Supply is the willingness *and* the ability of firms to provide a good or service at given prices. The higher the price of a product, the higher its supply tends to be.

4 Price elasticity

By the end of this chapter, you should be able to:
- define price elasticity of demand and supply and perform simple calculations
- demonstrate the usefulness of price elasticity in particular situations such as revenue changes and consumer expenditure.

Taken from Cambridge International Examinations Syllabus (IGCSE 0455/O Level 2281)
© Cambridge International Examinations

Price elasticity of demand

The law of demand (see Chapter 3) states that as the price of a product increases, the quantity demanded of that product will tend to fall. However, the responsiveness of change in the quantity demanded may vary depending on the customer's degree of ability and willingness to pay. For example, a rise in the price of a product with plenty of substitutes (such as bananas, greetings cards or chocolate bars) will have a larger impact on its level of demand than a rise in the price of a product that has fewer substitutes (such as petrol, toothpaste or haircuts).

Price elasticity of demand (PED) measures the degree of responsiveness of quantity demanded for a product following a change in its price. If a price change causes a relatively small change in the quantity demanded, then demand is said to be price inelastic: that is, buyers are not highly responsive to changes in price. For example, if the price of rice increases slightly, it is unlikely seriously to affect the demand for rice in countries like China, Vietnam and Thailand.

By contrast, demand is said to be price elastic if there is a relatively large change in the quantity demanded of a product following a change in its price: that is, buyers are very responsive to changes in price. For example, a small rise in the price of Pepsi Cola is likely to reduce its demand quite drastically as customers switch to buying rival brands such as Coca-Cola.

Demand for soft drinks is price elastic because there are many substitute products

As a staple food for billions of people, rice is highly price inelastic in Asia and the West Indies

Exam practice

Explain whether the price elasticity of demand for the following products is likely to be price elastic or price inelastic. Justify your answers.

1 Pineapples [4]

2 Tobacco [4]

3 Overseas holidays [4]

4 Textbooks [4]

The uses of price elasticity of demand

Knowledge of PED can give firms valuable information about how demand for their products is likely to change if prices are adjusted. This information can be used in several ways:

- Helping firms to decide on their pricing strategy – for example, a business with price inelastic demand for its products is likely to increase its prices, knowing that quantity demanded will be hardly affected. Therefore, the firm will benefit from higher revenue from selling its products at a higher price.

Theme parks charge different prices for essentially the same service. The difference is explained by PED

- Predicting the impact on firms following changes in the exchange rate – for instance, firms that rely on exports will generally benefit from lower exchange rates (as the price of exports become cheaper) and thus will become more price competitive. This assumes that the PED for exports is elastic, of course.

- Price discrimination – this occurs when firms charge different customers different prices for essentially the same product because of differences in their PED. For example, theme parks charge adults different prices from children and they also offer discounts for families and annual pass holders.

- Deciding how much of a sales tax can be passed on to customers – for example, products such as alcohol, tobacco and petrol are price inelastic in demand, so government taxes on these products can quite easily be passed on to customers without much impact on the quantity demanded.

- Helping governments to determine taxation policies – for example, the government can impose heavy taxes on demerit goods (see Chapter 5) such as petrol and cigarettes, knowing that the demand for these products is price inelastic. While demerit goods are harmful to society as a whole, the high level of taxes on such products does not significantly affect the level of demand (with minimal impact on sales revenues and jobs), but the government can collect large sums of tax revenues.

Activity

Discuss in pairs some examples of the ways in which multinational companies such as McDonald's, Microsoft, IKEA and Audi use PED in their businesses.

Calculating price elasticity of demand

Price elasticity of demand is calculated using the formula:

$$PED = \frac{\text{percentage change in quantity demanded}}{\text{percentage change in price}}$$

which can be abbreviated as:

$$PED = \frac{\%\Delta QD}{\%\Delta P}$$

For example, if a cinema increases its ticket price from \$10 to \$11 and this leads to demand falling from 3500 to 3325 customers per week, then the PED for cinema tickets is calculated as:

- percentage change in quantity demanded $= \dfrac{3325 - 3500}{3500} \times 100 = -5\%$

- percentage change in price $= \dfrac{11 - 10}{10} \times 100 = +10\%$

- $PED = \dfrac{-5}{10} = -0.5$

Worked example: Calculating PED

Assume the demand for football match tickets at \$50 is 50 000 per week. If the football club raises its price to \$60 per ticket and demand subsequently falls to 45 000 per week, what is the value of price elasticity of demand?

- First, calculate the percentage change in the quantity demanded – demand fell by 10 per cent from 50 000 to 45 000 match tickets per week.
- Next, calculate the percentage change in the price of match tickets – prices increased by 20 per cent from \$50 to \$60 per match ticket.
- Then, substitute these figures into the PED formula:
$$\frac{-10}{20} = -0.5$$

As the PED for match tickets is less than 1 (ignoring the minus sign), the demand for match tickets is price inelastic: in other words, football fans are not very responsive to the increase in match ticket prices. Consequently, there is a relatively small fall in the quantity demanded compared with the price rise.

Interpreting PED calculations

So what does a PED value of −0.5 actually mean? The cinema ticket example suggests that the demand for cinema tickets is *price inelastic* (i.e. relatively unresponsive to changes in price). This is because a 10 per cent increase in the price (from $10 to $11) only caused quantity demanded to drop by 5 per cent (from 3500 tickets per week to 3325).

The value of PED is negative due to the **law of demand** – an increase in the price of a product will tend to reduce its quantity demanded (see Chapter 3). The inverse relationship between price and quantity demanded also applies in the case of a price reduction – that is, a price fall tends to lead to an increase in the quantity demanded.

The calculation of PED generally has two possible outcomes:

● If the PED for a product is less than 1 (ignoring the minus sign), then demand is **price inelastic** (i.e. demand is relatively unresponsive to changes in price). This is because the percentage change in quantity demanded is smaller than the percentage change in the price (see Figure 4.1).
● If the PED for a product is greater than 1 (ignoring the minus sign), then demand is **price elastic** (i.e. demand is relatively responsive to changes in price). This is because the percentage change in quantity demanded is larger than the percentage change in the price of the product (see Figure 4.2).

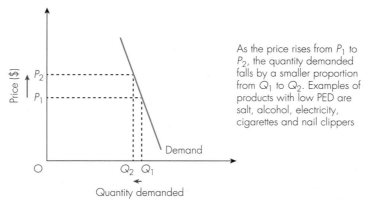

As the price rises from P_1 to P_2, the quantity demanded falls by a smaller proportion from Q_1 to Q_2. Examples of products with low PED are salt, alcohol, electricity, cigarettes and nail clippers

Figure 4.1 The price inelastic demand curve

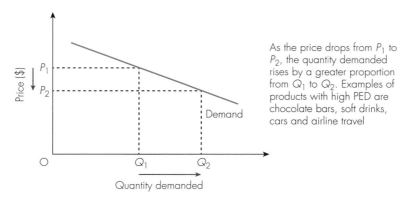

As the price drops from P_1 to P_2, the quantity demanded rises by a greater proportion from Q_1 to Q_2. Examples of products with high PED are chocolate bars, soft drinks, cars and airline travel

Figure 4.2 The price elastic demand curve

However, there are three special cases which are theoretical possibilities:

● If the PED for a product is equal to 0, then demand is **perfectly price inelastic**: that is, a change in price has no impact on the quantity demanded. This suggests that there is absolutely no substitute for such a product, so suppliers can charge whatever price they like (see Figure 4.3).

● If the PED for a product is equal to infinity (∞) then demand is **perfectly price elastic**: that is, a change in price leads to zero quantity demanded. This suggests that customers switch to buying other substitute products if suppliers raise their price (see Figure 4.4).

● If the PED for a product is equal to 1 (ignoring the minus sign), then demand has unitary price elasticity: that is, the percentage change in the quantity demanded is proportional to the change in the price (see Figure 4.5).

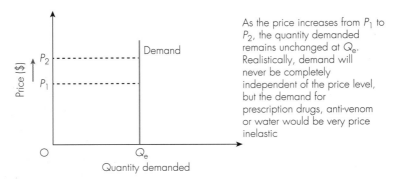

As the price increases from P_1 to P_2, the quantity demanded remains unchanged at Q_e. Realistically, demand will never be completely independent of the price level, but the demand for prescription drugs, anti-venom or water would be very price inelastic

Figure 4.3   The perfectly price inelastic demand curve

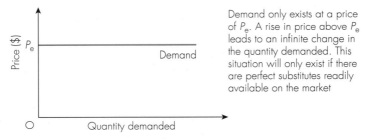

Demand only exists at a price of P_e. A rise in price above P_e leads to an infinite change in the quantity demanded. This situation will only exist if there are perfect substitutes readily available on the market

Figure 4.4   The perfectly price elastic demand curve

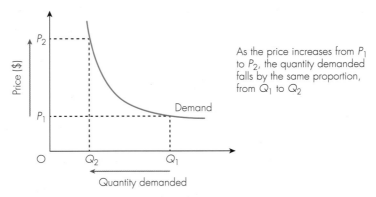

As the price increases from P_1 to P_2, the quantity demanded falls by the same proportion, from Q_1 to Q_2

Figure 4.5   The unitary price elastic demand curve

> **Activity**
>
> Many governments around the world raise taxes on tobacco, alcohol and petrol, on a regular basis.
>
> 1 As a class, discuss the economic reasons for doing so.
> 2 Use the concept of price elasticity of demand in your arguments.

Exam practice

1 Assume the price of a sack of rice falls from $25 to $24, resulting in an increase in quantity demanded from 850 sacks to 875 sacks per month. Calculate the value of price elasticity of demand for the product and comment on your finding. [4]

2 Explain two reasons why the demand for rice is price inelastic in countries like India, Vietnam and China. [4]

Determinants of price elasticity of demand

There are many interlinked determinants of the PED for a product:

- **Substitution** – This is the key determinant of the PED for a good or service. In general, the greater the number and availability of close substitutes there are for a good or service, the higher the value of its PED will tend to be. This is because such products are easily replaced if the price increases, due to the large number of close substitutes that are readily available. By contrast, products with few substitutes, such as toothpicks, private education and prescribed medicines, have relatively price inelastic demand.

- **Income** – The proportion of a consumer's income that is spent on a product also affects the value of its PED. If the price of a box of toothpicks or a packet of salt were to double, the percentage change in price is so insignificant to the consumer's overall income that quantity demanded would be hardly affected, if at all.

  By contrast, if the price of an overseas cruise holiday were to rise by 25 per cent from $10 000 to $12 500 per person, this would discourage many more customers because the extra $2500 per ticket has a larger impact on a person's disposable income (even though the percentage increase in the price of a cruise holiday is much lower than that of the box of toothpicks or packet of salt).

  Therefore, the larger the proportion of income that the price of a product represents, the greater the value of its PED tends to be. Of course, those on extremely high levels of income (such as Carlos Slim, Bill Gates and Warren Buffet – the three richest men on the planet) are probably not responsive to any change in the market price of goods and services!

- **Necessity** – The degree of necessity of a good or service will affect the value of its PED. Products that are regarded as essential (such as food, fuel, medicines, housing and transportation) tend to be relatively price inelastic because households need these goods and services, and so will continue to purchase them even if their prices rise.

  By contrast, the demand for luxury products (such as Gucci suits, Chanel handbags and Omega watches) is price elastic, as these are not necessities for most households.

  The degree of necessity also depends on the timeframe in question. For example, demand for fresh flowers on Valentine's Day and on Mother's Day is relatively price inelastic compared with other days. It also applies to peak and off-peak times. For example, many countries operate public transport systems that charge more for

Demand for fresh flowers on special days like Valentine's Day and Mother's Day is relatively price inelastic compared with other days

travelling during peak time. This is partly due to overcrowding problems during such times, but also because the transport operators know that peak-time travel is more of a necessity than off-peak travel.

- **Habits, addictions, fashion and tastes** – If a product is habit forming (such as tobacco) or highly fashionable (such as smartphones in many countries), its PED tends to be relatively price inelastic. Similarly, people who are extremely devoted to a particular hobby, such as sports or music, are more willing to pay, even at higher prices. Hence, the demand from these people is less sensitive to changes in price.

- **Advertising and brand loyalty** – Marketing can have a huge impact on the buying habits of customers. Effective advertising campaigns for certain products not only help to shift the demand curve outwards to the right, but can also reduce the price elasticity of demand for the product. Customers who are loyal to particular brands are less sensitive to a change in their prices, partly because these brands are demanded out of habit and personal preference – that is, they are the default choice over rival brands. Examples of brands with a loyal customer following include Coca-Cola, Apple, Samsung, Chanel, Toyota and Mercedes-Benz.

- **Time** – The period of time under consideration can affect the value of PED because people need time to change their habits and behavioural norms. Over time, they can adjust their demand in response to more permanent price changes by seeking out alternative products. For example, parents with children in private fee-paying schools are unlikely to withdraw their children from school if these establishments raise school fees because this would be very disruptive to their children's learning. Similarly, owners of private motor vehicles are not likely to get rid of their vehicles simply because of higher fuel prices. However, if there is a continual hike in prices over time, both parents and vehicle owners may seek alternatives. Hence, demand tends to be more price elastic in the long run.

- **Durability** – Some products, such as fresh milk, are perishable (do not last very long) and need to be replaced, so will continue to be bought even if prices rise.

  By contrast, if the price of consumer durable products (such as household furniture, LCD televisions or motor vehicles) increases, then households may decide to postpone replacing these items due to the high prices involved in such purchases. Therefore, the more durable a product is, the more price elastic its demand tends to be.

- **The costs of switching** – There may be costs involved for customers who wish to switch between brands or products. In the case of high switching costs, the demand for the product is less sensitive to changes in price – that is, it tends to be price inelastic.

  For example, manufacturers of smartphones, laptops and digital cameras make it more difficult for their customers to switch between rival brands by supplying different power chargers, memory cards and software. Similarly, mobile phone users and satellite television subscribers are bound by lengthy contracts, which makes switching between rival brands or services less easy. Such barriers to switching therefore make customers less responsive to higher product prices.

- **The breadth of definition of the product** – If a good or service is very broadly defined (such as 'food' rather than fruit, meat, apples or salmon), then demand will be more price inelastic. For example, there is clearly no real substitute for food or housing, so demand for these products will be very price inelastic. However, it is perhaps more useful to measure the price elasticity of demand for specific brands or products, such as carbonated soft drinks, Australian beef and IGCSE textbooks.

Study tips

Although there are many determinants of PED, the key factors can be remembered by THIS acronym:

- Time
- Habits, addictions and tastes
- Income
- Substitutes (availability and price of).

Case Study: Toyota Motor Corporation

Japanese car-maker Toyota has seen its fair share of troubles in recent times. It has had to deal with several cases of global product recalls for its cars due to safety concerns. The global financial crisis of 2008 also harmed global sales for several years. On top of that, much of the world's largest car-maker's stocks of new cars were destroyed in the tsunami of March 2011.

Nevertheless, customer loyalty remains strong in the USA, China and many other parts of the world. Toyota's closest rival, General Motors (GM), estimated the value of customer loyalty at $700 million for every percentage point of improvement in customer retention rates.

Market research from *Experian Automotive* revealed that 47.3 per cent of Toyota's current customers from the USA would purchase a Toyota, Scion or Lexus model as their next car. Globally, this figure stands at 58 per cent for Toyota and 52 per cent for GM.

Toyota's use of marketing slogans such as 'The best built cars in the world' can certainly go a long way to reassure Toyota's loyal customers about their cars.

Sources: adapted from *Wall Street Journal* and *TIME Business*

Activity

Discuss how the concept of price elasticity of demand and its determinants can help to explain why Toyota Motor Corporation is the world's largest car-maker.

PED, consumer expenditure and revenue changes

Knowledge of the price elasticity of demand for a product can be used to assess the impact on consumer expenditure and therefore sales revenue following changes in price. Sales revenue is the amount of money received by a supplier from the sale of a good or service. It is calculated by multiplying the price charged for each product by the quantity sold, i.e.

Revenue = price × quantity demanded

Note that this is not the same as profit, which is the numerical difference between a firm's sales revenues and its total costs of production.

For example, if Lenovo sells 5000 laptops at $700 each in the first quarter of the month, its sales revenue is $3.5 million. Suppose that the computer maker reduces its price to $650 and quantity demanded rises to 5200 units in the following quarter. Was this a good business decision?

A quick calculation of PED reveals that the demand for Lenovo laptops is price elastic:

- percentage change in quantity demanded $= \dfrac{5500 - 5000}{5000} \times 100 = +10\%$

- percentage change in price $= \dfrac{\$650 - \$700}{\$700} \times 100 = -7.14\%$
- thus, PED $= 1.4$

This means the PED for Lenovo laptops is price elastic. Hence a fall in price causes a relatively larger increase in the quantity demanded, so sales revenues should increase. This can be checked as follows:

> original sales revenue $= \$700 \times 5000 = \$3\,500\,000$
> new sales revenue $= \$650 \times 5500 = \$3\,575\,000$
> difference in sales revenue $= \$3.575\text{m} - \$3.5\text{m} = +75\,000$

Given that demand for Lenovo laptops in the above example is price elastic, a reduction in price was a sensible business decision. Therefore, it can be seen that knowledge of PED for a product can inform firms about their pricing strategy in order to maximise sales revenues. These relationships are summarised in Table 4.1 and and Figures 4.6 and 4.7.

Table 4.1   The relationship between PED and sales revenue

Price change	Inelastic	Unitary	Elastic
Increase price	Revenues rise	No change in revenues	Revenues fall
Reduce price	Revenues fall	No change in revenues	Revenues rise

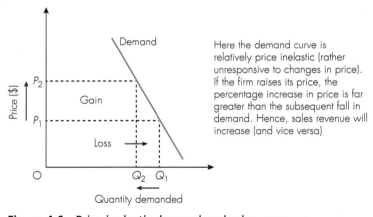

Here the demand curve is relatively price inelastic (rather unresponsive to changes in price). If the firm raises its price, the percentage increase in price is far greater than the subsequent fall in demand. Hence, sales revenue will increase (and vice versa)

Figure 4.6   Price inelastic demand and sales revenue

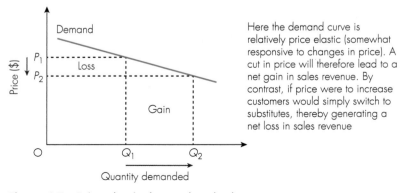

Here the demand curve is relatively price elastic (somewhat responsive to changes in price). A cut in price will therefore lead to a net gain in sales revenue. By contrast, if price were to increase customers would simply switch to substitutes, thereby generating a net loss in sales revenue

Figure 4.7   Price elastic demand and sales revenue

> **Activity**
>
> In small groups, discuss why firms use peak and off-peak pricing strategies, such as airline tickets being far more expensive during school holidays.
>
> 1 How many examples of price discrimination based on time (peak and off-peak) can your group come up with?
>
> 2 Does your group believe that price discrimination is beneficial? Justify your argument.

Exam practice

Suppose Sharma Fabrics sells 1350 units of wool per month at $4.00 each. Following an increase in price to $4.60 per unit, the firm discovers that the quantity demanded falls to 1215 units per month.

1 Calculate the price elasticity of demand for wool sold at Sharma Fabrics. [3]

2 Calculate the change in the total revenue following the increase in price of wool. [3]

3 Explain how knowledge of price elasticity of demand can be of use to Sharma Fabrics. [4]

Price elasticity of supply

Price elasticity of supply (PES) measures the responsiveness of the quantity supplied of a product following a change in its price. Supply is said to be price elastic if producers can quite easily increase supply without a time delay if there is an increase in the price of the product. This can help to give such firms a competitive advantage, as they are able to respond to changes in price.

By contrast, supply is price inelastic if firms find it difficult to change production in a given time period when the market price changes.

Calculating price elasticity of supply

Price elasticity of supply is calculated using the formula:

$$PES = \frac{\text{percentage change in quantity supplied}}{\text{percentage change in price}}$$

which can be abbreviated as:

$$PES = \frac{\%\Delta QS}{\%\Delta P}$$

For example, if the market price of beans increased from $2 per kilo to $2.20 per kilo, causing quantity supplied to rise from 10 000 units to 10 500 units, then the PES is calculated as:

- percentage change in quantity supplied $= \dfrac{10500 - 10000}{10000} \times 100 = +5\%$

- percentage change in price $= \dfrac{\$2.20 - \$2.0}{\$2.0} \times 100 = +10\%$

- $PES = \dfrac{+5\%}{+10\%} = 0.5$

What this means is that the supply of beans is hardly affected by the change in price – supply is relatively price inelastic. Note that the value of PES is positive due to the law of supply – that is, an increase in price tends to increase the quantity supplied (and vice versa).

The value of PES reveals the degree to which the quantity supplied of a product responds to changes in price. The calculation of PES generally has two possible outcomes:

- If PES > 1.0 supply is price elastic, i.e. supply is responsive to changes in price (the percentage change in quantity supplied is greater than the percentage change in price – see Figure 4.8).
- If PES < 1.0 supply is price inelastic, i.e. quantity supplied is relatively unresponsive to changes in price (percentage change in quantity supplied is less than the percentage change in price – see Figure 4.9).

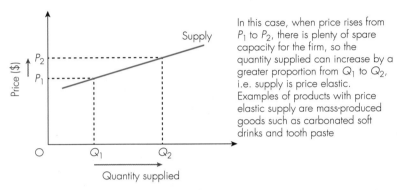

In this case, when price rises from P_1 to P_2, there is plenty of spare capacity for the firm, so the quantity supplied can increase by a greater proportion from Q_1 to Q_2, i.e. supply is price elastic. Examples of products with price elastic supply are mass-produced goods such as carbonated soft drinks and tooth paste

Figure 4.8 The price elastic supply curve

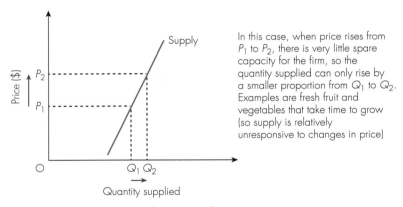

In this case, when price rises from P_1 to P_2, there is very little spare capacity for the firm, so the quantity supplied can only rise by a smaller proportion from Q_1 to Q_2. Examples are fresh fruit and vegetables that take time to grow (so supply is relatively unresponsive to changes in price)

Figure 4.9 The price inelastic supply curve

However, there are three special cases which are theoretical possibilities for PES:

- If the PES of a product is equal to 0, then supply is **perfectly price inelastic**: that is, a change in price has no impact on the quantity supplied. This suggests that there is absolutely no spare capacity for suppliers to raise output, irrespective of increases in price (see Figure 4.10).
- If the PES of a product is equal to infinity (∞) then supply is **perfectly price elastic**: that is, the quantity supplied can change without any corresponding change in price. For example, a software developer selling products online can very easily increase supply to match higher levels of demand, without any impact on the price level. Due to the spare capacity that exists, suppliers are able to raise output at the current price level (see Figure 4.11).

● If the PES for a product is equal to 1 then supply has **unitary price elasticity**: that is, the percentage change in the quantity supplied matches the proportional change in price (see Figure 4.12). Any upwards sloping supply curve that starts at the origin will have unitary price elasticity.

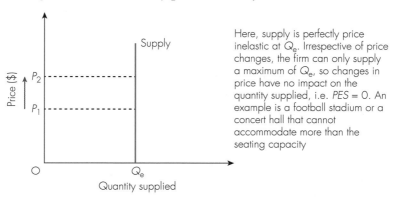

Here, supply is perfectly price inelastic at Q_e. Irrespective of price changes, the firm can only supply a maximum of Q_e, so changes in price have no impact on the quantity supplied, i.e. $PES = 0$. An example is a football stadium or a concert hall that cannot accommodate more than the seating capacity

Figure 4.10 The perfectly price inelastic supply curve

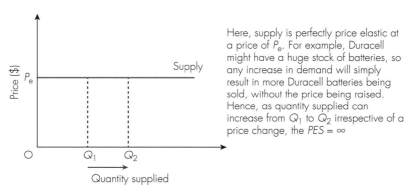

Here, supply is perfectly price elastic at a price of P_e. For example, Duracell might have a huge stock of batteries, so any increase in demand will simply result in more Duracell batteries being sold, without the price being raised. Hence, as quantity supplied can increase from Q_1 to Q_2 irrespective of a price change, the $PES = \infty$

Figure 4.11 The perfectly price elastic supply curve

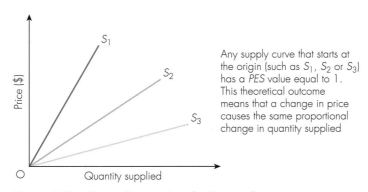

Any supply curve that starts at the origin (such as S_1, S_2 or S_3) has a PES value equal to 1. This theoretical outcome means that a change in price causes the same proportional change in quantity supplied

Figure 4.12 The unitary price elastic supply curve

> **Study tips**
>
> In reality, supply curves are likely to be non-linear, so will have a different PES value at different points. Supply is more elastic at lower prices and more inelastic at higher prices.

> **Activity**
>
> Discuss in pairs why the price elasticity of supply of the following products will differ:
>
> 1 Smartphones
> 2 Organic vegetables
> 3 Fresh flowers
> 4 Hotels
> 5 Ferrari cars.

Exam practice

Angry Birds is a highly popular video game created by Finnish company Rovio in December 2009 for the iPhone. Since then, over 12 million customers have paid $0.99 each to download the game from Apple's App Store. The game has become available for other platforms such as the Android and Windows operating systems and available for both video games consoles and personal computers.

Rovio has since launched variations of the video game, such as *Angry Birds Seasons*, *Angry Birds Rio*, *Angry Birds Space* and *Angry Birds Star Wars*. According to its website, the Angry Birds games have been downloaded over 1 billion times across all platforms, making it the most downloaded app of all time.

1 With the use of an appropriate diagram, explain why the high level of demand for *Angry Birds* games has no effect on the selling price.   [6]

2 Explain how knowledge of price elasticity of supply can help businesses such as Rovio.   [4]

Determinants of price elasticity of supply

There are several interlinked determinants of the PES for a product:

- **The degree of spare productive capacity** – If a firm has plenty of spare capacity then it can increase supply with relative ease: that is, without increasing its costs of production. This means that supply is relatively price elastic. For example, Coca-Cola's bottling plants can produce 10 000 cans of soft drink in just 60 seconds, so it is very easy for the world's largest beverage company with plenty of spare productive capacity to respond to changes in price. In general, the supply of goods and services is highly price elastic during an economic recession (see Chapter 20) when there are spare (unused) resources such as land, capital and labour.
- **The level of stocks** – If a firm has unused raw materials, components and finished products (collectively known as stocks or inventories) that are available for use, then the firm is more able to respond quickly to a change in price, as it can supply these stocks on to the market. Not all inventories are sold to consumers – raw materials and components (parts used in the production process, such as gearboxes and motors for cars) are used in the production process. In addition, some types of stock (such as pencils or ball bearings) are easier to store than others (such as fresh milk or organic vegetables), so it will be easier to increase supply if prices increase. This means that the higher the level of stocks of finished goods (such as cars) that are ready for sale, the more price elastic supply tends to be.
- **The number of producers in the industry** – The more suppliers of a product there are in the industry, the easier it tends to be for firms to increase their output in response to a price increase. For example, there is plenty of competition in the restaurant trade, so suppliers will be highly responsive to increases in price. Hence, the greater the number of firms in an industry, the more price elastic supply tends to be. By contrast, high barriers to entry in the pharmaceutical industry mean that there are very few suppliers in the industry, so supply tends to be price inelastic.

- **The time period** – In the short run, most firms are not able to change their factor inputs, such as the size of their workforce or the fixed amount of capital equipment they employ. For example, in agricultural farming, the supply of fresh fruit and vegetables is dependent on the time it takes to harvest the products and climatic conditions beyond the control of the suppliers. Hence, supply is less responsive to changes in price in the short run. Supply is more likely to be price elastic in the long run because firms can adjust their levels of production according to price changes in the market.
- **The ease and cost of factor substitution** – This refers to the extent to which it is possible to introduce factor resources (such as labour and capital) to the production process. If capital and labour resources are **occupationally mobile**, this means they can be substituted into the production process easily. An example of capital being occupationally mobile is a publishing company that can switch production quite easily between printing textbooks, magazines, trade journals, calendars or greetings cards. This means the ease of factor substitution in the publishing firm makes supply highly price elastic. By contrast, the PES for a product where capital equipment and labour cannot easily be switched, as the production process is inflexible, will be very low: that is, supply is price inelastic.

The value of PES to firms

In general, it is preferable for firms to have a high PES – to be highly responsive to changes in price (and other market conditions). This can help to make the firm more competitive and therefore to generate more sales revenue and profits. Firms can become more responsive to changes in market price in several ways, including:

- creating spare capacity
- keeping large volumes of stocks (inventories)
- improving storage systems to prolong the shelf-life of products
- adopting or upgrading to the latest technology
- improving distribution systems (how the products get to the customers)
- developing and training employees to improve labour occupational mobility (to perform a range of jobs).

Exam practice

Explain whether the price elasticity of supply (PES) of the following products is relatively elastic or inelastic.

1 Bananas   [4]
2 Fresh flowers   [4]
3 Computers   [4]
4 Coal   [4]

Chapter review questions

1 What is meant by price elasticity of demand (PED) and how is it calculated?
2 How might knowledge of PED be of value to firms?
3 How might knowledge of PED be of value to the government?
4 Why should firms raise prices for products with price inelastic demand?
5 Use a diagram to show the difference between perfectly price elastic demand, unitary PED and price inelastic demand.
6 What are the key determinants of PED?
7 What is meant by price elasticity of supply (PES) and how is it calculated?
8 Use a diagram to distinguish between price elastic PES and price inelastic PES.
9 If a product has a PES value of 0, what does this actually mean?
10 What are the key determinants of PES?

Key terms

Price discrimination occurs when firms charge different customers different prices for essentially the same product because of their differences in PED.

Price elastic demand describes demand for a product that is relatively responsive to changes in price, usually due to substitutes being available.

Price elasticity of demand (PED) measures the extent to which demand for a product changes due to a change in its price.

Price elasticity of supply (PES) measures the responsiveness of quantity supplied of a product following a change in its price.

Price inelastic demand describes demand for a product that is relatively unresponsive to changes in price, mainly because of the lack of substitutes for the product.

Stocks (or **inventories**) are the raw materials, components and finished goods (ready for sale) used in the production process.

Unitary price elasticity occurs when the percentage change in the quantity demanded (or supplied) is proportional to the change in the price, so there is no change in the sales revenue.

5 Market failure

By the end of this chapter, you should be able to:
● describe the concept of market failure and explain the reasons for its occurrence
● define private and social costs and benefits and discuss conflicts of interest in relation to these costs and benefits in the short term and long term through studies of the following issues:
   ○ conserving resources versus using resources
   ○ public expenditure versus private expenditure

Taken from Cambridge International Examinations Syllabus (IGCSE 0455/O Level 2281)
© Cambridge International Examinations

Market failure

Market failure occurs when the production or consumption of a good or service causes additional positive or negative externalities (spillover effects) on a third party not involved in the economic activity. In other words, the market forces of demand and supply fail to allocate resources efficiently.

Market failure may be caused by the following:

● Production of goods or services which cause negative side-effects on a third party. For example, the production of oil or the construction of offices may cause damage to the environment and a loss of green space.
● Production of goods or services which cause a positive spillover effect on a third party. An example is training programmes, such as first-aid or coaching skills for employees, which create benefits that can be enjoyed by others.
● Consumption of goods or services which cause a negative spillover effect on a third party. Such goods are known as demerit goods and include cigarettes, alcohol, gambling and driving a car.
● Consumption of goods or services which cause a positive spillover effect on a third party. Such goods are known as merit goods and include education, health care and vaccinations.
● Failure of the private sector to provide goods and services such as street lighting, road signs and national defence due to a lack of a profit motive. Such goods and services are known as **public goods** (see Chapter 15).
● The existence of a firm in a monopoly market (see Chapter 13) that charges prices which are too high and exploits customers.

Private and social costs

The private costs of production and consumption are the actual costs of a firm, individual or government. For example, the driver of a car pays for the insurance, road tax, petrol and cost of purchasing the car. The external costs are the negative side-effects of production or consumption incurred by third parties, for which no compensation is paid. For example, a car driver does not pay for the cost of the congestion and air pollution created when driving the car. This is an example of market failure because the private costs (of driving) do not represent the true costs (of driving) to society. The true cost of a car journey is called the social cost.

Social costs = private costs + external costs

Other examples of external costs are:

- air pollution caused by fumes from a factory
- noise pollution from a night club
- cigarette smoke
- litter
- too much advertising, which causes visual blight.

Government intervention

Governments try to solve market failure in a number of ways, such as by placing a tax on the price of a demerit good with the aim of reducing demand for the good.

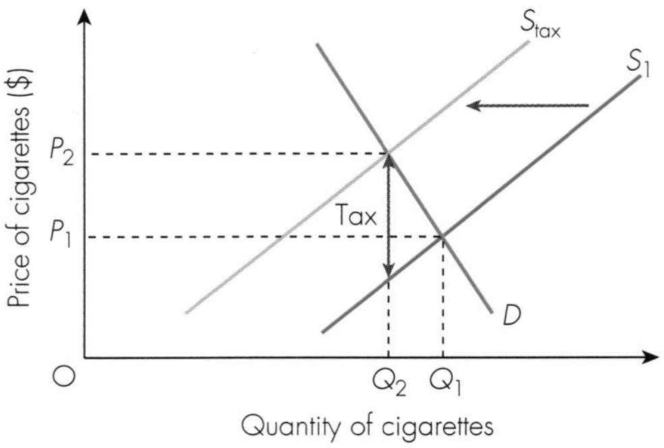

Figure 5.1 The impact of an indirect tax on cigarettes

Study tips

Remember that the level of taxation is measured by the vertical distance between the two supply curves. The consumer pays the increase in price ($P_2 - P_1$) and the producer pays the remainder. The more price inelastic the demand for the product, the greater the proportion of the tax paid by the consumer.

In Figure 5.1, the tax (see Chapter 3) imposed on a packet of cigarettes causes the supply curve to shift from S_1 to S_{tax}. The tax is the vertical distance between the two supply curves. As a result, price increases from P_1 to P_2 and the quantity of cigarettes demanded decreases from Q_1 to Q_2. The demand for cigarettes tends to be price inelastic (see Chapter 4) and therefore the percentage change in quantity demanded is less than the percentage increase in price.

The advantages and disadvantages of imposing a tax on a good or service are shown in Table 5.1.

Table 5.1 Advantages and disadvantages of taxing a good or service

Advantages	Disadvantages
• It increases the price and therefore should decrease the quantity demanded. • It creates tax revenue for the government which can be used on other goods and services.	• The demand for cigarettes, alcohol and petrol (gas for a car) tends to be price inelastic (see Chapter 4), which means that the increase in price may have little impact on consumption. The nicotine in cigarettes makes smoking highly addictive and therefore smokers will pay the higher price and consumption will change only slightly. • The indirect tax will be regressive (see Chapter 17) and have a greater impact on low-income earners than high-income earners.

Exam practice

Traffic congestion in central London has decreased since the introduction of a congestion charge for driving into the central business district. It costs £10 (approximately $15.20) each day to drive into the restricted area during peak hours (between 7a.m. and 6p.m. on weekdays). There is a penalty of between £60 (around $90) and £187 ($285) for late payment of the charge.

1 Explain, using an example, an external cost of driving a car. [2]

2 Assess the advantages and disadvantages of the congestion charge for two different groups in society. [6]

3 Discuss whether you think the congestion charge is a long-term or short-term solution to the problem of traffic congestion in London. [7]

Governments can also impose rules and regulations in an attempt to solve market failure. For example, imposing a minimum age that a person must be before they are legally allowed to purchase cigarettes or alcohol may reduce the consumption of such demerit goods (see Figure 5.2). Laws can also restrict where a person can smoke. In many countries, smoking is banned in public places such as shopping centres, bars, restaurants, airports, railways stations and even the beach!

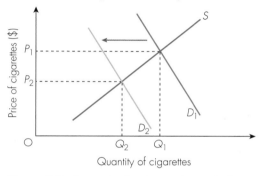

Figure 5.2 Impact of rules and regulations on the demand for cigarettes

Figure 5.2 illustrates the impact of a ban on smoking in public places on the demand curve for cigarettes. The demand curve shifts from D_1 to D_2, resulting in the quantity of cigarettes demanded falling from Q_1 to Q_2.

Other examples of laws and regulations imposed to correct market failures include:

- laws regulating where people can drive, cycle and gamble
- regulations imposed to make sure children are vaccinated against certain diseases
- laws making it illegal for people to smoke, eat or talk on a mobile phone while driving
- motorcyclists being made to wear a helmet and car passengers having to wear seat belts at all times
- airport authorities regulating the number of night flights
- banning of alcohol sales in Iran, Bangladesh, Brunei and Saudi Arabia.

Case Study: Compulsory education

Parents in the UK are fined if they do not send their children to school. This rule is designed to improve the uptake of education. From 2015, full-time education in the UK will be compulsory for children up to 18 years of age.

Activity

Investigate the laws and regulations in your country which are used to correct market failures. How effective have these laws and regulations been?

The advantages of imposing rules and regulations to correct market failures are as follows:

● Consumption of the good or service may be reduced.
● Awareness of the negative impacts of demerit goods (such as drinking and driving) may change the behaviour of people in the long term.
● Awareness of the positive impacts of consumption of merit goods (such as education) is raised.

The disadvantages of imposing rules and regulations to correct market failures are as follows:

● Restrictions cause underground (illegal) markets to develop where the good or service can be purchased, often at a very high price.
● The government has no control over the quality of the goods produced in underground markets, which in some cases can be dangerous for consumption, as with illegally distilled vodka and tainted baby milk powder.
● People break the rules: for example, under-age smokers and drinkers of alcohol can bypass the law by obtaining false identification cards. In the case of smoking, people may choose to smoke outside buildings and therefore inflict second-hand smoke on people entering and leaving the building.
● The fine or punishment for ignoring the ban must be enforced and set sufficiently high to discourage consumption of the good or service.

A third approach to correcting market failures is to use education and advertising. Many schools educate students about the negative side-effects of smoking and passive smoking. In many countries, cigarette packets must carry a government health warning that clearly explains the dangers of smoking. The Australian government has made it a legal requirement for cigarettes to be sold in packets covered in negative images about smoking. The images are graphic, aiming to educate and shock people in order to

Cigarettes in Australia are sold in identical olive-brown packets with the same typeface and covered with graphic images and health warnings. In the UK, a ban on tobacco products being displayed in shops came into effect in 2012

discourage them from smoking. If such methods are successful, the raised awareness of the dangers of smoking should reduce the demand for cigarettes (or any other demerit good), as shown in Figure 5.2.

Another example is the government using informative advertising and education to explain to people the benefits of eating at least five portions of fruit and vegetables each day. In Figure 5.3, the demand for fresh fruit and vegetables increases from D_1 to D_2 and the quantity demanded increases from Q_1 to Q_2. Healthier people in an economy should mean less absence from work and school, with fewer people using health services. Therefore healthy eating produces an external benefit for society.

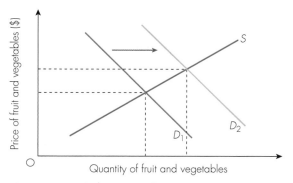

Figure 5.3 The impact of advertising on demand for fruit and vegetables

Schools around the world educate students about issues such as healthy eating, the negative impacts of driving gas/petrol-fuelled cars and the importance of conserving energy and recycling. Successful educational programmes should change the pattern of demand, thus helping to correct market failures.

Advantages of education and advertising to combat the problems of market failure include the following:

● Behaviour and consumption patterns of individuals and firms change – there is a rise in the consumption of merit goods and a fall in the demand for demerit goods. For example, people learn about the dangers of smoking, so fewer people smoke.
● Successful advertising may lead to a cultural change in the long term, such as healthier diets, an increase in use of electric cars, recycling, waste reduction and use of renewable energy.

Disadvantages of education and advertising to combat the problems of market failure include the following:

● Education and advertising have an opportunity cost – in other words, the money could have been spent on something else deemed more beneficial to the economy.
● Not all advertising and education is effective. For example, shock advertising tactics may not necessarily work on smokers and may be ignored.
● It can take a long time to educate people and for the advertised message to be accepted and acted upon.

> **Activity**
>
> Consider whether smoking is a problem in your country. Assess the degree of effectiveness of the measures taken by the government to reduce the number of smokers. What possible improvements could be made to the current situation? Take action by writing a letter to a local politician or a newspaper explaining your suggestions.

Conserving resources versus using resources

All economic activities involve social costs and benefits, at least to some extent, and every decision has an opportunity cost (see Chapter 1). For example, the decision to allow a firm to build a factory on a green field has a cost to the environment through the loss of green space, increased road traffic and potential pollution, but it also brings jobs to the area and creates business for related firms.

Production and consumption of goods and services uses the Earth's resources and can cause damage to the environment. It is therefore important that economic development is sustainable, which means that development today does not compromise the lives of future generations so that they cannot meet their own needs. Therefore, there is a potential conflict between the production of goods in the short term and the conservation of resources in the long term.

Case Study: The Deepwater Horizon disaster

On 20 April 2010 an explosion on an oil rig called Deepwater Horizon, owned by the company BP, caused approximately 4 million barrels of oil to spill into the Gulf of Mexico. Eleven oil rig workers died in the accident. The rig sank and the impact on the environment, people and businesses in the region was immense.

Many people, including fishermen, dock workers, restaurant owners and their employees, lost their livelihoods and jobs.

The damage to the surrounding coastline and wildlife was dramatic. There were endangered species of turtle and a rare species of sea horse living in the area, so measures had to be taken to ensure their survival.

Around 100 000 people have attempted to claim compensation from BP and many claims are still unresolved today. BP estimated that total damages would cost the firm $42 billion, and it was already committed to pay $32 billion.

Source: adapted from the *Guardian*, July 2010

Activity

Read the Deepwater Horizon disaster case study and identify as many examples of market failure and economic concepts as possible.

Exam practice

In Sri Lanka, economic growth has seen the increased use of pesticides and chemical fertilisers to increase the amount of crops produced. The growth of the tourism industry has brought about an increase in the construction of roads, hotels and guest houses. This has created jobs but at a cost to natural wildlife habitats.

1   Identify the social costs and benefits of economic growth in Sri Lanka.   [4]

2   Discuss the potential long-term impacts of economic growth in Sri Lanka and whether the benefits outweigh the costs.   [7]

Case Study: The Brazilian rainforests

According to Greenpeace, Brazilian supermarkets have banned the sale of meat produced from animals raised in rainforests. This is a move to reduce the amount of rainforest destroyed to make pasture for animals and soy plantations.

Private and social benefits

Private benefits are the benefits of production and consumption incurred by a firm, individual or government. For example, a car owner gains the benefits of driving the car and owning a means of private transport. Similarly, a person who owns a garden enjoys the personal benefits of having green space and plants, flowers and possibly vegetables to enjoy.

External benefits are the positive side-effects of production or consumption incurred by third parties, for which no money is paid by the beneficiary. For example, the sight and smell of a well-kept garden gives pleasure to a neighbour or a person walking past. The plants and trees also absorb carbon dioxide and therefore are good for the environment. Other examples of external benefits are education, training, health care and law enforcement.

When a person has a vaccination against tuberculosis, they receive the private benefit of being immune to the disease, but other people are also protected from this highly contagious disease. To eradicate diseases, many governments make it a legal requirement for children to be vaccinated against certain diseases before they can start school. Many governments provide such vaccinations free of charge to children.

This is an example of market failure because there are external benefits to society of vaccination programmes. If vaccinations were left to the choice of individuals, they would be under-consumed, mainly due to the price that would be charged for them. The true benefit of the vaccination is called the social benefit.

Social benefit = private benefit + external benefit

Activity

Discuss with a partner which of the following are examples of negative externalities and which are examples of positive externalities:
- dental health check-ups
- art museums
- consumption of soda/fizzy drinks
- overuse of antibiotics
- a person driving while smoking or eating
- family planning clinics

Study tips

Remember that the level of a subsidy is measured by the vertical distance between the two supply curves. The producer receives payment from the government and passes some of this income to consumers in the form of lower prices (shown by the distance $P_1 - P_2$ in Figure 5.4) and keeps the remainder.

Governments often subsidise goods and services to encourage consumption. For example, public transport might be subsidised to encourage people to use buses and trains rather than private cars. Figure 5.4 shows the impact of a subsidy on the demand for public transport. The bus and railway firms receive a sum of money from the government which lowers their production costs and causes the supply curve to shift from S_1 (pre-subsidy) to S_2 (post-subsidy). Price falls from P_1 to P_2 and the quantity demanded increases from Q_1 to Q_2. An increase in the use of public transport should lower congestion and reduce the amount of pollution caused by driving cars. Therefore the subsidy reduces external costs created by driving.

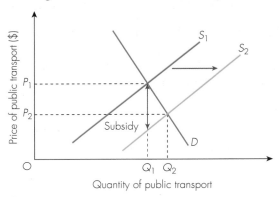

Figure 5.4   The effects of a producer subsidy

> **Case Study: Vaccinations in Hong Kong**
>
> The Hong Kong government subsidises the cost of annual flu vaccines for the very young and the elderly to encourage people in high-risk age groups to get vaccinated. The aim is to reduce the amount of flu in the wider community by targeting these age groups, so that fewer people need to be hospitalised for the treatment of flu. Vaccinations immunise people against certain diseases and therefore create positive spillover effects for the rest of the economy, resulting in less pressure on health care services.

Public expenditure versus private expenditure

In many countries, governments provide certain goods and services free of charge to their citizens (see Chapter 2), who may have paid for them indirectly through personal taxation. Examples include education, health care, public libraries, parks, museums, public roads and motorways (highways), garbage or refuse collection, street lighting, street signs and national defence.

Battleships are funded by the public sector from its national defence budget. HMS *Belfast* was used during the Second World War but has been decommissioned now and is used as a museum

There is a conflict between the provision of goods and services directly to people and asking them to pay for the goods and services. The law of demand (see Chapter 3) dictates that, as the price of a good or service rises, less of it will be consumed. Health care and education are under-consumed in some countries because people cannot afford to pay. In the short term this has a negative effect directly on the quality of their lives, and in the long term it causes a potential decrease in life expectancy and earnings potential (see Chapter 7). This impacts upon the whole of society because it means that human resources are not being used to their full capacity.

The advantages of government provision of goods and services are that:

- the goods and services are accessible to all people, regardless of their income or social status
- consumption of the goods and services has private benefits to the individual and external benefits enjoyed by third parties in society.

The disadvantages of government provision of goods and services are that:

- there is an opportunity cost, as the money could have been spent on something else, such as paying off government debt or possibly lowering the rate of taxation
- goods and services that are free of charge may be over-consumed, so long queues or shortages may arise (for example, the waiting list for a hip replacement operation in a government hospital may be very long)
- in the case of a shortage of supply due to excess demand, it can be difficult to decide who should be able to take advantage of the free government service
- some people (known as **free riders**) are able to take advantage of free goods and services without contributing to government revenue through paying taxes.

Exam practice

Scientific research has demonstrated the widespread social benefits of investment in health education and health care programmes to economies across the world, particularly in less economically developed countries such as Bangladesh.

1 Define the term 'social benefits'.   [2]
2 Discuss the short-term private costs and long-term social benefits of investing in health care in countries such as Bangladesh.   [7]

Chapter review questions

1 When and why does market failure occur?
2 What are the differences between merit and demerit goods?
3 How does traffic congestion cause a negative externality?
4 How can consumption of demerit goods be decreased?
5 What are the advantages and disadvantages of using taxation to deal with market failure?
6 How can a subsidy increase the demand for public transport?
7 What are the social benefits of the public provision of education?
8 What is the debate concerning the conservation of resources and the use of resources?
9 How do social benefits differ from private benefits of consumption or production?
10 What is the debate concerning public and private sector provision of goods and services?

Key terms

Demerit goods are goods or services which, when consumed, cause negative spillover effects in an economy (e.g. cigarette smoking, alcohol and gambling). Demerit goods are over-consumed due to imperfect consumer information about such goods.

External benefits are the positive side-effects of production or consumption incurred by third parties, for which no money is paid by the beneficiary.

External costs are the negative side-effects of production or consumption incurred by third parties, for which no compensation is paid.

Externalities (or **spillover effects**) occur where the actions of firms and individuals have either a positive or negative effect on third parties.

Free riders are people who take advantage of the goods or services provided by the government but have not contributed to government revenue through taxation.

Market failure occurs when the market forces of demand and supply fail to allocate resources efficiently and cause external costs or external benefits.

Merit goods are goods or services which, when consumed, create positive spillover effects in an economy (e.g. education, training and health care). Merit goods are under-consumed so government intervention is often needed.

Private benefits are the benefits of production and consumption enjoyed by a firm, individual or government.

Private costs of production and consumption are the actual costs of a firm, individual or government.

Social benefits are the true (or full) benefits of consumption or production: that is, the sum of private benefits and external benefits.

Social costs are the true (or full) costs of consumption or production: that is, the sum of private costs and external costs.

A **subsidy** is a sum of money given by the government to a producer to reduce the costs of production or to a consumer to reduce the price of consumption.

The individual as producer, consumer and borrower

Chapters

+3.96   98   18.76   2   58.92

+2.54   252   54.32   73   99.16

−2.13   86   98.65   8   34.18

+1.96   15   8.43   15   458.04

                       3.76   19   387.32

+3.32   24   65.12   7   673.54

+1.03   39   3   552.09

                       54   17.6   481.76

−3.45   15.31   2

               63   215.68

6 Money

The meaning of money

Money is any commodity which can be used as a **medium of exchange** that is accepted for the purchase of goods and services. In today's modern society, money includes officially issued banknotes and coins (collectively called **legal tender**), gold and bank account deposits. Money has the following characteristics:

- **Durability** – Money, such as banknotes and coins, should be fairly long lasting yet easily replaced if it becomes worn. Coins are highly durable and modern-day banknotes are made from polymer rather than paper. Polymer banknotes, first introduced in Australia in 1988, are significantly more durable and so are used extensively in countries such as Bermuda, New Zealand, Romania and Vietnam. Even so, a US dollar bill can be folded forward and back up to around 4000 times before it will tear. According to the USA's Federal Reserve, the typical $50 bill and $100 bill lasts 9 years

Polymer banknotes are widely used in Singapore, Brunei, Hong Kong and Australia

before it needs replacing and its coins survive in circulation for about 30 years.
- **Acceptability** – Money is widely recognised and accepted as a medium of payment for goods and services. Legal tender is the official money of a country (such as Canada's dollar or the UK's pound sterling).

  Other forms of money might also be accepted, such as tourists using US dollars. Gold is universally accepted as a form of money. By contrast, the Zimbabwean dollar ceased to be accepted as a medium of exchange in 2009 when the country, which had been suffering from civil unrest, experienced hyperinflation (see Chapter 18). In October 2008, Zimbabweans needed Z$2 621 984 228 to purchase US$1 worth of goods. Hyperinflation peaked a month later in November 2008 when average prices in Zimbabwe rose by 79 600 000 per cent within a month!
- **Divisibility** – As money is a measure of the value of goods and services, it must be divisible. Many economists and historians believe that cattle are the

Gold is universally accepted as a form of money

oldest form of money, with cows being used for trade as far back as 9000 BC. Cattle were still used as money in some African nations during the latter half of the twentieth century. However, cattle and livestock do not make 'useful' money as they are not truly divisible (a third of a cow is not really useful for any trader!).

- **Uniformity** – For money to be easily recognisable there must be uniformity within a country. This means all $50 banknotes will look virtually identical in terms of shape, size and design. The same applies to all legal tender denominations of banknotes and coins. Cows come in many sizes and shapes and each has a different value; cows are not a very uniform form of money. The first consistent form of money, cowry shells, was used in China over 3200 years ago. These seashells were used for mainly trading food, livestock and textiles.

- **Scarcity** – Money must be limited in supply in order for it to keep its value. Both seashells and salt have been used as money in the past, although the high level of supply meant that they soon lost much of their value as a medium of exchange. By contrast, silver and gold are better forms of money due to their scarcity. The supply of money, including banknotes and coins, is regulated by the country's central bank so that the money retains its value over time.

Cowry shells were used as money in sixteenth-century China

- **Portability** – Money must be conveniently portable. For example, the approximate weight of a banknote, regardless of its denomination, is just one gram. Whilst almost every country uses government-issued banknotes and coins as their official currency, there are other forms of money. For example, money in bank accounts and the use of credit cards enable payment to be made electronically, without the customer having to use cash. The first coins used as money appeared around 2000 BC. In those days, the value of coins was determined by their weight, which hindered their effectiveness as money due to the difficulties of portability.

Activity

1 Use the internet to find out about the hyperinflation experienced in Zimbabwe, which lasted around 5 years.
   a) Why did the Zimbabwean dollar cease to be used as money?
   b) Why do Zimbabweans today prefer to use currencies from other nations, such as the US dollar?
2 Discuss with a partner or as a class why the following products would not make 'good' money. Try to rank these in order of how many functions of money these products meet. Remember to justify your answers.
   a) Milk
   b) Cloth
   c) Fish
   d) Cigarettes

The functions of money

Economists suggest that there are four key **functions of money**:

- Money acts as a **medium of exchange** – For something to be considered as money it must function as a way to conduct trade. Money is widely recognised and accepted as a means of payment for goods and services.
- Money is a **measure of value** – Money is a unit of account, as it measures the market value of different goods and services. It is far more efficient for trading purposes to express the price of goods and services in dollars (or another monetary value) rather than using products such as cloth, shells, salt or livestock – all of which have been unsuccessful forms of money in history.
- Money is a **store of value** as it can be stored and used at a later date in the future. This means that money must be able to hold its purchasing power over time. Money therefore gives firms and households flexibility in the timing of their sales and their purchases, thus removing the urgency to trade straightaway.
- Money is a **standard of deferred payment** – This means that money is used as the standard for future (deferred) payments of debt. For example, loans taken out today are repaid in money at some time in the foreseeable future. Both the US dollar and the euro have been widely accepted standards for settling international debts.

> **Activity**
> To appreciate the need for money, try to explain why many economists argue that the invention of money is certainly one of the greatest inventions of all time.

Bartering and the need for exchange

In the absence of money, people have to use a barter system in order to trade goods and services. **Bartering** is the act of swapping items in exchange for other items through a process of bargaining and negotiation. For example, someone might trade five sacks of rice for one cow, or four chickens for a sheep.

- The key problem with a barter system is the need for a **double coincidence of wants** – the person with chickens must find a trader who wants chickens in exchange for their sheep. As two people engaged in a trade must both want what the other person is offering, bartering is highly inefficient.
- A second problem with bartering is that of divisibility – half a sheep or two-thirds of a chicken is not very useful for traders.
- A third problem is that of portability – compare the portability of a sheep or fish with that of paper money (banknotes).

The problems associated with bartering meant that countries around the world eventually developed the use of commodity money, such as cowry shells, grain and cloth. For much of history, precious metals such as gold and silver have served a monetary role.

> **Activity**
> Bartering still takes place in some parts of the world today. Discuss with a partner the problems associated with bartering as a means of trade and exchange in modern societies.

This print shows Scandinavian and Russian traders bartering their wares

Exam practice

1 Define the term 'bartering'.   [2]
2 With reference to the functions of money, explain why bartering is an
   ineffective method of trading.   [6]

The functions of central banks

The **central bank** of a country is the monetary authority that oversees and manages the nation's **money supply** and banking system. Examples of central banks are the European Central Bank (for the Eurozone countries), the USA's Federal Reserve, the Bank of England, the People's Bank of China and the Reserve Bank of India. These banks are responsible for overseeing the **monetary policies** (see Chapter 16) of their respective countries, including being responsible for the nation's entire money supply and the manipulation of interest rates to affect the economy.

> **Case Study: The Federal Reserve**
>
> The Federal Reserve (also known informally as the 'Fed') is the central bank of the USA. It was formed in December 1913, mainly in response to financial crises around that time. The main shareholders of the Federal Reserve are the major banks in the USA, although the exact shareholdings are not made public. According to the Federal Reserve's educational website:
> * The dollar was officially used as the USA's unit of currency in 1785, although the first dollar coin was issued in 1782.
> * The Federal Reserve produces approximately 26 million banknotes each day, with a face value of around $907 million.
> * Over 90 per cent of currency used in the USA consists of Federal Reserve banknotes.
> * The Secret Service was created during the USA's Civil War to fight against counterfeit money.
> * It costs the US government only about 6.4 cents to produce each banknote.
> * The average lifespan of a Federal Reserve $1 banknote is just 21 months whereas the lifespan of a $100 banknote averages 7.5 years.
>
> Source: adapted from **www.federalreserveeducation.org**

Activity

What interesting facts and figures can you find out about the central bank in your country?

Central banks tend to have the following four key functions:

- **The sole issuer of banknotes and coins** – In almost every country, the central bank has the sole right to issue legal tender in its own country: in other words, it is the only authority that can print banknotes and mint coins. This helps to bring uniformity to, and improves public confidence in, the country's monetary system.

    One rare exception to this function is in Hong Kong where three commercial banks (Standard Chartered, HSBC and Bank of China) have note-issuing rights, although the Hong Kong Monetary Authority maintains overall control of the country's banking system, including the circulation of banknotes and coins.

- **The government's bank** – The central bank operates as a banker to the government, performing the same functions as a commercial bank does for its customers. Hence, as the government's bank, it maintains the bank accounts of the central government, such as receiving deposits from government, making short-term loans to the government and making payments for items of government expenditure (see Chapter 16). The central bank also manages public-sector debt and represents the government in the international financial markets, such as foreign exchange. This has become an important function of central banks because such intervention can help to stabilise the external value of a nation's currency (see Chapter 24).

- **The bankers' bank** – The central bank acts as the bank for other banks in the country. This function includes overseeing the cash reserves of commercial banks. This means that all banks in the country must have their accounts with the central bank, enabling the central bank easily to manage the claims made by banks against each other. For example, payment made by a Citibank customer writing a cheque to another customer with an HSBC account goes through the central bank's clearing system – the central bank debits the account of the Citibank customer and credits the account of the HSBC customer. This cheque clearing function of the central bank reduces the need for cash withdrawals, thus enabling commercial banks to function more efficiently. In addition, it also allows the central bank to have a better overview of the liquidity position (the ability to convert assets into cash) of the country's commercial banks.

- **The lender of last resort** – Given that the authorities require all commercial banks to keep a certain percentage of their cash balances as deposits with the central bank, these cash reserves can be used by the country's banking system during financial emergencies. This function helps to build public confidence in the country's banking system. For example, if a certain commercial bank faces temporary financial difficulties, it can, as a last resort, seek financial assistance from the central bank. This helps to ensure the bank does not collapse, protects jobs and thus safeguards the nation's banking system and economic welfare.

Case Study: Bank bailouts

A **bailout** refers to a loan or financial assistance provided to a company (or country) which faces major financial difficulties or the threat of bankruptcy. The global financial crises of 1997 and 2008 caused the collapse of hundreds of banks all over the world, over a number of years. The financial bailout of many banks by central banks was seen as a necessity to prevent huge job losses and socioeconomic failures on a mass scale.

Central banks can bail out banks through various means, such as providing subsidies or low-interest loans to commercial banks in need of liquidity (cash assets). Bailouts in Indonesia (1997) and Cyprus (2012) proved to be the most expensive in economic history, with the latter country spending $10 billion bailing out its banks – this represents a huge 56 per cent of Cyprus's $18 billion GDP (see Figure 6.1).

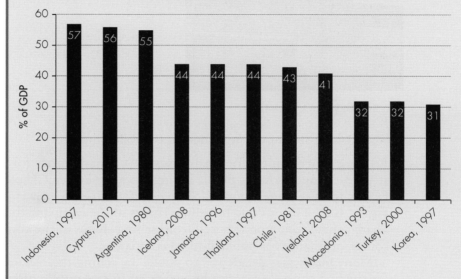

Figure 6.1   The biggest bank bailouts

Activity

1 Discuss as a group the reasons for and against central banks bailing out commercial banks facing a financial emergency.
2 Produce A3 coloured posters of the arguments (for and against) and use these as classroom displays.

The functions of stock exchanges

A **stock exchange** (also known as a **bourse**) is an institutional marketplace for trading the shares of public limited companies (see Chapter 10). It provides a platform for individuals, organisations and governments to buy and sell shares.

Examples of stock exchanges are the New York Stock Exchange (NYSE), London Stock Exchange, Frankfurt Stock Exchange, Shanghai Stock Exchange and Bombay Stock Exchange. The efficient functioning of a stock exchange helps to create business and consumer confidence, thereby boosting investment opportunities in the economy.

The Bombay Stock Exchange

Functions of a stock exchange include the following:

- **Raising share capital for businesses** – As a marketplace for buying shares, the stock exchange provides public limited companies (see Chapter 10) with the facility to raise huge amounts of finance for business growth and expansion (see Figure 6.2). This is done by selling shares in the company to the general public. Share capital (the money raised from selling shares in the company) is the main source of finance for public limited companies.

    Many businesses decide to 'go public' by selling their shares on a stock exchange for the first time – a practice known as an **initial public offering (IPO)**. Popular IPOs are heavily oversubscribed (the quantity demanded outstrips the quantity supplied) and this forces up the share price. Existing companies that are listed on a stock exchange can raise more share capital by selling additional sales in a share issue (or a share placement). However, by issuing more shares, ownership and control of the company become weakened.

Table 6.1   The world's largest initial public offerings

Company	Year	Share capital raised (US$bn)
Agriculture Bank of China	2010	22.10
Industrial and Commercial Bank of China	2006	21.97
American International Assurance	2010	20.51
Visa Inc.	2008	19.65
NTT Mobile Communications Network	1998	18.05

Source: adapted from Reuters.com and Forbes

- **Facilitating company growth** – In addition to making an IPO, existing companies can choose to sell additional shares to raise funds to finance their growth. This process is known as a share issue. For example, Petrobras – Brazil's largest oil company – managed to raise $70 billion from selling additional shares to the general public in September 2010.

The stock exchange also functions to facilitate the growth of companies through mergers and acquisitions (see Chapter 14). For instance, Walt Disney Company acquired Lucasfilm (creators of the best-selling Star Wars franchise) via the New York Stock Exchange in 2012 for $4.05 billion.

Darth Vader and other Star Wars characters ring the opening bell at the New York Stock Exchange

- **Facilitating the sale of government bonds** – Governments can raise capital to fund their development projects via the stock exchange, which sells securities known as bonds (a type of loan). Bondholders do not have ownership rights, but earn interest based on the number of bonds bought and the prevailing interest rate. Government bonds can be bought and sold through the stock exchange by the general public, such as individuals, companies and other governments. The finance raised is often used to fund infrastructure projects such as the construction of motorways (highways), sewage and water treatment systems, and public housing projects.
- **Price mechanism for trading shares** – Share prices are generally determined by the relative forces of demand and supply (see Chapter 3). Price fluctuations and the valuation of share prices are handled by the stock exchange. This function of the stock exchange provides important and up-to-date information to both buyers and sellers in the stock market.
- **Safety of transaction** – All companies that trade on a stock exchange are regulated. The share dealings of public limited companies are defined in accordance with the country's legal framework. This helps to boost the level of confidence in buying and selling shares. Thus, this function of a stock exchange can have a large impact on the economic growth prospects of a country as it facilitates capital formation (investment).

> **Activity**
> Use the internet to find out the world's five largest stock exchanges. What are the benefits to businesses that are listed (trade their shares) on large, well-known stock exchanges?

Exam practice

In May 2012, social media giant Facebook's initial public offering (IPO) on the New York NASDAQ Stock Exchange raised $16 billion (the third largest amount in US history) from investors buying shares at $38 apiece. This led to the company's valuation standing at $104 billion, the largest valuation of a newly listed public limited company to date.

1 Define the term 'initial public offering'. [2]

2 Explain two functions of a stock exchange such as the NASDAQ Stock Exchange. [4]

3 Comment on why Facebook might have decided to float its shares on the New York Stock Exchange. [4]

The functions of commercial banks

A **commercial bank** is a retail bank that provides financial services to its customers, such as accepting savings deposits and approving bank loans. Examples of commercial banks are listed in Table 6.2.

All commercial banks are responsible for maintaining the deposits of their account holders. Their transactions are socially and legally governed by the central bank. Commercial banking started over 200 years ago when goldsmiths (metal workers specialising in precious metals such as gold) operated as banks. Banking itself can be traced as far back as 2000 BC when merchants in Assyria and Babylonia used grain loans to farmers and other traders. Modern commercial banking using the internet (e-banking) did not start until 1995.

Table 6.2 The world's largest commercial banks, 2012

Rank	Bank	Country
1	Industrial and Commercial Bank of China (ICBC)	China
2	China Construction Bank	China
3	Wells Fargo & Co.	USA
4	Hong Kong and Shanghai Banking Corporation (HSBC)	UK
5	Agricultural Bank of China	China
6	JP Morgan Chase	USA
7	Bank of China	China
8	Itau Unibanco	Brazil
9	Citigroup	USA
10	Commonwealth	Australia

Source: **www.relbanks.com**

The functions of commercial banks can be split into two categories: primary and secondary (or general utility) functions.

The **primary functions** of commercial banks include the following:

- **Accepting deposits** – Commercial banks accept deposits from their customers, including private individuals, businesses and governments. Examples include **sight deposits** (which are payable on demand) and **time deposits** (which are deposits that are payable after a fixed time period such as 6 months or a year). Time deposits tend to attract higher rates of interest for deposit holders than sight deposits. Businesses deposit their cash in commercial banks for the convenience of their own financial operations, such as paying their suppliers and employees.

- **Making advances** – Commercial banks provide advances (loans) to their customers. These advances include overdrafts (a banking service that allows registered customers to withdraw more money than they actually have in their account) and mortgages (long-term secured loans for the purchase of assets such as commercial and residential property).

- **Credit creation** – This describes the process by which banks increase the supply of money in an economy by making money available to borrowers. Credit allows the borrower (or debtor) to gain purchasing power (money) now with the promise to pay the lender (or creditor) at a future time. Credit creation enables commercial banks to generate considerable additional purchasing power from their cash deposits. While central banks can print money, they do not create credit; this is a key function that distinguishes commercial banks from other financial institutions, such as insurance companies and investment banks.

The **secondary functions** (or general utility functions) of commercial banks include:

- collecting and clearing cheques on behalf of their clients
- offering additional financial services, such as tax advice, foreign exchange dealings and the buying and selling of shares
- providing safety deposit boxes for customers to safeguard highly valued possessions, including items of jewellery and important documents such as wills
- providing money transfer facilities, such as transferring money to an overseas bank account or paying various bills, such as telephone, electricity, gas and water bills
- providing credit card facilities for the convenience of customers – both private individuals and commercial clients
- providing internet banking facilities, such as online bill payments, online bank transfers between bank accounts and the online purchase of shares and foreign currencies.

Credit cards allow customers to buy now and pay later, so are widely used as a medium of exchange

Exam practice

According to *The Economist*, China's economy is expected to overtake the USA's by as early as 2018. Multinational companies hoping to make the most of this opportunity have been investing in China via the Shanghai Stock Exchange. Commercial banks such as the Industrial and Commercial Bank of China (ICBC) and the Hong Kong and Shanghai Banking Corporation (HSBC) also have an increasingly important role in the development of the Chinese economy. Nevertheless, the trading of the renminbi, China's official currency, is still closely monitored by the People's Bank of China – the central bank.

1   Describe the functions of a commercial bank such as ICBC or HSBC.   [4]
2   Explain the key functions of central banks such as the People's Bank of China.   [4]
3   Explain how the Shanghai Stock Exchange can play a key role in the economic development of the Chinese economy.   [4]

Chapter review questions
1   What is meant by money and what are its main characteristics?
2   What are the key functions of money?
3   What is a central bank and what are its key functions?
4   What is a stock exchange and what are its main functions?
5   What are commercial banks and what are their main functions?
6   How does a central bank differ from commercial banks?

Key terms

Bartering is the act of swapping items in exchange for other items through a process of bargaining and negotiation.

A **central bank** is the monetary authority that oversees and manages the supply of money and the banking system of the nation.

Commercial banks are retail banks that provide financial services to their customers, such as accepting savings account deposits and approving bank loans.

Functions of money describes the role that money plays in the economy: money is a *medium of exchange*, a *store of value* and a *measure of value* (or unit of account).

Money is anything that is widely accepted as a means of exchange (and acts as a measure and store of value).

Money supply refers to the amount of money in the economy at a particular point in time.

A **stock exchange** is an institutional marketplace for trading the shares of public limited companies.

(7) Labour markets

By the end of this chapter, you should be able to:
- identify the factors affecting an individual's choice of occupation (wage factors and non-wage factors)
- describe likely changes in earnings over time for an individual
- describe the differences in earnings between different groups of workers (male/female; skilled/unskilled; private/public; agricultural/manufacturing/services)
- describe the benefits and disadvantages of specialisation for the individual.

Taken from Cambridge International Examinations Syllabus (IGCSE 0455/O Level 2281)
© Cambridge International Examinations

Influences on an individual's choice of occupation

Most people work at some point in their lives. An individual's choice of occupation depends on many factors, which can be categorised as wage and non-wage factors.

Wage factors affecting choice of occupation

The level of **salary** or **wage** that a person receives in return for their labour is a major influence on their choice of occupation. Table 7.1 outlines the different methods of payment by which a worker may be paid in return for their labour.

Table 7.1 Different methods of payment for labour

Methods of payment	Explanation	Examples
Wages	Wages are paid hourly or weekly, so are a variable cost to firms	Part-time workers in a shop or restaurant (e.g. $7 per hour)
Salary	Salaries are paid monthly at a fixed value, so are fixed costs	Full-time job (e.g. teachers, shop managers and nurses)
Piece rate	A fixed amount paid per item produced or sold	Workers producing individual items in a factory (e.g. $2 per garment completed)
Commission	A percentage of the value of products or services sold	Real estate agents earning 1% of the value of each property that they sell
Bonus	An additional lump sum of money paid during year, usually dependent upon performance	Royal Bank of Scotland and Barclays paid 523 staff members more than £1m ($1.56m) in bonuses in 2013
Profit-related pay	Payment related to the profits earned by a firm	A partner in a law firm may receive 20% of the annual profits
Share options	Workers receive shares in the firm, so they have an incentive to work hard so that the firm is profitable	Public limited companies
Fringe benefits (or perks)	Additional benefits, which have a monetary value	Pensions, health insurance, company car, laptop, mobile phone, education for children, or membership of a health club

Non-wage factors

Non-wage factors are also a major influence on an individual's choice of occupation, as a person may be motivated by money in the short term but in the long term they will also want to feel happy and motivated at work. Non-wage factors that influence an individual's choice of occupation include the following:

- **Level of challenge** – does the job require thinking skills or is it repetitive and boring?
- **Career prospects** – will there be progression within the firm or will a person have to change jobs to be promoted?
- **Level of danger involved** – is the job dangerous? For example, some people face a high degree of risk at work, such as lifeboat rescue teams, firefighters, window cleaners and scaffold erectors.

Worker erecting bamboo scaffolding in Hong Kong

- **The length of training required** – Some jobs require few skills, such as cleaners and shop assistants. By contrast, other jobs require years of training, such as electrical engineers, plastic surgeons, pilots, accountants, lawyers and dentists.
- **The level of education required** – Some jobs require no or minimal education whereas other jobs require post-graduate levels of education (such as university professors).
- **Recognition in the job** – does the worker get praise and recognition for their performance at work? If a worker feels respected at work, they may be motivated to work harder.
- **Personal satisfaction gained from the job** – This is important because if a worker feels satisfied and happy in their work, they may work harder and stay in the job longer. Voluntary work might be carried out by people who are happy to work for no pay, as the reward they get is the personal satisfaction of working for a charity, such as taking care of the elderly or sick.
- **The level of experience required** – Some jobs require no or minimal experience whereas other jobs require a minimum amount of experience (such as judges and law-makers).

Activity

Interview several adults and ask them the financial and non-financial reasons why they chose their occupation. Share your findings with the rest of the class.

Changes in earnings over a lifetime

Earnings change over a person's lifetime (see Table 7.2) for the following reasons:

- The level of education a person has tends to affect, in most cases, their earnings and earning potential (see Table 7.3).
- Inexperienced workers, such as graduates in their first year of work, earn less than experienced workers.
- Salaries and wages usually increase with experience and time spent working at a firm.
- After workers reach the peak of their career, their salaries and wages tend to remain fairly constant.
- After retirement, earnings fall and people are dependent on their pensions and savings to cover their living expenses.

Table 7.2 Earnings by age, full-time workers (UK, 2010–2012)

Age category	2010 (£)	2011 (£)	2012 (£)
All employees	25 882	26 170	26 462
16–17	–	–	7 703
18–21	13 623	13 189	13 532
22–29	20 884	20 657	20 901
30–39	28 203	28 315	28 568
40–49	28 892	29 367	29 791
50–59	27 152	27 634	27 744
60+	23 585	24 000	24 715

Source: adapted from Office for National Statistics

Table 7.3 After-tax earnings by educational attainment (USA, 2011–2012)

	Less than college graduate		College graduate	
	Less than high school graduate	High school graduate	Bachelor's degree	Master's, professional, doctoral degree
Mean income after taxes ($)	32 564	45 903	89 354	108 532

Source: adapted from US Department for Labor

Exam practice

1 With reference to Table 7.2, explain why the potential earnings of an individual fall after the age of 60. [2]

2 With reference to Table 7.3, explain how education impacts upon earnings of an individual. [4]

Study tips

When you are answering questions about the demand for, and supply of, labour, remember that workers *supply* labour to firms and firms *demand* workers to produce goods and services.

Wage determination

Wages are determined by the interaction of demand for labour and the supply of workers in an industry. For example, the combination of the high demand (ability and willingness to pay) for, and the low supply of, neurosurgeons means their pay is very high.

The demand for labour

The **demand for labour** is a **derived demand**. This means that labour is demanded for the goods and services it produces and not for itself. For example, bakers are demanded for the bread they bake, not for the sake of hiring bakers.

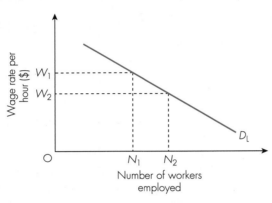

Figure 7.1 The demand for labour curve

Figure 7.1 shows a downward-sloping demand for labour (D_L) curve. When the wage rate falls from W_1 to W_2, the number of workers employed increases from N_1 to N_2. This is because firms (employers) can afford to hire more workers when the wage rate is lower.

The factors that influence the demand for labour include the following:

- The level of total demand in the economy (known as **aggregate demand**) – During a boom or period of economic growth, the demand for goods and services, and therefore the demand for labour to produce them, is higher than during a recession or period of declining growth.
- An increase in the productivity of labour (output per worker over a period of time) – The demand for workers increases as their productivity increases through training and changes to production methods (see Chapter 11). For example, allowing workers to make suggestions about how their working practices can be improved and putting the suggestions into practice can motivate workers, as they feel empowered to make changes. Recognition of workers' achievements can also be motivational and increase productivity. Consider how praise from your teachers or parents can impact upon your own attitude to learning!
- The **cost of labour** as compared with the cost of machinery and technology that could replace the labour – Although technology and machinery are expensive to purchase in the short run, they can save money for the business in the long run. For example, many firms have replaced security guards with security cameras. Cameras are cheaper in the long run and they do not need toilet breaks, although they do break down occasionally! Car manufacturers use robotic equipment and machinery that can operate 24 hours a day.

Security cameras can be more cost-effective than security guards in the long run

National minimum wage legislation

A **national minimum wage** (NMW) is the lowest amount a firm can pay its workers, as set by the government. Any firm that pays workers less than the legal minimum wage is breaking the law.

Since May 2013, the NMW in Hong Kong has been HK$30 (around $3.85) per hour for all workers. In Australia, the NMW is AUD15.96 (around $16.21) per hour or AUD606.4 (around $625.35) per week. For those aged below 21, the NMW is slightly lower (see Table 7.4).

Table 7.4   Minimum wage rates per hour in Australia, 2013 (US$)

Age of worker	NMW (US$)
Under 16	6.10
16	7.85
17	9.59
18	11.34
19	13.70
20	16.21

Source: Fair Work Ombudsman, Australia

In Figure 7.2 the **equilibrium wage rate** before the national minimum wage is W_1 and N_1 workers are demanded and supplied. If the government introduces a NMW which is above the equilibrium wage at W_2 then the quantity of labour supplied to the market increases from N_1 to N_2 as more workers are prepared to work for a higher wage rate.

However, the quantity of labour demanded falls from N_1 to N_3 because firms (employers) are less able or willing to pay as many workers at a higher wage rate. As the quantity supplied of labour is greater than the quantity demanded, there is a surplus of labour at a wage rate of W_2. Thus, if the NMW is set too high, this may lead to unemployment in the economy.

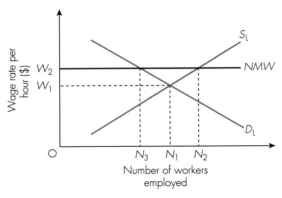

Figure 7.2 National minimum wage

Activity

1 Suggest reasons why the minimum wage in Australia may be less for younger workers than for workers aged 21 and over. Discuss possible reasons why the NMW is lower in Hong Kong than in Australia.

2 Find out the minimum wage in your country or a country of your choice and consider whether a job paying the NMW is sufficient to live on.

The advantages and disadvantages of a national minimum wage are listed in Table 7.5.

Table 7.5 The advantages and disadvantages of a national minimum wage

Advantages	Disadvantages
• Workers receive a fair wage for an hour's work and are not exploited by employers. • Unemployed people may have an incentive to work, as the wage may be more attractive than relying on welfare payments. • Low-income earners may have more money to spend and this may increase consumption in the economy, thus easing any fears that higher wages (costs of production) might cause unemployment.	• Workers who earn more than the minimum wage (perhaps due to their seniority) may request a higher wage rate to maintain the wage differential between them and workers who earn less than they do. For example, when cleaners in an office receive a pay rise as a result of an increase in the NMW, other office staff may ask for a wage increase to maintain the difference between their wages and that of the cleaners. This causes an even larger increase in the cost of labour for firms. • Unemployment might increase because firms could face higher wage bills as a result of increased wage rates. Therefore, their demand for labour (ability and willingness to employ workers) will fall. Alternatively, firms might purchase machinery and equipment to reduce the number of workers required. This might cause technological unemployment in the economy (see Chapter 19).

Government interference in labour market

- **Employment rights** – Governments impose laws to protect the rights of workers and employers, and these laws vary between countries. Laws are designed to prevent discrimination against workers due to gender, race, religion and disability, and also to protect the rights of employers and their ability to hire and fire workers.
- **Trade union legislation** – Governments can reduce the powers of trade unions in order to make labour markets more flexible and efficient (see Chapter 8). This happened in the UK during the 1980s when Margaret Thatcher was prime minister, and many countries have followed her lead. Trade unions now have less bargaining power and are less powerful generally.

1 May is still celebrated around the world as International Workers' Day. Indonesian workers hold a peaceful rally in Jakarta during the annual May Day march, demanding better pay and conditions of employment

> **Activity**
>
> Investigate the rights and responsibilities of employers and employers in your country. Share your findings with the rest of the class.

Factors affecting the supply of labour

The **labour supply** in an economy consists of people who are of working age and who are willing and able to work. This does not include those who are in full-time education or those who do not work by choice, such as housewives or househusbands.

Figure 7.3 shows an upward-sloping supply of labour (S_L) curve. If the wage rate in an industry increases from W_1 to W_2 the number of workers willing to work will increase from N_1 to N_2 because workers are attracted by higher wages.

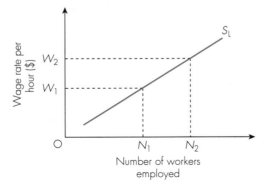

Figure 7.3 The supply of labour curve

It is possible, at least in theory, that the S_L curve can be backward bending. Figure 7.4 shows that high wage rates will cause workers to work longer hours to increase their earnings up to a certain point. As wage rates increase from W_1 to W_2 the number of hours worked increases from H_1 to H_2. However, as wages increase from W_2 to W_3 the number of hours worked falls from H_2 to H_3 because there is a trade-off between work and leisure time. At W_3 a person can work fewer hours yet have a higher income than at W_2. The **backward-bending supply of labour curve** therefore occurs when wage rates rise to a high enough point to allow people to work less and enjoy more leisure hours.

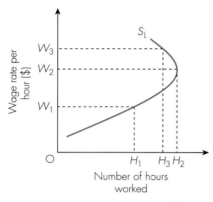

Figure 7.4   The backward-bending supply of labour curve

The structure of the labour supply varies between countries and depends on the following factors.

Labour force participation rate

The **labour force participation rate** is the percentage of the working population that is working, rather than unemployed. It is influenced by:

- the number of full-time and part-time workers in the labour force
- the number of women in the workforce
- the age distribution of the workforce (also see Chapter 22)
- the official retirement age of the country.

Table 7.6 shows examples of the labour participation rate, female labour participation rate (percentage of females working) and male labour participation rate in various countries.

Table 7.6   Labour participation rates, selected countries:

Country	Labour participation rate (%)	Male labour participation rate (%)	Female labour participation rate (%)
Vietnam	77	81	73
Bangladesh	71	84	57
Mauritius	60	76	44
Nigeria	56	63	48
Hong Kong	60	68	51

Source: adapted from the World Bank

Availability and level of welfare benefits

Welfare benefits are paid to the unemployed. However, if welfare benefits are high and readily available, this can discourage people from seeking work because the opportunity cost of not working and receiving welfare payments is too high. Governments try to regulate who can receive benefits to prevent disincentives to work. For example, in the UK a person must prove that they are actively seeking work if they are to continue to receive welfare payments.

Changing social climate

In many countries, more women are entering the workforce and delaying having families while more men are looking after the home and children. As a result of falling birth rates, some countries have ageing populations (see Chapter 22). These factors affect the composition of the workforce. Such countries may have to rely on immigration to ensure that they have workers with the required skills in the future.

Geographical mobility

Geographical mobility refers to the willingness and ability of a person to relocate from one part of a country to another for work. Some people may not be geographically mobile for the following reasons:

- **Family commitments** – People may not want to relocate as they want to be near their family and friends. There may be other commitments such as schooling arrangements for children (it can be highly disruptive to the education of children who have to move to a school in a different town or country).
- **Costs of living may vary between regions** – If costs of living are too high in a another location, it may be uneconomical for a person to relocate there. For example, a bus driver may find it impossible to relocate from the countryside to the city because house prices are much higher in the city and therefore they would not be able to purchase a home. By contrast, a banker may be offered a relocation allowance to move to another city and his or her potential earnings are much higher, so the banker has greater geographical mobility than the bus driver.

Exam practice

In some countries around the world there are shortages of people with particular skills. For example:
- There is a global shortage of doctors and nurses.
- Belgium and the UK have a shortage of chefs.
- Nordic countries have a shortage of psychologists.

In 2013 there were 200 million international migrants, including nurses trained in the Philippines, who were prepared to relocate to take advantage of employment opportunities.

Source: BBC News

1 Suggest two reasons why there is a global shortage of doctors and nurses. [4]
2 Analyse the reasons why nurses trained in the Philippines may relocate to take advantage of employment opportunities. [6]
3 Examine how countries can attract individuals to professions in which they have a shortage of workers. [6]

Occupational mobility

Occupational mobility refers to the ease with which a person is able to change between jobs. The degree of occupational mobility depends on the cost and length of training required to change profession (see the case study below).

> **Activity**
>
> Use the BBC Interactive Guide (**www.bbc.co.uk/news/business-21938085**) to investigate global employment opportunities in selected countries around the world.

> **Case Study: Occupational mobility**
>
> These cases demonstrate how varied people's occupational mobility can be:
> - A banker decides to retrain as an economics teacher. He takes a 12-month postgraduate teacher training course, which typically involves two 7-week blocks of teaching in a school. The banker is able to fund his training through savings earned while working in the banking industry.
> - An 18-year-old student decides to apply to university to become a doctor. She is willing to take out a student loan to pay for the 7-year course and cover her living expenses while she is at university because of her career prospects and high potential earnings in the future.
> - A coal miner loses his job in Chile when the mine closes. Having worked in the mine for over 30 years, he needs to consider retraining. He may find it difficult to be occupationally mobile as he lacks other skills and there are few jobs in the local area.

Wage determination

For the vast majority of jobs, wages are determined by the interaction of the demand for, and supply of, labour (see Figure 7.5).

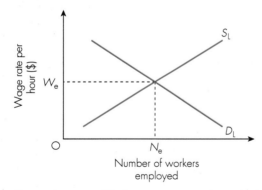

Figure 7.5 Equilibrium wage rate in an industry

The **equilibrium wage rate** is determined when the wage rate workers are willing to work for equals the wage rate that firms (employers) are prepared to pay: that is, the demand for labour is equal to the supply of labour. In Figure 7.5 the equilibrium wage rate is W_e and N_e workers are employed. Changes in the demand for, or supply of, labour in an industry will therefore change the equilibrium wage rate.

Differences in earnings

Differences in earnings between skilled and unskilled workers

In general, skilled workers earn more than unskilled workers due to their relatively higher demand and relatively lower supply. Table 7.7 shows some of the highest- and lowest-paid occupations in the UK (all figures expressed as pre-tax weekly earnings for the median full-time worker).

Table 7.7   Earnings for selected occupations in the UK, April 2012

Highest-paid professions			Lowest paid professions		
Rank	Occupation	Weekly wage (£)	Rank	Occupation	Weekly wage (£)
1	Aircraft pilots and flight engineers	1558.8	1	Leisure and theme park attendants	245.0
2	Chief executives and senior officials	1546.8	2	Hairdressers and barbers	246.1
3	Marketing and sales directors	1264.6	3	Bar staff	252.0
4	Information technology and telecommunications directors	1200.1	4	Waiting staff, launderers and dry cleaners	252.3
5	Air traffic controllers and legal professionals	1169.7	5	Kitchen and catering assistants	252.3

Source: adapted from Office for National Statistics

The data in Table 7.7 show that unskilled occupations (such as bar staff and waiters) earn less on average than skilled workers (such as medical practitioners and air traffic controllers). This is because there is a large supply of people able to work as waiters due to few skills being required, but to be a doctor requires a university degree and professional training. Therefore, the supply of doctors is lower than that of waiters. This is illustrated in Figure 7.6.

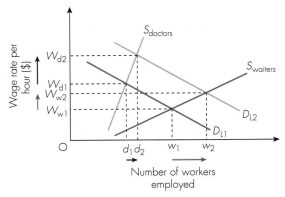

Figure 7.6 The difference in the equilibrium wage rates of waiters and doctors

Figure 7.6 shows the demand for, and supply of, waiters and doctors in an economy. Waiters are elastic in supply (S_{waiters}) because if the demand for waiters increases from D_{L1} to D_{L2} the percentage change in quantity supplied (w_1 to w_2) will be greater than the increase in wages (W_{w1} to W_{w2}), as indicated by the red arrows. This is because the job requires few skills and therefore it will be relatively easy to increase the supply of waiters in the short term.

By contrast, doctors are inelastic in supply (S_{doctors}). If demand for doctors increases from D_{L1} to D_{L2} the percentage change in quantity supplied (d_1 to d_2) of doctors in the short term will be less than the increase in wages (W_{d1} to W_{d2}). This is because the level of qualifications and length of training required make it difficult to increase the supply of doctors in the short term. A relatively large increase in wages is required to attract people to study and train as doctors, as illustrated by the blue arrows.

Differences in earnings between male and female workers

In literally all countries, the average earnings of males differ from the average earnings of females. Table 7.8 shows the differences in mean gross annual earnings (average pre-tax income) between male and female workers in the UK. The figures are for full-time workers.

Table 7.8 Differences in male and female working hours and earnings (UK, 2011–2012)

Gender	Males		Females	
Year	2011	2012	2011	2012
Median gross annual earnings (£)	28 393	28 713	22 765	23 074
Median gross weekly earnings (£)	538.4	545.80	442.6	448.60
Mean hourly earnings (£)	16.44	16.50	13.91	14.05
Median total weekly paid hours	40.20	40.10	37.1	37.30

Source: adapted from Office for National Statistics

Table 7.8 shows that there is a noticeable difference between the average wage of male and female workers. This pattern occurs throughout the world. Possible reasons for the difference in male and female earnings include the following:

- There are more women in part-time work than men, so their earnings are lower on average.
- Women take career breaks to have children and therefore miss out on promotional opportunities.
- Women may accept low-paid and part-time jobs, as hours are flexible and can fit in with childcare arrangements.
- Women may face discrimination at work.

However, times are changing for females, especially those in more economically developed countries such as the UK:

- In the UK's Financial Time Stock Exchange (FTSE) 100 firms, 17.3 per cent had female directors in April 2013 – an increase from 12.5 per cent in 2011.
- There are more females than males in the UK enrolled on veterinary science courses and in subjects associated with medicine at university.
- More than half of the headteachers (principals) in the UK are now females.

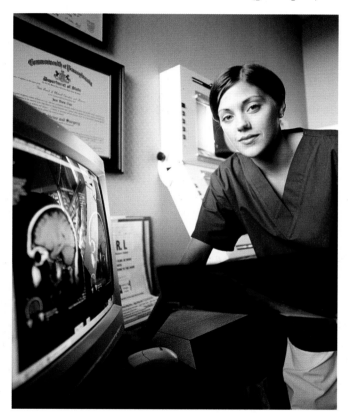

Female participation rates are increasing in many parts of the world

Differences in earnings between private and public sector workers

Workers in the private and public sectors tend to earn different wages. Table 7.9 shows the differences in earnings between full-time workers in the public and private sectors of the UK in 2012.

Table 7.9 Differences in private- and public-sector earnings (UK, 2012)

Sector	Private sector		Public sector	
Year	2011	2012	2011	2012
Median gross annual earnings (£)	24 895	25 240	28 774	28 930
Median gross weekly earnings (£)	474.10	479.10	555.80	564.60
Median hourly earnings (£)	11.55	11.75	14.86	15.07

Source: adapted from Office for National Statistics

> **Study tips**
>
> As Table 7.9 shows, it is incorrect to assume that those in the private sector get paid more than those in the public sector. This depends on many variables, such as the level of qualifications, skills and experience of the workers.

In theory, people in the private sector can earn more than workers in the public sector. In many countries, salaries in the public sector are typically less than those which can be earned in the private sector, but public-sector jobs are more secure and are accompanied by a pension in retirement. Examples of public-sector jobs are teachers, nurses, police officers, fire service officers and civil servants.

Private-sector jobs typically have higher earning potential as private individuals and firms strive for profit maximisation (see Chapter 10). For example, Lloyd Blankfein, the chief executive of the Goldman Sachs Group, received a 75 per cent pay rise in 2012 and earned $21 million, which included pay ($2 million), bonus ($5.7 million) and shares ($13.3 million).

However, this comes with more risk as jobs are less secure in the private sector and workers often have to save up for their own pensions in retirement. For example, the global financial crisis which started in late 2008 had caused over 11 000 job losses at Citibank Group by the end of 2013. US investment bank JP Morgan Chase cut 19 000 jobs during the same period.

Differences in earnings between industrial sectors

Table 7.10 shows the differences in per-hour earnings between full-time workers in the three industrial sectors (primary, secondary and tertiary) of the UK in 2012.

Table 7.10 Hourly earnings in selected industries (UK, 2012)

Primary sector (£)	
Agriculture, forestry and fishing	8.41
Mining and quarrying	17.06

Secondary sector (£)	
Construction	12.60
Manufacturing	12.19
Electricity, gas, steam and air conditioning supply	16.38
Water supply; sewerage, waste management	11.94

Tertiary sector (£)	
Wholesale and retail trade	9.66
Accommodation and food services	7.43
Information and communication	17.88
Financial and insurance activities	17.60

Source: adapted from Office for National Statistics

Table 7.10 shows that workers in the agricultural, fishery and forestry industries in 2012 earned the lowest wages in the UK with the exception of occupations in accommodation and food services, which generally offer unskilled work. The main reason for the low earnings in these industries is that the products produced, such as fish and food products, have a low sales value. In general, as the value of a good or service increases, so does the wage of the person who produces it.

Table 7.10 also shows that occupations in the finance, insurance, information and communication industries typically earn the highest wages. These tertiary sector occupations produce services of a higher value than those in the primary sector. A rise in the price of minerals and metals in recent years may help to explain the high earnings of people working in mining and quarrying. Skilled trades such as electricians and gas technicians have been in short supply in recent years in the UK, partly due to the lengthy training period required, and this may have led to increased earnings for workers in these occupations.

People in tertiary sector professions tend to have high earnings because to become a fully qualified accountant, doctor or lawyer requires postgraduate level study, professional examinations and many years of experience. The reward for this time and effort is higher wages, which attract people to those professions. In many economies, students have to take out loans for university and postgraduate training and they would only be prepared to do this because of the potential reward of high future earnings.

> **Activity**
>
> Discuss in small groups the possible reasons why people who produce food, which is essential for life, get paid the lowest wages on Earth, while bankers, who produce nothing of substance, get paid the highest.

Earnings of people with special talents or celebrity status

There are some people with special talents or qualities who earn exceptionally high wages. Examples are supermodels, top footballers and tennis players, and famous celebrities and actors. This is because their skills are exceptional and are in short supply, thus their labour supply curve is price inelastic, as shown in Figure 7.7.

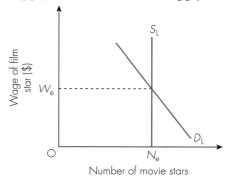

Figure 7.7 Price inelastic supply of Hollywood movie stars

There are only a finite number of top Hollywood movie stars (N_e), so the equilibrium wage rate will be relatively high (W_e). Such special talents allowed Johnny Depp to be paid \$35 million for the movie *Pirates of the Caribbean* in 2011, and J. K. Rowling, the author of the Harry Potter books, to earn £45.4 million (\$71m) in 2012.

J. K. Rowling earned £45.4 million ($71m) in 2012. She earns money from box-office takings, Harry Potter book rights and merchandising spin-offs

---

Activity

1 Investigate the highest-earning male and female:
   a) film stars
   b) tennis players
   c) pop singers
   d) individuals in another category of your choice.
2 Discuss the possible reasons for any differences in their earnings.

Specialisation of labour

Specialisation of labour occurs when a worker becomes an expert in a particular profession, such as a landscape architect, a psychiatric nurse, an electrical engineer or an economics professor.

Specialisation of labour can also occur when a worker becomes an expert in a part of a production process. Examples are supermarket checkout operators, waiters serving people in a restaurant, and factory workers who operate machinery.

Advantages of specialisation for the individual (worker) include the following:

● Workers become experts in their field, so their productivity increases.
● The quality of the product or service increases.
● Workers can become very skilful, so their earning potential may increase.

Disadvantages of specialisation for the individual include the following:

● The work may become repetitive and boring.
● Workers may become alienated, especially those specialising in low-skilled work.
● The production process may become overspecialised – that is, too dependent on an individual worker or group of workers.
● The workers may become deskilled in other areas – in other words, there is a lack of flexibility.

The advantages and disadvantages of specialisation for regions and countries are outlined in Chapter 23.

Chapter review questions

1 What are the wage and non-wage factors that affect people's choice of occupation?
2 Why do an individual's earnings change over their lifetime?
3 What are the factors that affect the demand for labour?
4 What are the factors that affect the supply of labour in an economy?
5 What are the advantages and disadvantages of a national minimum wage?
6 How might the government intervene in labour markets?
7 What is meant by geographical and occupational mobility?
8 Why do male workers in general earn more than female workers?
9 Why might a public-sector worker earn less than a worker in the private sector?
10 What are the advantages and disadvantages of specialisation of labour?

Key terms

Demand for labour is the number of workers firms are willing and able to employ at a given wage rate.

Derived demand means the demand for labour is not demanded for itself but for the goods and services labour is used to produce.

The **equilibrium wage rate** is determined when the wage rate workers are willing to work for equals the wage rate that firms are prepared to pay.

Geographical mobility occurs when a person is prepared to relocate to another area for a job.

The **labour force participation rate** is the percentage of the working population that is working.

Labour supply consists of people who are of working age and are willing and able to work at prevailing wage rates.

A **national minimum wage** is the lowest amount a firm can pay its workers and is set by the government.

Occupational mobility is when a person can easily move from one type of job to another.

A **salary** is a fixed monthly payment in return for labour services.

Specialisation of labour occurs when a worker becomes an expert in a particular profession or in a part of a production process.

A **wage** is the return for labour services, paid hourly or weekly. Payment depends on the amount of time worked.

8 Trade unions

By the end of this chapter, you should be able to:
● describe trade unions
● analyse the role of trade unions in an economy.

Taken from Cambridge International Examinations Syllabus (IGCSE 0455/O Level 2281)
© Cambridge International Examinations

The role of trade unions

A **trade union** (or **labour union**) is an organisation that exists to protect the rights of workers. Trade unions originated in the nineteenth century in the UK and the USA. Workers often worked in very poor conditions, so trade unions were created to bargain for better terms and working environments for their members. A worker becomes a member of a trade union by paying a weekly, monthly or yearly subscription fee. The membership fees help to pay for the administrative and legal expenses of the union.

Employees (workers) and employers often have different aims and objectives. For example, in addition to maintaining a happy and well-motivated workforce, employers may want to:

● maximise profits
● minimise costs
● maximise sales.

On the other hand, employees may want to:

● maximise wages/salaries
● work in a safe and healthy environment
● have good terms and conditions at work
● maximise their non-wage benefits
● enjoy job security.

There is often a conflict between the aims of employees and employers. For example, an increase in wages along with a decrease in working hours will increase costs to employers but improve the terms of employment for workers.

> **Study tips**
>
> It is possible for the aims of both employees and employers to be met at the same time. For instance, firms may agree to the demands of trade unions in return for productivity gains from their workforce.

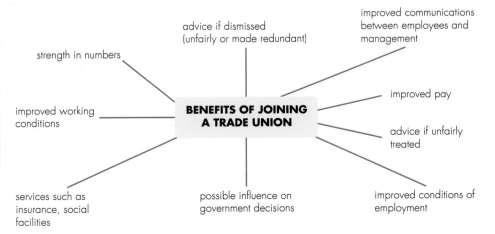

Figure 8.1 The benefits of joining a trade union

Article 23 of the United Nations Universal Declaration of Human Rights supports trade unions and decrees that all people should work in a safe environment for a fair amount of pay. It states the following:

1 Everyone has the right to work, to free choice of employment, to just (fair) and favourable conditions of work and to protection against unemployment.
2 Everyone, without any discrimination, has the right to equal pay for equal work.
3 Everyone who works has the right to just and favourable remuneration (pay and benefits), ensuring for himself and his family an existence worthy of human dignity.
4 Everyone has the right to form and to join trade unions for the protection of his interests.

According to the declaration, membership of trade unions is therefore a basic human right and individuals should have freedom of association – they cannot be discriminated against for being a member of a trade union. However, firms (employers) are not obliged to recognise and negotiate with trade unions. Instead, they can set their own terms and conditions and rates of pay. In some countries, such as the United Arab Emirates, the law does not allow trade unions to exist.

Types of trade union

Trade unions can be classified as follows:

- **Craft unions** – These are the oldest type of labour unions, which were originally formed to organise workers according to their particular skill. For example, engineers and printers formed their own unions, as did carpenters, plasterers and electricians. Craft unions try to restrict membership to only those with the particular skills.
- **Industrial unions** – These trade unions represent all workers in their industry, irrespective of their skills or the type of work done. An oil workers' labour union would include workers involved in exploration, extraction, storage, refining and any other jobs associated with the oil industry. The United Auto Workers Union of the United States (UAW) is an example of an industrial union.
- **General unions** – These trade unions are usually prepared to accept anyone into membership regardless of the place they work, the nature of their work or their industrial qualifications. These labour unions have a very large membership of unskilled workers. The Transport and General Workers' Union (TGWU) is a very large general union in the United Kingdom. Its members include drivers, warehouse workers, hotel employees and shop workers. In Australia the largest general union is called the Australian Workers' Union.
- **'White collar' unions** – These labour unions recruit professional, administrative and clerical staff (salaried workers) and other non-manual workers. They are common in teaching, banking, the civil service and local government.

Some professions, such as law, accountancy, engineering and medicine, do not have trade unions because their work is governed by a professional body which sets entry requirements in terms of examinations, training and level of experience. The entry requirements are high and therefore the number of workers in each profession is controlled.

The role of trade unions

The primary role of a trade union is to protect the interests of its members. Examples of labour union roles and responsibilities include:

- bargaining with employers for pay rises and better terms and conditions
- ensuring that equipment at work is safe to use (supported by health and safety legislation) and that workers are given sufficient training to enable them to perform their role at work safely
- ensuring members are given legal advice when necessary
- giving support to members when they are made redundant
- providing financial and legal support to workers who may have been unfairly dismissed or disciplined
- persuading the government to pass legislation in favour of workers, such as laws covering minimum wages, maximum working hours, pension rights and the retirement age.

Trade unions act as a means of communication and negotiation between employers and employees through a process called **collective bargaining**. This occurs when a trade union representative, who is voted into the position by colleagues, negotiates on behalf of the union's members (the workers) with the employer for better pay and working conditions. A collective voice is more powerful than each worker negotiating individually with the employer. Trade unions can therefore be an effective means of communication between the employer and employees.

Trade unions with high membership tend to be more powerful than unions with a small number of members. If trade unions make full use of their bargaining strength, they could succeed in getting larger and/or more frequent wage increases than the weaker unions. This highlights the importance of 'unionisation' to trade unions: the larger and more united the union, the better its bargaining position tends to be.

Unions may be affiliated to a larger organisation which negotiates with the government: for example, the Trade Union Congress (TUC) in the United Kingdom and the American Federation of Labor and Congress of Industrial Organisations in the USA. These organisations push for legal protection of rights for workers, such as the imposition of a national minimum wage or an increase in its level (see Chapter 7).

The basis for wage claims

Trade unions normally base claims for higher wages on one or more of the following:

- A rise in the cost of living due to inflation (see Chapter 18) has reduced the real income of trade union members.
- Workers in comparable occupations have received a wage increase.
- The increased profits in the industry justify a higher return to labour.
- The productivity of labour has increased, again possibly justifying an increase in wages.

Types of industrial action

As part of the collective bargaining process, trade unions can call upon their members to take **industrial action**. Table 8.1 outlines some of the actions in which trade union members can engage, in order to get what they want from their employers.

Table 8.1 Types of industrial action

Type of industrial action	Definition	Impact on employers	Impact on workers
Strike	Trade union members refuse to work, i.e. they stop working.	Production of goods and services ceases temporarily and this has an immediate impact on the firm.	Workers do not get paid when they do not work, so they lose wages/earnings.
Work-to-rule	Trade union members literally work to fulfil the minimum requirements of their job and will not do anything outside what is written in their contract of employment.	Bus drivers drive extremely slowly and stop at every bus stop regardless of whether there are any passengers who wish to get on or off. A school teacher does not take part in any extra-curricular activities or refuses to meet with students outside of lesson time.	Workers are meeting their contractual responsibilities and therefore cannot be disciplined.
Go-slow	Trade union members complete their work very slowly.	Productivity and efficiency fall.	Morale may drop as a result of low targets and productivity.
Sit-in	Trade union members turn up to work and occupy the premises but do not undertake their normal work.	Production of goods and services ceases temporarily and this has an immediate impact on the firm.	There is a loss in wages and, as a consequence, living standards fall.

Exam practice

In February 2013 the region of Kerala in India came to a standstill due to a nationwide strike called by a central trade union. The members of the trade union belonged to all sectors of the workforce, from banking to transport. Workers demanded price controls to bring a halt to the increasing price of necessities, enforcement of labour laws in all places of work and an increase in the minimum wage.

Source: adapted from NDTV

1 Identify the factors that have caused the trade union members in Kerala to strike. [3]

2 Discuss how effective you think the strike will be in successfully getting the demands of the trade unions met. [6]

Trade unions and the economy

Trade unions can have both positive and negative impacts on the economy, as outlined in Table 8.2.

Table 8.2 Positive and negative effects of trade unions

Positive impacts	Negative impacts
• Act as a channel of communication between employers and employees. Through negotiations and collective bargaining, they help to solve disputes and settle pay claims efficiently. • Offer legal support and advice to employees. • Negotiate on behalf of their members with employers for better pay and working conditions and can therefore help to raise living standards. • Negotiate with the government for an increase in the minimum wage, which can also help to increase standards of living.	• Trade unions are often portrayed in the media as having a negative role in an economy when they take industrial action which results in lost productivity. Strikes are the most extreme form of industrial action and can cause serious disruption to the wider economy. • From an employer's point of view, a trade union's demands for better pay and working conditions for its workers may increase the costs to the firm and therefore reduce profits. However, others might argue that increases in pay and improvements in working conditions lead to a better motivated workforce and thus an increase in productivity and profits.

Case Study: Hong Kong dock workers' strike

On 28 March 2013 a group of workers belonging to the Union of Hong Kong Dockers went on strike because their demands for a pay increase of 20 per cent had been rejected by Hong Kong International Terminals (HIT). The workers had demanded the pay rise to maintain a reasonable standard of living at a time of rising prices. HIT, their employer, offered a pay rise of between 3 and 5 per cent.

HIT is part of the Hutchinson Whampoa Group of companies, which belongs to Li Ka-shing, Asia's richest man. On 18 April the dock workers protested outside the office building of Li Ka-shing.

The International Transport Workers' Federation, which represents the interests of 4.5 million transport workers worldwide, became involved in discussions to see how it could support the strike. A small group of Australian dock workers flew to Hong Kong to support the workers and to show solidarity with the strikers.

> **Activity**
>
> Investigate the number and types of unions that exist in your country. Find a recent example of industrial action that has taken place and determine whether the action was successful or not in achieving its aim.

Exam practice

In September 2012, the Australian Education Union (AEU) in the state of Victoria called upon teachers working in the public sector to take part in two 1-day strikes. The teachers had asked the government for a 30 per cent pay increase over a 3-year period. The union, without consulting its members, decreased the teachers' demands and asked the government to increase wages by 12 per cent over 3 years. The government did not agree to the demands and instead introduced a maximum pay increase of 2.5 per cent per year for public-sector workers and called for the introduction of performance-related pay and further increases in productivity. The wage ceiling was part of a government strategy to decrease public-sector spending in the Victoria region.

Source: adapted from the World Socialist Web Site

1 Suggest two reasons why the trade union decreased the demands for a pay increase without consulting with its members. [4]
2 Explain the impact of a strike on the teachers, school children and the wider economy. [6]
3 Discuss reasons why the government did not agree to the 30 per cent pay increase. [7]

Trade union membership

Trade union membership is growing in some countries, such as China. In others, such as the United Kingdom, membership is declining (see Figure 8.2). Possible reasons for increasing trade union membership in some countries include:

- growth in manufacturing jobs, as manufacturing industry is typically unionised
- an increasing number of workers experiencing low pay and poor working conditions in manufacturing
- an increasing wealth gap and higher costs of living, which have caused workers to petition for higher wages and better working conditions.

Possible reasons for declining trade union membership in some countries include:

- changing government legislation, which seeks to reduce union influence
- a decline in manufacturing, which is traditionally unionised
- growth in part-time employment, as part-time workers are less likely to join a trade union
- firms independently agreeing fair terms and conditions with their employees without negotiating with trade unions
- an increase in unemployment (see Chapter 19)
- an increase in employment in small firms, as it is more difficult to organise unions within such firms

● an increase in the number of self-employed people (people who work for themselves and not for a firm), who are therefore not trade union members.

In response to falling membership in some countries, unions have tried to improve their image by making their services more appealing and relevant to today's world. For example, the Association of Teachers and Lecturers (ATL) in the United Kingdom has a 'no strike' policy to which all members agree. Many unions now offer their members financial services such as loans, mortgages, insurance, credit cards, discount holiday vouchers and discount car hire as incentives to join. Some trade unions also provide grants for college courses or arrange retraining programmes (to develop new skills) for their members who have been made redundant.

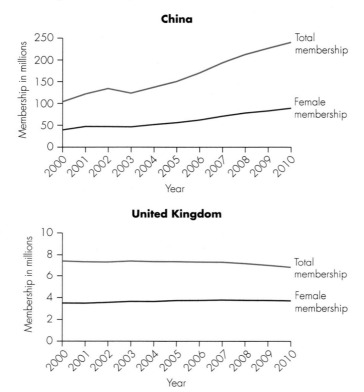

Source: International Labour Organisation

Figure 8.2 Trade union membership in China and the UK, 2000–10

Exam practice

1   With reference to Figure 8.2, suggest two possible reasons for the changes in the number of female members of trade unions in the UK and China.   [4]

2   With reference to Figure 8.2, describe and account for the trends in trade union membership in the UK and China.   [6]

Chapter review questions

1 What are the reasons why a worker might join a trade union?
2 Why might the aims of employees and employers conflict?
3 What are the main types of trade union?
4 What are the main roles of trade unions?
5 What are the key reasons why trade unions demand higher wages?
6 What are the different types of industrial action?
7 How do trade unions affect the economy?
8 Why has trade union membership decreased in many countries?

Key terms

Collective bargaining occurs when a trade union representative negotiates on behalf of the union's members with the employer to reach an agreement that both sides find acceptable.

A **go-slow** occurs when workers decide to complete their work in a leisurely way and therefore productivity falls.

Industrial action is any deliberate act to disrupt the operations of a firm in order to force the management to negotiate better terms and conditions of employment, e.g. strike action.

A **sit-in** is when union members go to their place of work, occupy the premises but do not undertake their normal work.

A **strike** occurs when union members withdraw their labour services by refusing to work.

A **trade union** is an organisation that aims to protect the interests of its members: namely, the terms of pay and conditions of employment.

Work-to-rule means that workers literally work to fulfil the minimum requirements of their job and do nothing outside what is written in their contract of employment.

9 Income and expenditure

By the end of this chapter, you should be able to:
- analyse the different motives for spending, saving and borrowing
- discuss how and why different income groups have different expenditure patterns (spending, saving and borrowing).

Taken from Cambridge International Examinations Syllabus (IGCSE 0455/O Level 2281)
© Cambridge International Examinations

Consumer spending

Consumer spending and income

Consumer spending – the amount that individuals spend on goods and services – largely depends upon their level of **income**. Most people exchange their labour services for wages or salaries (see Chapter 7), but people may also earn income from the other factors of production, for example:

- interest on savings (return on capital)
- rent earned from leasing property (return on land)
- dividends (a share of a company's profits) from shares owned in a company (return on enterprise)
- profits earned from running a business (return on enterprise).

Disposable income refers to the income earned by an individual after income tax and other charges such as pension contributions and trade union fees (see Chapter 8) have been deducted. It is therefore the amount of income a person has available to spend on goods and services. There is a positive relationship between the level of spending and the income earned – higher levels of disposable income usually lead to higher spending.

There is a positive relationship between the level of spending and the income earned

Direct taxation (see Chapter 17) reduces the amount of income a person receives. So higher income tax rates can lower the level of disposable income and therefore consumption. Table 9.1 shows the reasons why different income groups have different expenditure patterns (spending, saving and borrowing).

Table 9.1 Reasons for different expenditure patterns

Income group	Spending	Saving	Borrowing
Low	• Spend most of their income on necessities (e.g. food, clothing and housing)	• Tends to be low as there is not much income left over after spending on necessities	• Borrow to fund their expenditure on capital items (e.g. furniture, cars and computers) • In extreme circumstances, people may borrow to fund current expenditure on necessities • Banks less likely to lend money to low-income earners as they represent higher risk
Middle	• Spend on necessities and some luxuries • Spend a lower proportion of their income on food and other necessities	• Able to save some money from their wages or salaries	• Borrow money to fund expenditure on capital items (e.g. furniture, cars and computers) • Use credit cards to pay for both capital and current expenditure • Take out a **mortgage** (long-term secured loan) to purchase a home
High	• Spend the smallest proportion of income on necessities (compared with other income earners) • Purchase luxury goods and services	• High level of savings possible • Save a greater proportion of their income than other income groups	• Borrowing occurs but there is only a small risk of not being able to repay loans and mortgages • Banks lend money rather easily to high-income earners • Generally, there is less of a need to borrow money to fund items of capital expenditure

Low-income earners spend a greater proportion of their income on food and necessities, whereas high-income earners will spend a lower proportion of their income on food and necessities.

> **Activity**
> Identify all your sources of income and list the factors that influence how much of your income you spend.

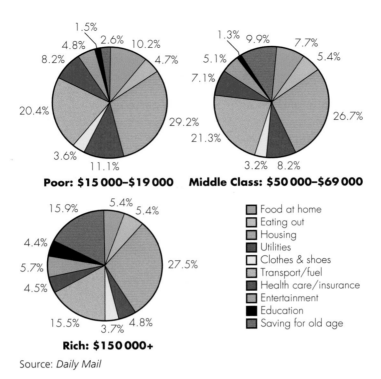

Poor: $15 000–$19 000   **Middle Class: $50 000–$69 000**

Rich: $150 000+

Food at home
Eating out
Housing
Utilities
Clothes & shoes
Transport/fuel
Health care/insurance
Entertainment
Education
Saving for old age

Source: *Daily Mail*

Figure 9.1   What Americans spend their money on (2012)

Figure 9.1 shows the proportion of income spent by low- and high-income households on food eaten at home in the USA (10.2 per cent and 5.4 per cent respectively). A low-income household spends 54.1 per cent of its income on necessities (food, housing, utilities, clothing and shoes) and only 2.6 per cent on savings for retirement. By contrast, a high-income earner is able to save 15.9 per cent of their salary and spend 4.4 per cent on education. Remember that 15.9 per cent of a $150 000 income is much greater than 2.6 per cent of a $19 000 income!

Figures 9.2–9.5 show the recent trends in real household disposable income and consumer spending in the United States, Japan and the United Kingdom.

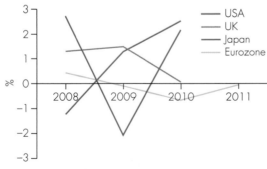

Source: adapted from *OECD Factbook 2013*

Figure 9.2   Real household disposable income in the USA, UK, Japan and the Eurozone, 2008–11 (% annual growth rates)

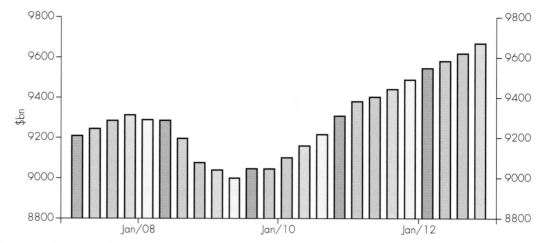

Source: Trading Economics

Figure 9.3   Consumer spending in the United States (US$bn), 2008–13

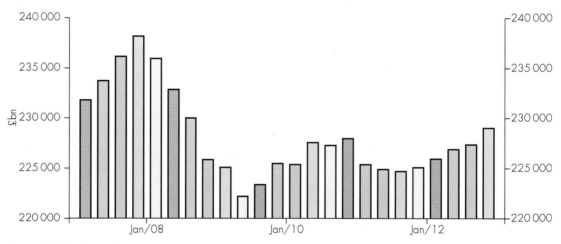

Source: Trading Economics

Figure 9.4   Consumer spending in the United Kingdom (£bn), 2008–13

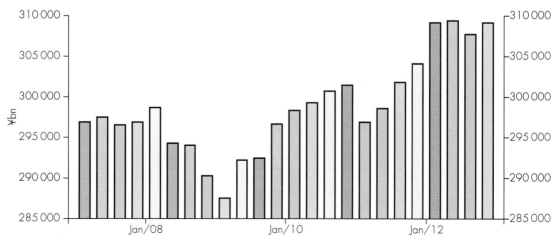

Source: Trading Economics

Figure 9.5   Consumer spending in Japan (¥bn), 2008–13

Activity

1 With reference to Figures 9.2–9.5, compare the trends in real household disposable income in the United States, Japan and the United Kingdom from 2008 to 2012 with consumer spending in these countries.

2 Determine whether there is a positive relationship between the two variables.

The **wealth** of an individual is measured by the amount of assets they own minus their liabilities (the amount they owe). When the value of assets, such as property and other investments, increases there is said to be a **positive wealth effect**. This causes people to spend more and, in some cases, causes owners of assets to borrow against the value of their assets such as residential or commercial property. Alternatively, if the value of an asset decreases, the wealth effect can become negative. For example, a severe recession can cause some people to experience **negative equity** – when the value of their secured loan or mortgage exceeds the value of the property.

Conspicuous consumption occurs when people purchase goods and services that they feel increase their status or image. For example, a person may buy a very expensive car, yacht, diamond ring or designer handbag as a status symbol. Wealthy people tend to engage in conspicuous consumption.

The Chinese are known for their love of luxury brands like Louis Vuitton, Gucci and Burberry. Conspicuous consumption in China shows no sign of a slowdown

Case Study: Negative equity

Louis Chow bought an apartment in Los Angeles for $900 000 in the year 2000. He borrowed $850 000 from the bank and paid a deposit of $50 000. In December 2008 the property market crashed due to the global financial tsunami, causing Louis's apartment to fall in value to $700 000. Louis still owes the bank $800 000. He is in negative equity as the value of the mortgage is greater than the value of the property.

Activity

With reference to the case study above, in pairs:

1 Discuss the impact of negative equity on Louis's consumer spending, saving and borrowing.

2 Investigate the options available to Louis to repay his mortgage.

Other determinants of consumer spending

Apart from levels of income, there are several other determinants of consumer spending, saving and borrowing.

Inflation

The general level of prices in the economy influences consumer spending because an increase in inflation (see Chapter 18) reduces the purchasing power of individuals. Therefore, inflation tends to cause reduced spending, less savings and more borrowing, and vice versa (see Figures 9.6 and 9.7).

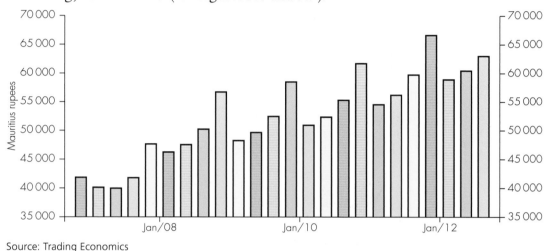

Source: Trading Economics

Figure 9.6 Consumer spending in Mauritius, 2008–13

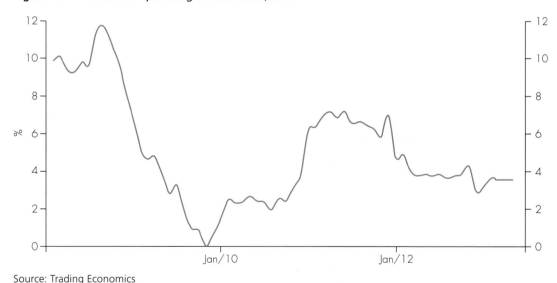

Source: Trading Economics

Figure 9.7 Inflation rates in Mauritius, 2008–13

> **Activity**
> With reference to Figures 9.6 and 9.7, compare and contrast the trends in consumer spending in Mauritius with inflation rates between 2008 and 2013.

Interest rates

The interest rate refers to the cost of borrowing or lending money. An increase in interest rates (see Chapter 16) may lead to decreased consumer spending, less borrowing and more saving because:

- borrowing has become more expensive and therefore the demand for loans falls, which leads to less consumer spending
- saving may become more attractive due to the higher return, so individuals may save more and spend less
- if an individual has a loan or mortgage, the increase in interest repayments may lead to a decrease in demand for other goods and services, so spending falls.

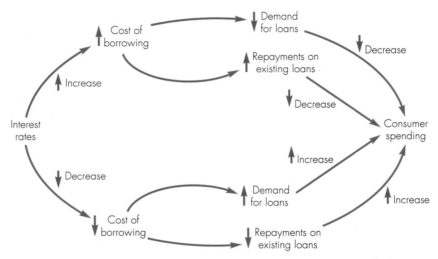

Figure 9.8 The effects of a change in interest rates on consumer spending

Confidence levels

The level of personal spending in an economy is heavily influenced by the level of consumer and business confidence. During a recession or a period of low economic growth (see Chapter 20), people may prefer to save rather than spend as they lack confidence about the future of the economy – for example, fearing that they may lose their job. By contrast, during an economic boom or a period of high economic growth, people and firms feel confident about the future and therefore purchase more goods and services. The sale of luxury items such as restaurant meals, spa treatments and foreign holidays increases. Firms may invest more in new equipment and technology because they feel confident about the future. This creates jobs and fuels spending, borrowing and savings.

The sale of luxury items such as bespoke jewellery increases during an economic boom or period of high economic growth

Age

A person's age impacts upon their level of consumer spending. A young single person may earn a relatively low income and may spend most of it on goods and services to support their lifestyle. As a person gets older, their earnings will typically rise and they may start to save a greater proportion of their income to buy a property or in anticipation of marriage and children. During the family stage of a person's life they will spend more of their income on their children but will also have to save to build up a pension to support them when they retire. They may also be saving for their children's university education. After retirement, people **dissave** as they have no earned income and so must spend from their savings.

Activity

Copy and complete the following table using the words: high, low or moderate.

Age	Spending	Saving	Borrowing	Dissaving
16–25	High	Low	Low	–
26–35	Moderate			
35–45	Moderate			
45–65	Moderate			
65 onwards				Yes

The size of households

The average size of households has changed over time. In economically developed countries, birth rates are falling (see Chapter 22) as people choose to marry and have children later in life. There has also been an increase in single households. This influences expenditure patterns as a family with three children will usually consume more goods and services than a single-person household.

Exam practice

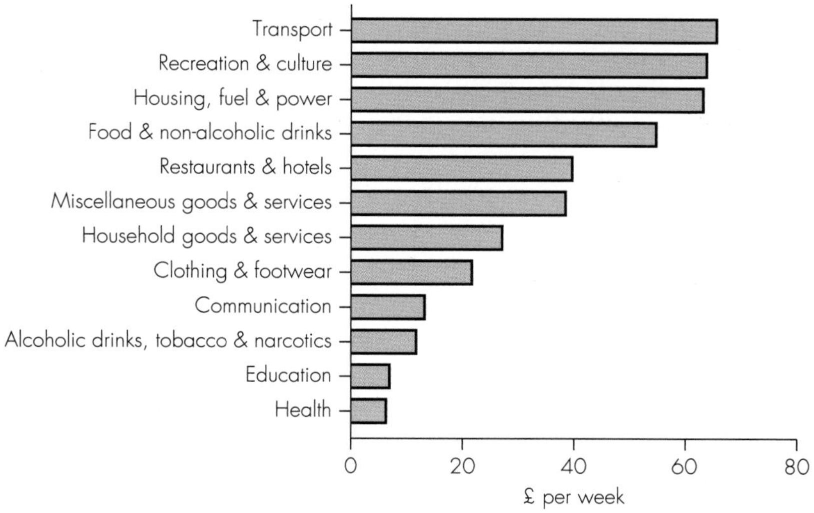

Source: Living Costs and Food Survey, December 2012 (Office for National Statistics)

Figure 9.9   The amount spent on goods and services in a week in the UK, 2011

1   With reference to Figure 9.9, discuss how spending patterns might be different
    in a less economically developed country such as Haiti or Bangladesh.   [4]

2   Spending on education and health is a small proportion of overall spending in
    the UK. Explain two reasons why this might be the case.   [4]

Savings

Saving occurs when a person puts away part of their current income for future
spending. Reasons for saving include the following:

- A person may decide to sacrifice current spending so that they have funds to spend
  in the future. For example, people may save for a holiday or for their retirement.
  Parents may save money for their children's education.

- A person may choose to save a portion of their income in a bank or other
  financial institution in order to earn interest. Banks also provide a secure place for
  depositing savings.

- A person may save for precautionary reasons so that they have money put aside
  in case of an emergency, such as an accident, job loss or unforeseen event in the
  future.

The level of savings is affected by the following factors:

- **Age** – In many modern economies, people from about the age of 25 start to save
  for their future. They will be likely to have secured permanent employment and
  paid off any student loans. The amount a person will save is influenced by the
  amount of support a government gives its citizens in terms of old-age pensions and
  health care provision. If people have to fund their own health care and pensions,
  they will have to save more during their working lives.

- **Attitude to saving** – As every person is different, they each have a different
  attitude to saving. For example, in the USA and the UK many consumers borrow
  to fund expenditure by using credit cards to make purchases or by getting loans to
  buy large item such as cars. In other countries, such as
  Japan, the use of credit cards is low. The Chinese also
  tend to be cautious and conservative with money, so
  like to save for a 'rainy day' (unforeseen emergencies).

- **Consumer and business confidence** – If people
  and firms have confidence in the performance of the
  economy, the level of savings will usually fall as people
  will be more willing to spend money. Savings tend to
  rise during recessions when consumers are feeling less
  optimistic about the future.

- **Interest rates** – A rise in interest rates means that
  people with existing debts have higher repayments to
  make to the lender. This will therefore reduce their
  level of spending in other areas. At the same time,
  people may save more in a bank to take advantage of
  the higher rate of return. When interest rates are low,
  people have a disincentive to save and may choose
  to spend their money instead or find an alternative
  means of increasing the value of their savings – by
  purchasing shares in a firm, for example.

Case Study: Saving in China

In China the level of personal savings as a percentage of total household income was approximately 20 per cent in 2013. Possible reasons for China's high level of savings are:

- Household incomes have risen due to China's phenomenal economic growth over recent decades. Many people have a surplus of income over their expenditure so are able to save.
- The one-child policy has been in place since 1979 and this has reduced family size and therefore the level of household spending (and hence encouraged higher levels of saving).
- People are accustomed to saving up to buy large items they wish to own instead of borrowing money from banks in order to do so. Culturally, Chinese people buy what they can afford and do not wish to get into debt to make purchases.

Exam practice

Figure 9.10 shows the net savings rates of households in Canada, France, Germany, Japan and the United States.

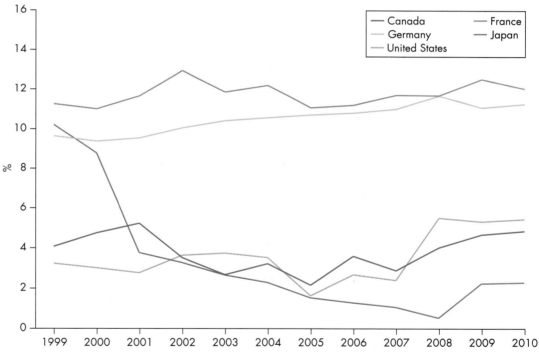

Source: *National Accounts at a Glance*, 2013 (OECD)

Figure 9.10 Household net savings rates, 1999–2010 (% of household disposable income)

1 Study Figure 9.10 and analyse the similarities and differences in the net savings rate between the countries. [6]

2 Explain possible reasons for the changes in the net savings rate in Japan. [4]

Borrowing

Borrowing occurs when an individual, firm or the government takes out a loan from a bank or financial institution, paying it back over a period of time with interest. Borrowing leads to debt, which is manageable if monthly repayments are affordable and interest rates are relatively low. An increase in interest rates causes repayments to rise and this can affect the purchasing power of individuals, firms and governments.

Case Study: The cost of borrowing

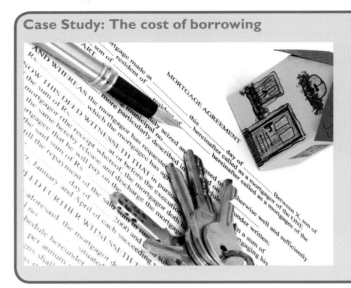

Laura Brown borrows $500000 to buy a property when current mortgage interest rates are 6 per cent. In the first year, interest repayments are $30000 (or $2500 per month). In the second year of the loan, interest rates increase to 7 per cent and interest repayments rise to $35000, which increases Laura Brown's monthly loan repayments to around $291). The higher cost of borrowing will therefore reduce her disposable income.

Individuals and firms may borrow for different reasons, including:

● to fund expensive items, such as a car, a motorcycle or an overseas holiday
● to purchase property or land, such as a factory, office or home
● to start up a new business
● to fund large projects such as a business expansion in foreign countries
● to fund private and tertiary education
● to fund current expenditure in the event of job losses or economic decline.

Factors that affect the level of borrowing in an economy include the following:

● **Availability of funds** – Banks and other financial institutions lend money to individuals and firms in the form of loans. The central bank (see Chapter 6) of a country controls the amount of funds which are available for borrowing by setting the **cash reserve ratio** (the percentage of a bank's assets which must be kept in cash in bank vaults or with the central bank). A decrease in the cash reserve rate ratio means that more funds are available for lending and an increase in the money supply can therefore lead to an increase in borrowing.

● **Credit cards** – Credit allows people to purchase goods and services with deferred payment. People or firms take ownership of the goods and services immediately and must repay the amount to the credit card company several weeks later – in other words, they 'buy now and pay later'. If the full amount owed to the credit card company is repaid in full each month then no interest is charged, but if only a portion is repaid then interest is charged on the remainder. Interest rates on credit card borrowing are extremely high: for example, the annual percentage rate charged on Citibank credit cards in 2013 was 35.81 per cent.

- **Store cards** – These are issued to regular customers of large retail stores in many countries to encourage spending. Store cards act as a credit card that can be used only in the individual retail outlet. Firms offer discounts and free gifts as an incentive for people to sign up for a store card. Customers can also accumulate loyalty points on the card, which can be used in the future to purchase goods and services in the store. Store cards can give people an incentive to overspend and can raise their level of debt. If debts are cleared when payment is requested, no interest is charged – but just as in the case of credit cards, if repayments are not made then interest is charged on the outstanding debt.
- **Wealth** – The wealth of a person may affect their level of borrowing, as a bank will be more willing to lend money to wealthier individuals or highly profitable firms. This is because they have valuable assets and so are more likely to repay the loan, whereas less wealthy customers have a higher risk of defaulting on the loan (being unable to repay their borrowing). To avoid **bad debts** (debts that cannot be repaid), banks often make sure that they have some guarantee of getting their money back. A large business may own several stores or have valuable assets that can be taken as **collateral** (security) for a loan. In the case of a mortgage, the property purchased provides security for the loan and if the borrower defaults on the loan, the bank will take ownership of the property.

Exam practice

The household debt-to-disposable income ratio in South Korea is one of the highest in the world. In 2012, disposable income rose by 5.8 per cent and debt rose by an average of 1.7 per cent. This lowered the debt-to-disposable income ratio to 152.3 per cent from 158.5 per cent.

The reasons for the high levels of debt are, firstly, that in the early 2000s the South Korean government lent money to small firms to encourage their growth and development and, secondly, because there was a housing boom in 2011. The acceleration in house prices provided an incentive for people to increase borrowing to buy property, as they believed that prices would continue to rise.

There is a low **savings ratio** in South Korea, which means that banks have a limited amount of funds to lend to borrowers. As a result they have borrowed from overseas. Households are worried about their level of debt, despite the recent growth in real disposable income.

Source: Reuters

1. Identify two reasons why borrowing might have increased in South Korea in the early 2000s. [2]
2. Analyse the effect on the economy of a high borrowing-to-disposable income ratio. [6]
3. Explain two problems which may arise because of a low savings ratio in South Korea. [4]
4. Discuss reasons why some people spend more of their income and others save more of their income. [7]

Chapter review questions

1 What are the main factors that affect the level of consumer spending in an economy?
2 How might the spending, borrowing and saving patterns of a young family with two children under the age of 5 compare with those of an old-aged pensioner?
3 How do spending and savings patterns of low-income earners differ from those of high-income earners?
4 How does wealth affect a person's level of spending, saving and borrowing?
5 How do changes in interest rates influence consumer spending, saving and borrowing?
6 What are the main determinants of the level of savings in an economy?
7 What factors affect the level of borrowing in an economy?
8 Why might one person save more of their income than another?

Key terms

Bad debts occur when people and businesses cannot repay a loan.
Borrowing occurs when an individual, firm or the government takes out a loan from a financial institution, paying back the debt with interest over a period of time.
Collateral means security for a loan, e.g. property in the case of a mortgage, or the car purchased in the case of a car loan.
Conspicuous consumption occurs when people purchase highly expensive goods and services due to status or a desired image.
Consumer spending refers to the amount of household expenditure per time period.
Disposable income refers to the earnings of an individual after income tax and other charges have been deducted.
Dissaving occurs when people spend their savings.
Income is the total amount of earnings an individual receives in a period of time. It may consist of wages, interest, dividends, profits and rental income.
Mortgage is a secured loan for the purchase of property.
Saving occurs when a person puts aside some of their current income for future spending.
Savings ratio refers to the proportion of household income which is saved instead of consumed in an economy.
Wealth is measured by the value of assets a person owns minus their liabilities (the amount they owe to others).

The private firm as producer and employer

10 Business organisation

By the end of this chapter, you should be able to:
- describe the types of business organisation in the public and private sectors: sole proprietors, partnerships, private limited companies, public limited companies, multinationals, co-operatives and public corporations
- describe and evaluate the effects of changes in the structure of business organisations.

Taken from Cambridge International Examinations Syllabus (IGCSE 0455/O Level 2281)
© Cambridge International Examinations

Types of business organisations

The main types of business organisation in the private sector are classified as:

- sole traders
- partnerships
- private limited companies
- public limited companies
- multinationals
- co-operatives.

Public corporations exist in the public sector. Each type of organisation has its merits and drawbacks, which help the owners to determine the best type of legal form for their business organisation.

Sole traders

A **sole trader** is a business owned by a single person, also known as a **sole proprietorship**. This person can employ as many people as needed, but remains the only owner of the business. Examples of sole proprietors are market traders, hairdressers, physiotherapists, and owners of small shops such as a bakery, café or stationery shop.

A food stall in China is an example of a sole trader

The advantages of being a sole trader are detailed in Table 10.1.

Table 10.1 Advantages of being a sole trader

Advantage	Explanation
Can set up the business easily	Sole proprietorships are the cheapest and easiest type of business to set up. There are very few legal procedures needed to start the business.
Has autonomy in decision making	The owner is the boss and does not need to consult anyone about their decisions. This makes the business relatively easy to run.
Keeps all the profits made by the business	This gives an incentive for the sole trader to work hard as they are rewarded with more profits as the business becomes more successful.
Enjoys tax advantages	In many countries small businesses pay a lower rate of tax on profits than large companies.
Enjoys privacy	The business does not need to publish its accounts to the general public. Only the tax authorities need to see the financial information of the sole trader.
Can be flexible in what the business does	For example, the owner has some flexibility in the choice of working hours. Also, if one business idea does not work out, the sole trader can quite easily introduce new trading activities or close down the business and start another one.
Has a sense of achievement	Sole traders are motivated by running their own business. There is a real sense of personal achievement if the business is successful.

The disadvantages of being a sole trader are listed in Table 10.2.

Table 10.2 Disadvantages of being a sole trader

Disadvantage	Explanation
Bears all the risks	There is no one else to share the burden, problems, decision making or responsibilities.
Has added workload and pressures from having to run the business as a sole proprietor	As the only person in the business, the sole trader often has to work long hours, especially during the early stages after the business has been set up.
Limited specialisation	Unlike large companies, sole traders cannot rely on the marketing, finance, production and human resource management expertise of others. This limits the extent to which sole proprietors can benefit from large-scale specialisation and the division of labour (see Chapter 7).
Limited access to sources of finance	Being a small business, the sole proprietorship represents high risk. This limits the extent to which the sole trader can raise finance from banks and other sources.
Lack of continuity	If the owner is sick or wishes to go on holiday, the business will struggle to continue. If the owner dies, the business will cease to operate in its current legal form.
Has restricted ability to exploit economies of scale	Large businesses are usually able to enjoy **economies of scale** (see Chapter 14), i.e. lower unit costs of production resulting from large-scale operations. This means that sole traders struggle to gain cost advantages and therefore have to charge higher prices for their products.
Has **unlimited liability**	This means that if the business goes into debt and makes a loss, the sole trader is personally liable for repaying the debts, even if this means personal belongings have to be sold to do so. This is because there is no legal difference between the owner (the sole trader) and the business itself (the sole proprietorship).

Partnerships

A **partnership** is a business organisation owned by more than one person. In an **ordinary partnership**, there are between 2 and 20 owners, known as **partners** (the co-owners of the partnership). At least one of these partners will have unlimited liability, although it is usual practice for all the partners to share responsibility for any losses made by the business. The government does allow some businesses, such as law and accountancy firms and health clinics, to operate with more than 20 partners.

Examples of businesses that are run as partnerships

It is possible for a partnership to have a **sleeping partner** (or **silent partner**) who invests money in the partnership but does not take part in the daily management of the business. It may also be possible for a partnership to be a **limited liability partnership (LLP)** where the partners have limited liability and the partnership has a legal identity separate from its owners. An example is KPMG, an accountancy firm that operates globally. The rules governing this type of partnership vary between countries.

To prevent potential misunderstandings and conflict, most partnerships draw up a legal contract between the partners, known as a **deed of partnership**. The contents of this agreement include the names of all partners, the amount of capital invested by each partner, their responsibilities, voting rights, arrangements for dismissing a partner or approving a new partner, and how profits are to be shared between the owners.

The advantages of partnerships are as follows:

- As there are up to 20 owners, a partnership is usually able to raise far more capital than a sole trader.
- Similarly, as there are more owners, the business can benefit from having more ideas and expertise. Most partnerships can therefore benefit from specialisation and division of labour.
- Like sole traders, the business affairs of partnerships are kept confidential. Again, only the tax authorities need to know about the financial position of the business. This makes the partnership an appropriate form of organisation for businesses such as private health care providers, accountancy firms and law firms, as they need to keep their business affairs confidential.
- As partnerships tend to be small businesses, there tend to be good working relationships with both colleagues and customers. One of the potential drawbacks of being a large organisation is the lack of clear communication between staff, because there are simply too many of them (see Chapter 14 – diseconomies of scale).

- There is more continuity than for the sole trader, as the partnership can remain in business if a partner is ill or goes on holiday.
- In some cases, additional finance can be raised from silent partners. These partners simply invest in the business without taking an active role in the running of it.

The disadvantages of partnerships include the following:

- As there is more than one owner, there might be disagreements and conflict between the owners. This can undoubtedly harm the running of the partnership.
- Although the business can operate on a larger scale than a sole trader, any profits made must be shared between all the owners.
- In most cases, the partners have unlimited liability. Although it is possible to have limited liability partnerships, limited liability usually applies only to sleeping partners, as they are not directly involved in the daily running of the partnership and so are not personally liable for any debts incurred.

Limited liability companies

Limited liability companies are owned by shareholders. The owners have the benefit of **limited liability**, which means that in the event of the company going bankrupt they would not lose more than the amount they had invested in the company – they cannot be forced to sell their personal belongings to repay the debts of the company. In legal terms, there is a **divorce of ownership and control**, since the *owners* (shareholders) are treated as separate legal entities from those who *control* and run the business (the directors and managers).

Limited liability companies can raise finance by selling shares. However, a **private limited company** cannot sell shares to the general public whereas a **public limited company** can raise finance in this way. When a firm becomes a public limited company it offers shares to the general public in an Initial Public Offering (IPO) on a stock exchange. To attract investors the firm will publicise the IPO in newspapers and on media websites.

Table 10.3 outlines the key differences between public and private limited companies. Examples of private limited companies are IKEA, Mars, Ernst & Young, LEGO, Rolex, Toys R Us and the Virgin Group. Examples of public limited companies are Walmart, Toyota, Samsung, Apple and the Walt Disney Company.

Examples of private limited companies

Examples of public limited companies

Case Study: Google floats on the NASDAQ

On 19 August 2004 Google Inc. became a public limited company through an IPO. Prior to the firm's flotation on the NASDAQ stock market, its shares were valued at $85 each. In 2013 the shares traded for over $800.

All limited liability companies must be registered with a government agency that keeps records of all public limited and private limited companies in the country. In the UK, for example, the agency is called the Registrar of Companies, and to set up a limited liability company, the owners must submit two important documents:

● The **Memorandum of Association** – a document that records the name, registered business address, amount of share capital and outline of the company's operations (what it does).
● The **Articles of Association** – a lengthier document that contains information about:
  ○ the details and duties of the directors of the company
  ○ shareholders' voting rights
  ○ the transferability of shares
  ○ details and procedures for the company's Annual General Meeting
  ○ how profits are to be distributed (dividend policy)
  ○ procedures for winding up (closing) the company.

Once the Registrar of Companies (or equivalent) is satisfied with the paperwork, a **Certificate of Incorporation** is issued to the limited liability company so that it can start trading.

The shareholders elect a **Board of Directors** (BOD) to represent their interests. The BOD is in charge of the strategic management of the company on behalf of its shareholders. The top director on the BOD is known as the **Managing Director** (MD) or **Chief Executive Officer** (CEO), who oversees the operations of the company. It is at the Annual General Meeting that shareholders vote in the BOD to represent their interests.

A private limited company selling beads in Hong Kong

Table 10.3 Differences between private and public limited companies in the UK

	Private limited company	**Public limited company**
Legal status	Carries the initials 'Ltd' after its name in official business communication	Carries the initials 'PLC' after its name in official business communication*
Buying shares	Shares are not available on an open stock exchange, thereby limiting the amount of funds	Shares are tradable on a stock exchange, so the general public can buy shares in the company
Selling shares	Shares can only be sold to family, friends and employees with the prior approval of the majority of the shareholders; hence it can be difficult to sell shares in the company	Shares can be sold instantaneously to anyone via a stock exchange such as the London Stock Exchange or the New York Stock Exchange
Minimum start-up share capital	$3.04 (£2)	$76 219 (£50 000)
Number of shareholders	No upper limit, but likely to have far fewer shareholders than a public limited company	No upper limit, but likely to have far more shareholders than a private limited company
Raising further finance	The sale of more shares in the company must first be approved by the directors	A subsequent 'share issue' can be used to sell more shares and raise more funds

*Public limited companies in other countries have different initials after the company name. Examples include:

- USA – Inc. or Corp. (short for 'incorporated' or 'corporation')
- Germany – AG (short for 'AktienGesellschaft', meaning 'shareholder corporation')
- Sweden – AB (short for 'Aktie Bolag', meaning 'limited liability company')
- Australia – Pty Ltd (short for 'proprietary limited company')

Activity

Produce a table like Table 10.3 for public and private limited companies in your country. The following website: www.corporateinformation.com/Company-Extensions-Security-Identifiers.aspx will help you complete the task.

The advantages of limited liability companies are as follows:

- Since shareholders have limited liability, it is usually easier to raise a large amount of finance from selling shares. For example, the Agricultural Bank of China raised a record $22 billion its initial public offering in the summer of 2010.
- The vast sum of money that can be raised from selling shares allows limited liability companies to enjoy the benefits of being large, such as economies of scale (see Chapter 14), market power and market presence/dominance.
- Additional finance can be raised through a share issue, which is the process of selling more shares in the company. In 2010, Brazil's state oil company Petrobras raised $70 billion in the world's largest share issue.

The disadvantages of limited liability companies include these:

- Companies have to file their financial accounts and have these audited (checked) by an external accountant. This is both time consuming and potentially expensive.
- These completed documents can be accessed and examined by all shareholders and the general public – the affairs of the business cannot be kept private.
- Companies are more administratively difficult, time consuming and expensive to set up compared with sole proprietorships and partnerships.
- The preparation, publication and distribution of company annual reports to shareholders can be highly expensive. The internet has gone some way to reducing this cost to companies that offer online annual reports (although shareholders can demand a printed version of the report).

For public limited companies, there are further potential drawbacks. These include the following:

- There are high costs in complying with the rules and regulations of the stock exchange.
- There is a potential threat of takeover by a rival company that purchases a majority stake in the business (as shares are openly available for purchase on the stock exchange).
- As they tend to be the largest form of business organisation, there is the possibility that they will become too large to manage efficiently and therefore will suffer from **diseconomies of scale** – that is, higher average costs of production (see Chapter 14).
- The firm is subject to fluctuations in value caused by investor speculation (buying and selling of shares to make a profit) on the stock market.

Multinationals

A **multinational corporation** (MNC) is an organisation that operates in two or more countries. For example, Levis Strauss & Co. sells its products in over 55 000 locations in 110 countries. It also has 1500 of its own retail stores across the globe.

Various factors have made it easier for businesses to operate on a global scale. These include lower transportation costs, advances in technology such as e-commerce, more efficient communication systems, and trade liberalisation (the removal of barriers to international trade – see Chapter 26).

The advantages of being a multinational company include the following:

- MNCs operate on a very large scale, so they are able to exploit economies of scale. This means that the MNC can pass on cost savings to customers in the form of lower prices, thereby enhancing its international competitiveness.
- Through job creation, MNCs are able to help improve standards of living in the countries where they operate. For example, Walmart, the world's largest retailer, employs over 2.1 million people worldwide.
- By operating in overseas markets, MNCs are able to generate more profit by selling to a larger customer base.
- MNCs are able to spread risks by operating in overseas markets. For example, adverse trading conditions in one part of the world can be offset by more favourable circumstances in other parts of the world.
- By producing in a foreign country, a MNC is often able to avoid any trade restrictions. For example, Japan's Honda is able to avoid import taxes in the European Union because it has manufacturing plants in the UK, Belgium, Italy and France.
- The MNC can set up factories in new markets and benefit from lower transport costs. For example, the Japanese car manufacturers Honda, Nissan and Toyota all have factories in China – the world's largest market for private cars.
- Multinationals might choose to move or expand operations in foreign countries to benefit from lower rates of corporation tax. For example, corporation tax rates in Japan, Australia and the UK are far higher than those in Hong Kong, Singapore and Bahrain.

A Levi's store at AlphaOne shopping mall in Amritsar, India

Multinational corporations suffer from the following disadvantages:

- MNCs face an array of issues to deal with, such as different legal systems, tax regulations and environmental guidelines. The lack of local knowledge can also cause major problems for an MNC.
- The sheer size and geographic spread of an MNC makes it harder to manage the overall business. It becomes more difficult for managers to ensure everyone works well together and to the same standard. Effective communication can also be an issue if workers are located in countries with different languages, national cultures and time zones.
- Fluctuating exchange rates (see Chapter 25) can make it difficult to measure and compare the value of an MNC's sales and profits in overseas markets.
- Multinational corporations have often been criticised for their cost-cutting practices, resulting in poor working conditions and low wages paid to workers in some countries.
- Since many MNCs earn far more revenue than the gross domestic product (see Chapter 15) of the host country, they are often in a powerful negotiating position with foreign governments over location decisions and access to finance (government subsidies, grants and loans).
- While jobs might be created, MNCs can force local firms that are less competitive to close down. Their huge market power and ability to exploit economies of scale (see Chapter 14) mean that local firms might struggle to compete.
- The overreliance on MNCs in low-income countries means that there are major consequences should an MNC choose to relocate its operations to another country. For example, in 2010 French supermarket chain Carrefour pulled out of Thailand, Malaysia and Singapore, creating unemployment in these countries.
- MNCs may be unsuccessful in a country as the goods and services offered may not appeal to local tastes and customs. For example, British retailer Tesco closed all of its US 'Fresh & Easy' supermarkets in April 2013.

Activity

Research the global operations of an MNC that operates in your country and assess the advantages and disadvantages to the firm and the host country. Make a judgement about whether the benefits to the host country outweigh the costs.

Exam practice

MNCs are attracted to the United Arab Emirates (UAE) because of low taxes, political stability and high GDP per capita. Examples of MNCs in the UAE are Microsoft, Marriott Group, DHL and Ericsson, along with a number of international engineering, law and accountancy firms. An influx of MNCs to the area brings workers from many countries and this creates a demand for international goods, services and schools. There are many shopping malls filled with international brands and Dubai (one of the seven Emirates that make up the UAE) has gained a reputation as a destination for shopping. This has attracted many tourists who visit Dubai for a shopping and leisure trip.

1   Describe the characteristics of a multinational corporation.   [3]
2   Discuss the benefits and costs of MNCs locating in the UAE.   [6]

Co-operatives

Co-operatives are business organisations that are owned and run by their members (who may be employees or customers) and have a common aim of creating value for their members in a socially responsible way. The employees (members) work together towards a shared goal and each has a vote, so they can contribute to decision making. Co-operatives share profits between their members and they are distributed according to how much each person contributes to the co-operative.

Co-operatives operate in many areas of business, such as retail shops, financial services, credit unions, child care services, housing and agriculture. For example, Canada has approximately 8500 co-operatives and credit unions, and more than 17 million co-operative members.

Co-operatives around the world follow the values and principles set out by the International Co-operative Alliance. These are:

- voluntary and open membership
- democratic member control
- member economic participation
- autonomy and independence
- education, training and information
- co-operation among co-operatives
- concern for community.

Source: International Co-operative Alliance

Examples of co-operatives include:

- Crédit Agricole Group – France's largest bank and credit union
- Xinjiang Quanliang – a dairy farmers' co-operative in China
- Aurora Wine Cooperative – a producer co-operative in Brazil
- Sunkist Growers – farmer-based co-operative in the USA that produce the famous Sunkist brand of fruit juice
- Ocean Spray – a leading producer of cranberry and grapefruit juice drinks, owned by a grower-owned cooperative.

At the Ocean Spray Plant in Middleboro, Massachusetts, USA

Types of co-operative

Consumer co-operatives are co-operatives that are owned by the customers who purchase the goods or services. Examples are child care, housing, health care services, telecommunications and utilities. The members of these co-operatives can get access to goods and services at prices usually less than those charged by a for-profit firm.

Worker co-operatives are co-operatives set up, owned and organised democratically by the employees. Examples include small shops, cafés, printers and other business enterprises. Mondragon Corporation is a Spanish co-operative that produces food and industrial products. It is one of the largest business organisations in Spain with approximately 50 000 members.

Producer co-operatives exist when firms co-operate and support each other in several ways. For example, farmers might create a co-operative to buy equipment, fertiliser and seeds, and to market and sell their produce collectively.

> **Activity**
>
> Investigate whether there are any co-operatives in your country or in a country of your choice. Choose one co-operative and research its aims and objectives and how it operates. Create a table of the differences and similarities between a co-operative and a similar-sized profit-seeking firm.

The advantages and disadvantages of co-operatives are listed in Table 10.4.

Table 10.4 Advantages and disadvantages of co-operatives

Advantages	Disadvantages
• Employees have a share in the business and therefore are interested in how it performs. This may lead to high levels of staff motivation and engagement in their work.	• Decision making may be slow as all members of the co-operative can contribute to the decision-making process and this may be time consuming.
• The employees also have a say in how the business is run (voting rights are equal between members) and how the capital in the business is used. This, too, may lead to higher levels of commitment and motivation.	• It can be difficult to settle disputes because of the number of people involved in decision making.
• Productivity may be high as workers are motivated by the values of the co-operative and the desire to add value to their members and the wider community.	• Co-operatives may suffer from a lack of capital as they cannot raise funds through selling shares and so are limited to the amount contributed by their members.
• Co-operatives tend to be run on socially responsible principles and therefore may create positive externalities that are enjoyed by the wider society.	• Productivity and profitability may be low as people are not motivated by self-interest.
	• There may be inefficient managers because the co-operative is unable to use high salaries to provide incentives to work harder.
	• Only a small amount of the profits is shared between members as the rest is re-invested in the co-operative.

Public corporations

Public corporations (or **public-sector organisations**) are wholly owned by the government and are therefore funded through tax revenues. They are organisations that provide goods and services for the general public. Examples of public-sector organisations are: water suppliers, sewerage providers, utilities (electricity and gas boards), the post office and state-owned news and broadcasting organisations (such as ABC in Australia).

It should be noted that in the USA 'public corporation' is another term for a public limited company that can trade shares on the stock exchange. In the USA, public corporations are referred to as public-sector organisations.

Case Study: The Bank of England

The Bank of England became an independent public organisation in 1998. This means it is wholly owned by the Treasury Solicitor on behalf of the UK government, with independence in setting monetary policy (see Chapter 16).

In some countries, some goods and services are supplied by private-sector firms. For example, water, electricity and gas are all supplied by the private sector in the UK. In other countries they are supplied by the government, as in the case of Amtrak, the state-owned railway in the USA. Education and health care in many countries are provided by both the private and public sectors (see Chapter 2).

The advantages of public-sector corporations include the following:

● Essential goods and services, such as housing and education, are under the control of the state, ensuring adequate provision for the general public.
● Prices can be regulated by the government and therefore essential goods and services, such as health care, are made affordable to all.
● Government can fund unprofitable services so that everybody has access to essential services such as postal services or bus services to remote areas of the country.
● Public corporations can generate revenue for the government. For example, Petróleos de Venezuela (PDVSA) is the state-owned oil company of Venezuela. All profits made by PDVSA form part of the Venezuelan government's revenue.

> **Activity**
> Find some examples of public corporations in your country or a country of your choice.

The disadvantages of public sector corporations include the following:

● Public corporations are funded using taxpayers' money, so there is an opportunity cost (see Chapter 1) – in other words, the money could have been used for other purposes, such as welfare benefits, government debt repayment or to improve the economy's infrastructure.
● A public-sector corporation could be inefficient, as there is little incentive to maximise profits because the aim of the organisation is to provide a service to the general public.
● A public corporation may be a **monopoly** (see Chapter 13), so it could charge high prices and provide a poor service as it is not subject to any competition.

> **Activity**
> Investigate the number of public corporations in your country or a country of your choice. Consider whether there are any goods and services which are provided by both the private and public sectors of the economy.

Nationalisation

Nationalisation is the process of taking assets into state ownership – it is when the government takes over private-sector corporations. For example, this occurred during the global financial crisis of 2008–09 when several banks were partially or entirely nationalised and taken into government ownership in the UK (see Table 10.5). These have since been privatised – that is, sold back to private investors. For example, Northern Rock was nationalised on 22 February 2008 but sold to the Virgin Group on 1 January 2012.

Table 10.5 Nationalised banks in the UK

Bank	Government ownership (%)
Northern Rock	100
Royal Bank of Scotland	83
Lloyds	41

Factors affecting the choice of business organisation

People setting up a business have to decide which legal form of business organisation they wish to establish. This will depend on numerous factors, as outlined below and in Table 10.6:

- **Ownership** – Does the owner want to be in complete control of the business? Can the owner(s) afford to risk having unlimited liability? Do they want to be held accountable to the shareholders of the company?
- **Control** – How many people will own the business? Do they want complete privacy of their financial accounts? Do the owners prefer to work alone or with others, perhaps to share the workload?
- **Sources of finance** – How much money is needed to set up the business? Do the owners have the necessary money to start the business or are additional funds required? Are the owners prepared to share the profits in return for greater sources of finance to fund the organisation's business operations?
- **Use of profits** – Does the owner want to keep all the profits of the business? Are the profits going to be reinvested in the business or distributed to shareholders?

Table 10.6 Choice of business organisation

Type of organisation	Access to finance	Liability	Privacy	Control
Sole trader	Owner's capital	Unlimited	Yes	Owner has full control
Partnership	Partners' capital	Unlimited	Yes	Partners share control
Private limited company (Ltd)	Shares sold to private individuals	Limited	Financial accounts are prepared and audited but do not have to be made available to the general public	Divorce of control and ownership, run by directors of company
Public limited company (PLC)	Shares sold to general public	Limited	Financial accounts are prepared, audited and made available to the general public	Divorce of control and ownership, run by directors of company
Co-operative	Capital invested by members	Limited	Financial accounts are prepared, audited and made available to members	Controlled by the members, who have one vote each
Public corporation	Government funded	Unlimited	Financial accounts are prepared, audited and made available to the general public	Controlled by directors (individuals) appointed by the government

Activity

Conduct a survey of a local business area and record the number of sole traders, partnerships, private and public limited companies, multinationals and co-operatives. Analyse your findings. What is the dominant type of business organisation? Why do you think that this is the case? Be prepared to share your findings.

Exam practice

Water supplies in the USA are provided by both private firms and public corporations. Housing is provided in the public sector and the private sector, and by housing co-operatives.

1 Distinguish between the aims of a public limited company and a public corporation. [3]

2 Discuss how housing provided by a housing co-operative might differ from that provided by a private-sector firm. [6]

Chapter review questions

1 What are the benefits of being a sole trader?
2 Why might a sole trader decide to become a partnership?
3 What are the disadvantages of being an ordinary partnership?
4 What are the differences between a public limited company and a private limited corporation?
5 What are the benefits of limited liability?
6 How does a business change from being a private limited company to a public limited company?
7 What are the two documents that limited liability companies must register with the government before trading?
8 What are the characteristics of a co-operative?
9 Why might a firm wish to operate in more than one country?
10 Why are some goods and services provided by a public-sector organisation?

Key terms

Co-operatives are business organisations set up, owned and run by their members, who may be employees and/or customers.

Limited liability means that in the event of a company going bankrupt the owners would not lose more than the amount they had invested in the company.

Multinational corporations are businesses that operate in two or more countries. Examples are Apple, BMW, HSBC, Marks & Spencer, Nike and Sony.

Nationalisation is the process of taking assets into state ownership. A nationalised organisation is also known as a public-sector organisation.

Partnerships are businesses owned by between 2 and 20 owners, who pool funds and take risks together, but have to share profits between themselves.

A **private limited company** has limited liability and can sell shares to raise finance, but not to the general public.

Public corporations (public-sector organisations) are organisations that are wholly owned and funded by the government, such as the postal office.

A **public limited company** has limited liability and can sell shares to the general public to raise finance.

A **sole trader** is a person who owns and runs a business as a single proprietor. Sole traders take all the risks but keep any profit made by the business.

Unlimited liability means that if a business goes bankrupt, the owner(s) is (are) personally liable for the debts, even if it means that personal belongings have to be sold.

(11) Production

By the end of this chapter, students should be able to:
- describe what determines the demand for factors of production
- distinguish between labour-intensive and capital-intensive production
- define productivity and recognise the difference between productivity and production.

Taken from Cambridge International Examinations Syllabus (IGCSE 0455/O Level 2281)
© Cambridge International Examinations

The demand for factors of production

Factors of production (see Chapter 1) are the resources used to produce goods and to provide services. The four factors of production, or **factor inputs**, are:

- **Land** – natural resources used in the production process, such as raw materials, fish and physical land.
- **Labour** – the physical and mental human input into the production process. This includes the level of skills, qualities and qualifications of the workforce, and not only the number of workers.
- **Capital** – manufactured goods used to produce other goods and to provide services, such as tools, machinery, vehicles, computers, factories, roads and money.
- **Enterprise** – risk-takers who provide the ideas and resources to organise the other three factors of production in the pursuit of profit.

In general, the demand for any factor of production is a **derived demand**. This means that the demand for factors of production depends on the demand for the goods and services that they will be used to produce. For example, economics lecturers at university are hired only if there is demand for economics courses from undergraduates.

On a macroeconomic scale, the demand for the factors of production in a country results from the total level of demand for goods and services in an economy. For instance, during an economic recession (see Chapter 20), firms will demand less labour.

In addition to the derived demand for factors of production, the demand for land, labour and capital also depends on their cost, availability and quality.

- The **cost** of factors of production – The higher the cost of land, labour and capital, the lower their demand tends to be. For example, Apple outsources the production of its iPhones and iPads to Foxconn, a Taiwanese manufacturer based in China, due to the relatively lower costs of land and labour.

  Similarly, if labour costs are relatively high compared with the cost of capital then workers might be replaced by machinery and technology. Also, the demand for capital depends on the cost of borrowing money – that is, interest rates.
- The **quantity** (or availability) of land, labour and capital – The greater the availability of factors of production, the lower their cost tends to be, and hence the higher their demand. For example, the relatively large size and availability of the workforce in India and China has boosted the demand for labour from multinationals seeking to expand their operations. In general, the greater the quantity of a factor of production, the lower its cost tends to be.
- The **quality** of land, labour and capital – Higher-quality resources tend to demand a higher price. For example, surgeons, pilots and barristers are in high demand

due to their highly valued skills and qualifications. China, India, Vietnam and Thailand have good-quality land to grow rice, whereas Scandinavian countries do not have the natural climate to do so.

Workers on an assembly line at a Foxconn plant in Shenzhen, China

Activity

Foxconn is a Taiwanese company that makes electronics products such as the iPhone, PlayStation, Kindle and Wii. It has operations throughout the world, including in China, Brazil, India, Malaysia and Mexico.

Investigate the various reasons why companies such as Apple, Sony, Amazon and Nintendo might choose to use manufacturers such as Foxconn to make products on their behalf.

Labour-intensive and capital-intensive production

The production or provision of different goods and services requires varying amounts of factors of production. In **labour-intensive** industries, the use and cost of labour is proportionately higher than the cost of other factors of production. Examples are teaching, psychiatry, sports coaching and management consultancy.

By contrast, in **capital-intensive** industries the use and cost of capital is more than that of any other factor of production. Examples are car manufacturing, soft drinks production and oil extraction.

Labour-intensive production

A labour-intensive firm is one that spends proportionately more on labour as a percentage of its total costs of production. Traditional forms of agricultural farming and fishing are examples of labour-intensive production. It is also commonplace in economically developed nations that specialise in the output of services, such as accountancy, physiotherapy, real estate services and tourism.

Labour-intensive production can be very expensive. For example, in private fee-paying schools and health clinics, labour costs account for the largest proportion of production costs, so the price charged to customers is relatively high.

Labour-intensive production processes tend to be used to produce individual or personalised products (such as a Hollywood movie or a custom-made wedding dress) on a relatively small scale.

Fishing for scallops is labour intensive in China

Case Study: Professional football

Professional football (soccer) is highly labour intensive. The top-earning players in the world enjoy celebrity status and are rewarded generously for their services. The ten highest-paid footballers during the 2012–13 season are listed in Table 11.1.

Cristiano Ronaldo and Lionel Messi consistently feature in the highest-paid footballers list

Table 11.1 Highest-paid footballers, 2012–13

Rank	Player	Club	Total earnings
1	David Beckham	LA Galaxy	$46m
2	Cristiano Ronaldo	Real Madrid	$42m
3	Lionel Messi	Barcelona	$39m
4	Wayne Rooney	Manchester United	$24m
5	Kaka	Real Madrid	$21m
6	John Terry	Chelsea	$18m
7	Yaya Toure	Manchester City	$18m
8	Fernando Torres	Chelsea	$17m
9	Frank Lampard	Chelsea	$16m
10	Steven Gerrard	Liverpool	$16m

Source: Forbes

Exam practice

Study the hypothetical data below for two firms and answer the questions that follow. The figures show the amount of money spent by each industry on factors of production.

Firm	Labour costs ($)	Capital costs ($)	Other costs ($)
A	20 000	10 000	10 000
B	40 000	40 000	20 000

1 What is meant by labour-intensive production? [2]
2 Use the data in the table to explain why Firm A might be considered to be more labour intensive than Firm B, despite the latter spending twice as much on labour costs. [4]

Capital-intensive production

Capital-intensive production takes place if a firm spends more on capital costs than on any other factor of production. This will include the expenditure on capital equipment such as tools, equipment, machinery and vehicles. Capital-intensive firms, such as aircraft and motor vehicle manufacturers, therefore need a lot of money to fund their operations. This can act as a barrier to entry into the industry, since it is difficult for new firms to enter such industries.

There are significant entry barriers into the car and aircraft manufacturing industries

Despite the initially high costs of capital-intensive production, there are potentially huge cost savings in the form of **technological economies of scale** in the long run (see Chapter 14). Firms that become more capital intensive usually do so to increase the levels of output and productivity by mass producing their products. In this situation, unit costs of production are relatively low. As countries such as India and China industrialise, their production is also tending to become more capital intensive.

Exam practice

Educational services are exploiting the use of technology in the twenty-first century. For example, long-distance learning technology (such as e-learning and video conferencing) allows students to study courses from the comfort of their own homes without physically attending a university campus, replacing the traditional lecture-style experience.

1   Outline two benefits of capital-intensive technologies in the provision of educational services.   [4]

2   Discuss whether technology could ever replace the traditional labour-intensive nature of teaching and learning.   [8]

Whether firms choose more capital- or labour-intensive production methods depends on several related factors:

● **The cost of labour compared with the cost of capital** – Firms will tend to choose more capital-intensive methods of production if labour costs are relatively high (assuming that it is possible to substitute factors inputs in the production process), and vice versa.

● **The size of the market** – Capital-intensive production tends to take place for mass-market products such as soft drinks, passenger vehicles and consumer electronics. Labour-intensive methods are often used for personalised services, such as a private tutor, counsellor, adviser, instructor or coach.

● **The firm's objectives** – Profit-maximisers operating in mass markets tend to opt for capital-intensive production methods in order to minimise their unit costs of production. Other firms might choose to use labour-intensive methods as they operate on a smaller scale or to safeguard jobs. Black & Decker, operating in Shenzhen, China, uses labour-intensive production methods to create jobs in the special economic zone (see Chapter 16), benefiting from tax incentives from the government.

Productivity

Productivity is a measure of how well resources are used in the production process: that is, the economic efficiency of land, labour, capital and enterprise. For example, **labour productivity** measures the efficiency of the workforce in terms of output per worker. It can be improved by having a better-skilled workforce (through education and training) or by allowing workers to use better, more efficient technologies to increase their output.

By contrast, the use of automation, such as the robotics and specialised computer equipment used in car manufacturing, can help to raise **capital productivity** without the need to hire more workers.

Figure 11.1   The input–output process

Higher productivity is important for an economy for several reasons:

- **Economies of scale** – Higher levels of output, whether through capital-intensive or labour-intensive methods of production, help to reduce unit costs of production (see Chapter 14). These cost-saving benefits can be passed on to consumers in the form of lower prices. For example, the mass production of flat-screen televisions and digital cameras has made these products much more affordable to many customers around the world. In addition, cost savings from higher productivity levels can help firms to earn more profit on each item sold.

- **Higher profits** – Productivity gains are a source of higher profits for firms. These efficiency gains can be reinvested in the business to fund research and development or used to expand the operations of the business. Either way, higher profits help to fund the long-term survival of the firm.

- **Higher wages** – Highly productive firms that enjoy cost savings and higher profitability can afford to pay higher wages to their workers, especially if they become more efficient. Such firms also tend to attract the best workers, as people prefer to work for firms with better prospects and profitability.

- **Improved competitiveness** – Productive firms can gain advantages beyond economies of scale. For example, they are more efficient, so they can compete more effectively on a global scale. Samsung's efficiency gains during the late 2000s ensured that the South Korean company took market share from Nokia and Apple to become the market leader in the smartphones industry.

- **Economic growth** – Productivity is a source of economic growth because it increases the productive capacity of an economy, thus shifting its production possibility curve outwards (see Chapter 1). This helps to raise employment and standards of living in the economy. Higher wages, from improved efficiency of firms and higher labour productivity, also mean that the government collects more tax revenues to fund its expenditure on the economy (see Chapter 16).

The difference between productivity and production

Productivity is a measure of the degree of efficiency in the use of factor inputs in the production process. It takes an average measure of this efficiency, such as output per worker, revenue per sales person or output per machine hour. Alternatively, productivity can be measured as a ratio, such as the value of output compared with the cost of the inputs (factors of production).

By contrast, **production** refers to the total output of goods and services in the production process. Production can be increased either by using more factor inputs or by raising the productivity of existing factors of production.

> **Study tips**
>
> Higher productivity increases the output of goods and services. However, increasing the number of workers or any other factor input does not necessarily increase output unless these resources are used efficiently. Firms that operate on a larger scale can suffer from diseconomies of scale (see Chapter 14).

Exam practice

Study the data below for two real estate firms selling residential property over a typical weekend. The number of units sold and the number of sales staff involved are also shown.

Firm	Total sales ($)	Units sold	Sales staff
Charnley Realty	3 950 000	10	8
Tsang Realty	3 800 000	14	10

1 Calculate the labour productivity as measured by sales per worker for both Charnley Realty and Tsang Realty. [3]

2 Use the information in the table to comment on why it might be difficult to decide whether Charnley Realty or Tsang Realty is the more productive firm. [4]

Determinants of productivity

The five main determinants of productivity growth are as follows:

- **Investment** – This is the expenditure on physical capital such as machinery, vehicles and buildings. For example, investment in the latest technologies generally helps workers to do their jobs better – that is, to produce more output and of better quality. The degree of investment in turn is determined by the level of interest rates (see Chapter 16). In general, the higher the interest rate, the more expensive capital expenditure will be, thus discouraging investment in the economy.
- **Innovation** – This refers to the commercialisation of new ideas and products. The invention of tablet computers and smartphones has transformed the way many people work, as they are able to conduct their business while mobile rather than at the office. Such innovations have increased the speed of work, improved communications and enhanced organisation at work. Thus, innovation helps to boost productivity.

Innovation has helped business people boost productivity by working while on the move

- **Skills and experience** – The productivity of labour is determined by its quantity and quality. The latter can be increased by improving the skills and experience of the labour force. Education and training, for example, enhance the **human capital** (skills and experience of the workforce) in the economy, thus boosting productivity.
- **Entrepreneurial spirit** – Entrepreneurs take risks in the production process in the pursuit of profit. They plan and organise the various factors of production in the production process. Productivity is dependent on the drive (motivation) of entrepreneurs, such as their willingness and ability to exploit new business opportunities.
- **Competition** – This creates an incentive for firms to be more productive. Without competition, firms might lack the incentive to be efficient or innovative (see the Exam Practice below). By contrast, competition forces firms to be more efficient, thus helping to boost the economy's overall productivity.

Exam practice

Kodak, once the largest firm supplying photographic camera film, became complacent as rival firms switched to the production of digital camera technology from the late 1990s.

Founded in 1888, the American firm had dominated throughout most of the twentieth century, with its market share reaching 90 per cent in 1976. Having failed to make any profit for five consecutive years, however, Kodak ceased its output of digital cameras and filed for bankruptcy in early 2012.

1   What is meant by 'market share'?   [2]
2   Explain why productivity is important for the survival of firms such as Kodak.   [4]

> **Activity**
> Investigate the ways in which the level of productivity in your school might be improved. Try to make your recommendations realistic and be prepared to share your suggestions with the rest of the class.

Chapter review questions

1 What is meant by the 'derived demand' for factors of production?
2 What are the main factors that determine the demand for factors of production?
3 Distinguish between capital-intensive production and labour-intensive production.
4 What are the factors that determine whether firms choose more capital- or labour-intensive production methods?
5 What is meant by 'productivity' and how does it differ from 'production'?
6 Why is productivity important for the economy?
7 What are the main determinants of productivity in an economy?

Key terms

Capital-intensive production happens when a firm spends proportionately more money on capital costs than on any other factor of production.

Derived demand means that factors of production are not demanded for their own sake, but for the goods and services that they are used to produce.

Innovation is the commercialisation of new ideas and products. It is a vital source of productivity.

Labour-intensive production occurs when labour costs account for proportionately more of a firm's costs than any other cost of production.

Production refers to the total output of goods and services in the production process.

Productivity is a measure of efficiency that involves calculating the amount of output per unit of a factor input (such as output per worker or output per machine hour).

12 Costs, revenues and profits

By the end of this chapter, you should be able to:
- define total and average cost, fixed and variable cost, and perform simple calculations
- analyse particular situations to show changes in total and average cost as output changes
- define total and average revenue and perform simple calculations
- describe the principle of profit maximisation as a goal and recognise that business organisations may have different goals.

Taken from Cambridge International Examinations Syllabus (IGCSE 0455/O Level 2281)
© Cambridge International Examinations

Costs of production

Costs are the payments made by firms in the production process. Examples of costs of production include:

- wages and salaries paid to employees
- rent paid to landowners for hiring of business premises
- advertising expenses
- purchases of raw materials and components from suppliers
- utility bills for telephone, gas and electricity services
- dividend payments to shareholders (see Chapter 10)
- taxes paid to the government based on the value of company profits made.

Costs of production can be categorised in four different ways.

Fixed costs

Fixed costs are the costs of production that have to be paid regardless of how much a firm produces or sells. For example, salaries for senior managers, insurance payments and rent all have to be paid regardless of the firm's output level. This relationship is illustrated in Figure 12.1.

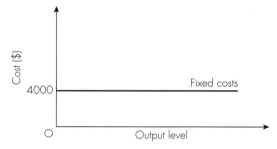

Figure 12.1 Fixed costs for a firm (with $4000 of fixed costs)

Variable costs

Variable costs are costs of production that change when the level of output changes. Examples are the costs of raw materials or components needed to build houses – the more houses that are built, the higher these variable costs become. The total variable cost line (see Figure 12.2) starts at the origin because when there is no output, no variable costs are incurred.

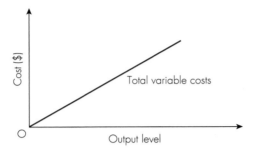

Figure 12.2   Variable costs of a firm

Total costs

As the name suggests, the **total costs** of production are the sum of all fixed and variable costs. The total cost line, shown in Figure 12.3, starts at the same value as fixed costs because even when nothing is produced, fixed costs still have to be paid by the firm.

Total costs = fixed costs + variable costs

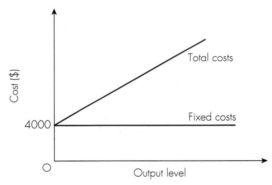

Figure 12.3   Total costs for a firm

Average costs

Average costs refer to the total cost of making *one* product – it is the unit cost of production.

Average costs = total costs ÷ output level

Firms that operate on a large scale are able to reduce their average costs of production (see Chapter 14). For example, Coca-Cola's bottling plants can produce 10 000 cans of soft drinks per minute. This enables Coca-Cola to benefit from lower unit costs of production, as shown in Figure 12.4. Here, the firm is able to enjoy **economies of** scale (lower average costs as it expands output from O*a* to O*b*). If the firm becomes too large, by operating beyond O*b*, it will suffer from inefficiencies, thus leading to **diseconomies of scale** (see Chapter 14).

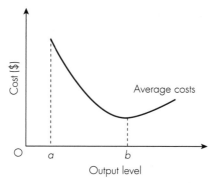

Figure 12.4 Average costs of a firm

Figure 12.5 Summary of business costs

Exam practice

1 The table below shows a firm's fixed and variable costs of production at different levels of output. Calculate the level of output where average costs are at their lowest. [2]

Output (units)	Fixed costs ($)	Variable costs ($)
20	300	40
30	300	75
40	300	120
50	300	250

2 Johnson's Candles has fixed costs of $4000 each month. Its average variable costs are $3 per candle. The firm's current level of demand is 2500 candles per month. The average price of its candles is $6.

    a) Using an example, explain what is meant by a fixed cost of production. [2]

    b) Calculate the firm's current average costs. [2]

    c) Calculate the firm's current total costs of production each month. [2]

    d) Calculate the profit if demand increases to 3000 candles per month. [3]

3 Juke Engineering produces batteries for a major car-maker. Juke's monthly cost structure is shown in the table below. Assume that the firm's average variable costs of production remain constant at all levels of output shown.

Output level (batteries)	Total costs ($)
1000	50 000
2000	80 000
3000	110 000

a) Calculate the average variable costs of production for Juke Engineering.   [2]

b) Calculate the value of its monthly total fixed costs.   [2]

c) Calculate the change in average costs of production if Juke Engineering increases its production from 1000 batteries per month to 3000 batteries per month.   [2]

Revenues

Revenue refers to the money payable to a business from the sale of its products. For example, Nike and Adidas receive most of their revenues from the sale of sports apparel and sports equipment. According to its website, McDonald's – the world's largest restaurant chain, with over 34 000 restaurants worldwide – earned around $28 billion of revenue in 2013 from the sale of fast food.

McDonald's has over 34 000 restaurants worldwide and earned around $28 billion of revenue in 2013. This is a branch in Tokyo, Japan

Revenue is often referred to as **sales revenue** or **sales turnover**. It is calculated by using the formula:

Revenue = price × quantity sold

For example, if a cinema charges an average price of $10 for a movie and manages to sell 5500 tickets in a week, its total revenue will be $55 000 (that is, $10 × 5500).

Average revenue refers to the typical price received from the sale of a good or service. It is calculated using the formula:

Average revenue = total revenue ÷ quantity sold

So, if instead the cinema earns $60 000 from the sale of 7500 tickets, the average revenue (or average price) would be $60 000 ÷ 7500 = $8 per ticket.

Profit and profit maximisation

A firm earns **profit** if its total revenues exceed its total costs of production. Profit is calculated by using the formula:

Profit = total revenue − total costs

Profit provides an incentive for entrepreneurs to take risks. Without profit, firms will struggle to survive in the long run.

ExxonMobil, the world's largest oil company, earns annual profits in excess of $41 billion

Profit maximisation and business objectives

Profit maximisation is the goal of most private-sector firms. Profits are maximised when the positive difference between a firm's sales revenues and its costs of production is at its greatest.

Study tips

Students often use the terms 'cost' and 'revenue' interchangeably, although the terms have different meanings. Firms always pay the 'cost' (of production) whereas customers always pay the 'price'. To make a profit, a product's price must exceed its cost.

Exam practice

1   Copy and complete the information below for a firm that sells pizzas.   [5]

Units sold (pizzas per week)	Sales revenue ($)	Total fixed costs ($)	Total variable costs ($)	Total costs ($)	Profit/ loss ($)
0	0				−4000
400			4000	8000	
800		4000			
1200	18 000				

2 The following data refer to the monthly costs and revenues of Mintjens Curtains Ltd when operating at 300 units of output per month.

Item	Cost/revenue ($)
Price	50
Raw materials per unit	15
Advertising costs	200
Rent	3500
Salaries	3000

   a) Explain why advertising costs are an example of fixed costs of production for Mintjens Curtains Ltd. [2]

   b) Calculate Mintjens Curtains Ltd's monthly total fixed costs of production. [2]

   c) Calculate Mintjens Curtains Ltd's total cost of producing 300 units per month. [2]

   d) Calculate the profit made by Mintjens Curtains Ltd if it sells all its output. [2]

3 The table below shows the total costs of a firm.

Output (units)	20	30	40	50
Total costs ($)	120	150	190	230

   a) Calculate the total revenues at each level of output if the selling price is $5. [4]

   b) From the above calculations, identify the number of units that the firm should produce in order to maximise profits. [1]

4 On Valentine's Day 2013, US Airways and American Airlines merged in a deal worth $11 billion to create the largest airline on the planet, with 6700 daily flights and annual revenues of around $40 billion. Critics of the merger were concerned that with less competition, the US airline industry would have fewer incentives to keep prices at a competitive level. Others believed that the intensity of competition between Delta Air Lines and United Airlines would simply force American Airlines to offer better customer service for passengers.

   a) Define the term 'sales revenue'. [2]

   b) Discuss whether the merger between American Airlines and US Airways would lead to lower costs and higher profits for the firm. [8]

Alternative business objectives

Businesses have a variety of **objectives** and do not necessarily strive to maximise profit. Other business objectives include:

- **Survival** – While business survival is a vital objective for new businesses, even well-established firms will need to focus on this, especially during unfavourable trading times. To survive in the long run, firms need to earn a profit.
- **Market share** – This refers to a firm's sales revenues as a proportion of the industry's total sales revenue. An increase in sales revenues will, other things being constant, lead to greater market share for the firm. Higher market share has several advantages, such as economies of scale (see Chapter 14) and customer loyalty.

- **Image and reputation** – Businesses might aim to improve how the general public perceives them. A bad image can turn suppliers and customers against the firm's products and services. For example, German car-maker BMW recalled 720 000 cars worldwide in 2013 due to potential electrical problems. Resolving such problems, although costly to BMW, prevents problems for the firm in the long run.
- **Ethical objectives** – This refers to the moral principles (values and beliefs) that guide business activity. These objectives focus on what is considered to be socially responsible. Ethical businesses strive to improve the treatment of workers, customers, shareholders and the natural environment. Not-for-profit organisations such as charities aim to provide services to enhance the welfare of people in society.

Activity

Investigate the objectives of any two organisations of your choice. Compare and contrast your findings and be prepared to share these with the rest of the class.

Chapter review questions

1. Using examples, distinguish between total, average, fixed and variable costs of production.
2. How might total and average costs change when the level of output changes?
3. What is the difference between total and average revenue?
4. What is profit maximisation?
5. Explain the alternative objectives that businesses might have.

Key terms

Average cost is the total cost of making one unit of product – that is, the unit cost of production.

Costs refers to a firm's expenditure on, for example, wages, salaries, rent, loan repayments, fuel bills, marketing expenses, taxes, accountancy fees and legal costs.

Fixed costs are costs that a firm has to pay irrespective of how much it produces or sells, such as management salaries, administrative costs, bank loan repayments and rent.

Objectives are the goals or targets of an organisation, such as business survival, growth, higher market share and profit maximisation.

Profit is the positive difference between a firm's total revenues and its total costs of production: that is, profit = total revenue – total costs.

Sales revenue is the payment received by a firm from the sale of its goods and/or services.

Total costs are the sum of all fixed costs of production and all variable costs of production.

Variable costs are those that change as the level of output changes, such as raw material costs, payment for components used in production and the payment of wages.

Perfect competition and monopoly

Perfect competition

In economics, the term **market structure** refers to the key characteristics of a particular market. These features include the number and size of firms in the market, the degree and intensity of price and non-price competition, and the nature of barriers to entry. The two extreme market structures in economics are perfect competition and monopoly.

The model of **perfect competition** describes a market where there is immense competition. A real world example is the wet markets (fresh food markets) commonly found in Asian countries such as Hong Kong, Singapore, South Korea, Taiwan and Macau.

A wet market in Hong Kong – an example of perfect competition

The main characteristics of firms in perfect competition are as follows:

- There are **many buyers and sellers** in the industry, none of which has any significant market power to influence the market supply or demand (see Chapter 3).

- Hence, firms are said to be **price takers** – the price they charge is determined by the market forces of demand and supply rather than firms setting their own prices.
- As there are literally **no barriers to entry** in perfect competition, there is freedom of entry to, and exit from, the market.
- Firms produce a **homogeneous product**. This means that the products being sold are identical, such as bananas or strawberries being sold in fresh fruit markets.
- Both buyers and sellers have **perfect knowledge**. This means that customers and firms have ease of access to information about the product and the prices being charged by competitors.

However, perfect competition is a theoretical possibility only and in reality the vast majority of markets are imperfect. For example:

- In most industries, there are market leaders (those with a high market share) who have significant power to influence the market supply and hence prices. An example is Apple and Samsung, which dominate the tablet computer industry. Hence, these firms are **price makers** (or price setters) rather than price takers.
- In reality, barriers to entry exist in virtually all markets. For example, there may be legal entry barriers to some industries, such as the professional qualifications needed to practise law and medicine, or the high **set-up costs** to enter other markets, such as the airline or pharmaceutical industries.
- Consumers and suppliers are likely to have **imperfect knowledge** rather than perfect knowledge. This means that customers and rival firms do not have easy access to information about the products and the prices being charged by competitors. For example, mobile phone network providers use very confusing pricing packages for their services. Similarly, banks offer a variety of interest rate charges for their various types of loan.
- Firms are likely to produce **differentiated products**, rather than homogeneous ones. For example, sports apparel firms such as Adidas and Nike use branding, different product designs, colours and slogans to differentiate their products. Many successful and large businesses develop memorable slogans (catchphrases) as a form of product differentiation (see Table 13.1).

Table 13.1 Some examples of business slogans

Slogan	Business
Impossible is nothing	Adidas
The ultimate driving machine	BMW
The world's online marketplace	eBay
The world on time	FedEx
The world's local bank	HSBC
Because I'm worth it	L'Oréal
I'm lovin' It	McDonald's
Where do you want to go today?	Microsoft
Just do it	Nike
Ideas for life	Panasonic
I don't wanna grow up	Toys R Us
It's everywhere you want to be	VISA
Always low prices	Walmart

Pricing and output policies in perfect competition

A high degree of competition in a market can benefit consumers. This is because they get good-quality products and good customer service, all at the right prices. In addition, competition brings about greater choice, higher output and more competitive prices (see Figure 13.1).

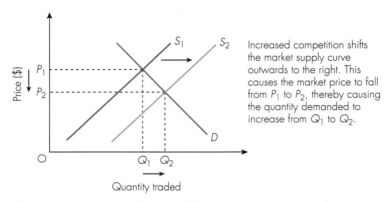

Figure 13.1 Impact of competition on market price and output

Exam practice

Supermarket chains such as Walmart, Carrefour and Tesco use an extensive range of pricing and non-pricing strategies to compete. Market research published by *Which?* (a consumer campaigning organisation in the UK) showed that most shoppers believe supermarkets deliberately try to mislead them by using confusing pricing strategies.

The *Which?* findings showed that supermarkets often use poor labelling and puzzling prices for their products. For instance, a 600 g jar of mayonnaise might be priced at £3.49 while a 400 g jar of the same brand is priced at £2.35 – so which one offers better value? Similarly, pre-packed fruits and vegetables are found to have very different prices compared with loose varieties of the same produce.

1. Price is one way in which supermarkets compete. Explain *three* non-pricing strategies that supermarkets use to compete with each other. [6]
2. To what extent do supermarkets operate in a competitive market? [6]
3. Do consumers benefit from the competitive strategies used by supermarkets? Give reasons for your answer. [8]

Monopoly

There are different interpretations of what is meant by a monopoly. In general, a **monopoly** is a market structure where one supplier dominates the market. Examples are Coca-Cola (carbonated soft drinks), YKK (zip fasteners) and Mabuchi (which makes around 90 per cent of the micro-motors used to adjust rear-view mirrors in cars).

A **pure monopoly** exists if only one firm supplies the whole market. In the USA, this would include the United States Postal Service (the only service provider of first class postage) and the Federal Reserve (the sole supplier of banknotes and coins).

The word 'monopoly' comes from the Greek language, with *monos* meaning one and *polein* meaning to sell. Hence, monopoly can be defined as a market structure where there is only one supplier of a good or service.

Microsoft enjoyed a monopoly position in the software industry during the 1990s

Features of monopoly include:

- **Single supplier** – As its name suggests, a monopolist is the sole supplier of a product in a given market. This is due to high barriers to entry (see below), which result in a lack of substitutes.
- **Price maker** (or price setter) – The monopolist has significant market power, controlling enough of the market supply (see Chapter 3) that it can charge higher prices yet produce lower output than would be the case if it faced real competition.
- **Imperfect knowledge** – A monopolist is able to protect its prestigious position because customers and rivals have imperfect knowledge, partly as a result of the monopolist's ability to protect its trade secrets.
- **High barriers to entry** – A monopolist can remain so only if in the long run there are very high barriers to entry. These obstacles effectively prevent other firms from entering the market. Examples include: economies of scale of existing firms, ownership of essential resources, the existence of intellectual property rights (namely, patents, trademarks and copyrights), advertising expenditure and legal barriers to entry.

Study tips

It is incorrect to claim that monopolists can charge 'whatever' price they want because they are the single supplier of a good or service. While monopolists have the ability to control market supply, they cannot control the level of market demand. Customers will switch to, or seek, alternatives if prices rise too high. Hence, monopolists must lower prices if they want to sell more.

Exam practice

The advertising budgets of large firms can act as a barrier to entry. America's most watched sporting event, the annual Super Bowl, is a magnet for firms with huge advertising budgets. The average cost of a 30-second advert during the Super Bowl was $4 million in 2013. Marketers believe that the best Super Bowl adverts earn a permanent place in history, being broadcast on television and internet websites such as YouTube for years to come.

1 Define the term 'barriers to entry'. [2]
2 Explain why advertising expenditure can act as a barrier to entry. [4]

Pricing and output policies in monopoly

Due to the lack of competition, the monopolist is able to restrict market supply. This is shown in Figure 13.2 by the shift in supply from S_1 to S_2, which reduces output from Q_1 to Q_2. Alternatively, we can say that supply would be higher at S_1 in the absence of monopoly power. As the monopolist limits the supply of its good or service, the price is higher (at P_2 rather than P_1).

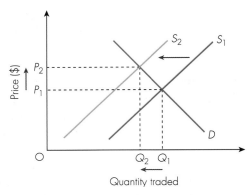

Figure 13.2 Impact of monopoly power on market price and quantity traded

Monopolists are also able to use **price discrimination**. This is the practice of charging different prices to different customers for essentially the same product. For example, public transport operators, theme parks and cinemas charge students different prices compared with other adults. Another example, often used by supermarkets, is price discrimination based on the quantity sold. For example, supermarket customers who buy 'multipacks' of a product usually get to enjoy a lower price for each unit bought. This discriminates against those who buy in smaller quantities.

Exam practice

Theme parks such as Disneyland, Universal Studios and SeaWorld are experts at using price discrimination. An example of such pricing policies is shown below.

	Admission price ($)
Adult (aged 12 and above)	28
Child (aged 3–11)	14
Family (2 adults, 2 children)	75
Family (1 adult, 2 children)	50
Annual pass (adult)	75
Annual pass (child)	35
Free admission is granted to children under 3 years old and local senior residents aged 65 years old or above with proof of identity and age.	

1 Define the term 'price discrimination'. [2]
2 Using examples of the above data, explain how organisations such as theme parks use price discrimination. [6]

Other pricing policies that might be used by firms include:

● **Cost-plus pricing** – This involves working out the average cost of each unit of output and then adding a certain amount or certain percentage on top to earn profit.

   For example, if the cost of producing a commercial aeroplane is $120 000 and the firm wants a 100 per cent profit margin, the selling price will be $240 000. Whilst cost-plus pricing is easy to calculate, the price setter must ensure that the chosen price is still competitive.

- **Competition-based pricing** – This occurs when a firm sets its price according to the prices being charged by its rivals. This allows the firm to be competitive in terms of price, but also means it may need to rely on non-price factors to maintain its market share.

  For example, many airline companies will set similar prices for their flights but choose to compete on other aspects of their service, such as baggage allowance, amount of leg room (space), flight times and connection times, the quality of the food, the variety of their in-flight entertainment, and the overall level of customer service.

- **Penetration pricing** – This involves setting a low price in order to enter a new market. This pricing policy is often used by firms when launching new products in untested markets in order to gain market recognition and market share. It can help to give a product a competitive edge.

- **Loss leader pricing** – This happens when the price is set below the costs of production, thus making a loss in the short run.

  Supermarkets often use loss leader pricing for some of their products (such as toilet tissue or carbonated soft drinks) in order to attract more customers to buy other products sold at the supermarket.

- **Price skimming** – This pricing policy involves a firm setting an initially high price in order to maximise profits and to recover its pre-launch costs, such as marketing and R&D (research and development). Price skimming is often used when selling new innovative products with few, if any, substitutes. The price is continually reduced (or 'skimmed') as competitors enter the market to launch rival products and compete for market share.

  While novelty for a new product can cause high demand and hence a high price, customers eventually look for newer versions or better alternatives. For example, when Apple launched the iPhone 4S it was priced at $399 in the USA, although the launch of the iPhone 5 in 2012 led to the price of the iPhone 4S falling to just $99.

- **Promotional pricing** – This commonly used pricing policy involves firms temporarily reducing their prices to attract more customers. Promotional pricing can be used to clear excess stock when a product is being withdrawn from the market or to boost demand for products in a new market.

  This pricing policy is often used to encourage brand loyalty (when customers stick to a certain brand due to their personal preference) and can thus increase the firm's market share in the long run.

Note that if monopolies exploit their market power and act against the public interest, perhaps by deliberately charging unreasonably high prices, then the government can intervene to break up their monopoly powers. For example, a merger between the two largest firms in a market can be prohibited by the government if there is reason to believe that the monopolist's resulting gain in **market share** (or **market dominance**) will act against the interest of the general public. In 2013, Visa and Mastercard were fined a record $7.25 billion for colluding to fix the credit card fees that they charged retailers.

> ### Case Study: Prices through the roof
>
> With a large degree of monopoly power, firms are able to charge astronomical prices for some of their products. For example:
> - The most expensive can of Coca-Cola, made for astronauts, is priced at $1250 per can.
> - The world's fastest car, Bugatti's Veyron World, costs a cool €1.95 million, before taxes are applied.
> - The most expensive Barbie doll, which comes with a one-carat pink diamond, sold in 2010 for a record price of $302 500.
> - The world's most expensive barbecue is the 24-karat gold-plated BeefEater Barbecue, and for that privilege you have to pay $165 000.
> - At $25 000 the world's most expensive dessert is a chocolate sundae, containing gold flakes, sold with a golden spoon! Customers can keep the spoon, which is made by luxury jeweller Euphoria New York.
>
>

Disadvantages of monopoly

Monopolies have a number of disadvantages:

- Private-sector monopolies can be inefficient in terms of resource allocation. In pursuit of profit maximisation, the monopolist can restrict the output of a product and/or charge a higher price for it. This creates a loss in the welfare of consumers (see Figure 13.2).
- High barriers to entry prevent new firms from entering the market. This limits the degree of competition and ensures monopolists can continue to charge relatively high prices.
- As there are no substitutes for the products supplied by monopolists, demand is price inelastic (see Chapter 4). However, as monopolists are price makers, they can charge higher prices to maximise profit from the relatively low PED (see Figure 4.6).
- Imperfect knowledge about prices and products means that consumers may not necessarily make rational choices. For example, the confusing pricing policies used by utilities companies (gas, telephone, water and electricity) mean that customers find it troublesome to switch between suppliers, especially as they might not know

if they would be better off. Thus, imperfect knowledge enables monopolists to maintain market power.

● Monopolists may have less incentive to innovate than firms in competitive markets. Innovation is the commercial exploitation of an invention. The lack of competitive pressures means that monopolists can become complacent (as there is no need to be worried about competition), rather than focus on innovations to ensure their survival.

Advantages of monopoly

● As monopolists control market supply, they operate on a very large scale, thus benefiting from huge economies of scale (see Chapter 14) – that is, lower average costs of production. This means that monopolists can actually supply larger quantities of output and at lower prices. This market power can be a source of international competitiveness against foreign competitors.

● Monopolists have the financial resources to invest in innovation. Research and development expenditure can help to generate new ideas, products and production processes. Innovation can therefore act as a source of profit and improve the productive capacity of the economy. For example, Apple's innovative products, such as the iPhone and iPad, have made the company the most valuable business on the planet. Only Boeing and Airbus have the financial resources to commercialise passenger aircraft such as the 787 Dreamliner and A380.

● Some monopolies can eliminate wasteful competition. For example, it makes more economic sense to have one monopoly supplier of postal services in a town, state or country rather than allowing private-sector firms to compete to provide such services. This is because profit-seeking firms may not have much of a financial incentive to provide services to remote areas of the country and a single provider can gain huge economies of scale. The same applies to suppliers of water pipes, railway tracks, telephone lines and electricity grids.

Activity

According to Wikipedia, the top five suppliers in the sugar and tobacco industries account for 99 per cent of the market in the UK.

1 Use the internet to research the industries which are most dominated by monopolists in your own country.

2 In small groups, discuss whether monopolies offer more or less choice for customers. Think of real-world examples to aid your discussions. Is choice a good thing?

3 Discuss the information you would need in order to assess whether a particular monopolist benefits consumers.

Chapter review questions

1 What is meant by 'perfect competition'?
2 What are the main characteristics of a perfectly competitive market?
3 What is meant by a 'monopoly'?
4 What are the main characteristics of a monopoly?
5 How do barriers to entry to an industry limit the degree of competition in a market?
6 What are the advantages and disadvantages of a monopoly?

Key terms

Barriers to entry are the obstacles that prevent other firms from effectively entering the market. Examples are the existence of intellectual property rights, large advertising budgets of existing firms, and legal constraints to prevent wasteful competition.

Market structure refers to the key characteristics of a particular market, such as the number and size of firms in the market, the degree and intensity of price and non-price competition, and the nature of barriers to entry.

Monopoly is a market structure where there is only one supplier of a good or service, with the power to affect market supply or prices.

Perfect competition describes a market where there is immense competition due to the absence of barriers to entry. This means there are many small firms competing in the market, none of which has any power to influence market supply or price.

Price discrimination is the practice of charging different prices to different customers for essentially the same product.

A **price maker** is a firm with significant market power, which means that it can control enough of the market supply to affect the price level.

Price takers are firms that set their price according to the market forces of demand and supply, rather than determining their own prices.

14 Business growth

By the end of this chapter, you should be able to:
- describe the main reasons for the different sizes of firms (size of market, capital, organisation)
- describe and evaluate integration, economies and diseconomies of scale.

Taken from Cambridge International Examinations Syllabus (IGCSE 0455/O Level 2281)
© Cambridge International Examinations

Size of firms

In every economy there are firms of different sizes. Small firms, such as local grocery stores or sole proprietors (see Chapter 10), co-exist alongside large multinational companies such as Walmart and Apple. It may be the objective of a firm to increase its market share or to operate in several countries, and it will therefore put strategies in place to achieve these aims. A business may start as one store and grow over time. For example, Starbucks opened its first coffee shop in Seattle, USA, in 1971 and now has around 20 890 stores in 62 countries. Alternatively a business may choose to stay small, such as a wedding dress designer, a hairdresser or an owner of a small gift shop.

The size of a firm can be measured in the following ways:

- The **number of employees** – In 2013, GlaxoSmithKline, a large pharmaceutical company, had over 100 000 employees. A small local grocery shop may have only five employees.
- The **size of the market (market share)** – For example, Hertz, Enterprise and Budget car hire companies collectively had 95 per cent of the car hire market in the USA in 2013. Nestlé dominates the food and beverages market in Pakistan, as it is the leading company in milk production and related products including yogurt, milk powder and butter. It also dominates the bottled water market in Pakistan.
- The **capital employed** in a firm – This is the difference between the assets of a firm (what it owns) and its liabilities (what it owes). For example, in January 2013 Walmart's capital employed was $203.1 billion, making it the world's largest retailer.
- The **sales turnover (sales revenue)** of the firm. This is measured by multiplying the unit price of a product by the quantity sold (see Chapter 12). For example, in 2012 ExxonMobil had sales turnover of $433.5 billion and was the world's largest firm by this measure.

Firms of all sizes exist in local, national and international markets, and industries are often dominated by large firms. For example:

- The sports clothing industry is dominated by Nike, Adidas and Puma.
- The tennis racket industry is dominated by Wilson, Prince and Head.
- The chocolate industry is dominated by Kraft, Mars, Nestlé and Ferrero Rocher.

The structure of a firm influences its size. Small businesses tend to be sole traders or partnerships, while large firms tend to be public limited companies that can sell shares on stock markets to obtain finance (see Chapter 10).

Exam practice

Study Table 14.1.

Table 14.1 The world's largest companies

Rank	Company	Country	Sales ($bn)	Profits ($bn)	Assets ($bn)	Market value (billion)
1	ExxonMobil	USA	433.5	41.1	331.1	4407.4
2	JPMorgan Chase	USA	110.8	19.0	2265.0	170.1
3	General Electric	USA	147.3	14.2	717.2	213.7
4	Royal Dutch Shell	Netherlands	470.2	25.1	340.5	227.6
5	ICBC	China	82.6	16.2	2039.1	237.4
6	HSBC Holdings	UK	102.0	16.2	2550.0	164.3
7	PetroChina	China	310.1	20.6	304.7	294.7

Source: Forbes

1 With reference to the data in the table, identify the industries within which the world's largest firms operate.   [3]
2 Explain why you think these industries can support very large firms.   [6]

How do firms grow?

Internal growth (organic growth)

- Firms can grow by **increasing the number of branches** (stores) within a particular country or by opening branches in different countries. They can also expand by selling their products in a greater number of countries and can finance this expansion using profits earned within the business. Coca-Cola now sells its cola drink in all but two countries in the world: North Korea and Cuba.
- Firms can grow by **franchising**. This means that an individual or a firm purchases a licence from another firm to trade using the name of the parent company. The Subway sandwich chain, established in the USA, has approximately 141 stores in the United Arab Emirates (UAE) and this expansion is due to franchising.
- Firms may **attract investment from larger businesses**. For example, the sandwich chain Pret a Manger funded its expansion through investment in the company by the fast-food giant McDonald's. Innocent, originally a small UK-based fresh fruit juice and smoothie manufacturer, is now large enough to supply supermarkets in the UK and some overseas shops through investment funding from Coca-Cola, which owns 90 per cent of the drinks company.

External growth (inorganic growth)

- Takeovers – A firm can instantly increase its size by buying a majority stake (share) in another business. For example, the Indian car-maker Tata Motors took over the UK-owned Jaguar and Land Rover in 2008. Tata Motors is part of the much larger Tata Group of companies. Kraft Foods took over Cadbury in 2011 and now has Cadbury's share of the global chocolate market in addition to its existing share. Microsoft bought Skype in 2011 and the purchase enabled the software giant to gain a larger share of the internet communications industry. Takeovers can be hostile, which means that the firm being taken over does not agree to the buyout. Takeovers can also be agreeable to both firms.

- Mergers – Two firms can merge together to form one new company. For example, the MTRC and KCRC railway companies in Hong Kong merged in 2007 to become one company, which now is the only provider of railway and underground railways services in Hong Kong. They have formed a natural monopoly (see Chapter 13) and any fare increases must be approved by the government. Another example of a merger is pharmaceutical giants Glaxo Wellcome and SmithKline Beecham (forming GlaxoSmithKline) in a deal worth $75.96 billion back in 2000.

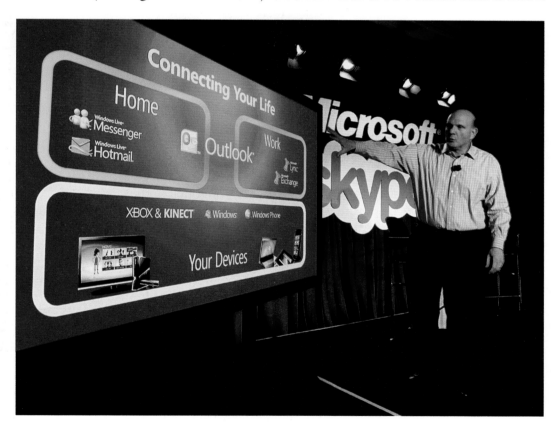

Microsoft's purchase of Skype enabled the software giant to gain a larger share of the internet communications industry

Types of integration

Integration refers to the combining of two or more firms, either through a merger or a takeover.

Horizontal integration

Horizontal integration occurs when two firms in the same sector of industry integrate together, by either a merger or a takeover. For example, AG Barr is a Scottish manufacturer of the soft drinks Irn Bru, Tizer and Rubicon, and wishes to merge with Britvic, another soft drinks manufacturer that makes Robinsons Barley Water, J2O and Fruit Shoots.

The proposed merger of Barr and Britvic would create one of Europe's largest soft drinks companies

The two combined businesses can benefit from:

- getting an increased market share
- gaining skilled employees from one another
- operating with fewer employees (as there is no need to hire two finance departments, for example), so this may reduce costs
- taking advantage of economies of scale.

However, the potential costs or drawbacks include the following:

- There may be duplication of resources and therefore some workers may be made redundant – that is, lose their jobs. Redundancies can cause anxiety, lead to demotivated staff and cause a decrease in productivity.
- The newly formed larger firm may face increasing costs arising from diseconomies of scale (see below).
- The combined firm may suffer from a culture clash if the two businesses are very different. This may initially cause communication and organisational problems.

Vertical integration

Vertical integration occurs when a firm from one sector of industry merges with, or is taken over by, a firm from another sector of industry. There are two types of vertical integration: backward and forward.

Backward vertical integration

Backward vertical integration occurs when a firm from the secondary sector of industry merges with a firm from the primary sector, or a firm from the tertiary sector merges with a firm from the secondary sector. For example, a factory in China that makes chicken nuggets for McDonald's might buy a chicken farm. The chicken farm supplies the factory directly with live chickens and the eggs produced are sold to McDonald's outlets for their breakfast products.

The benefits of backward vertical integration in the previous example include the following:

- The firm in the secondary sector has control over the quality of raw materials with which it is supplied.
- There is no wastage as all produce from the primary sector can be used.
- The price of raw materials falls as the manufacturer does not have to pay another (external) firm for the raw materials.

However, there are also costs of backward vertical integration in the example:

- Costs of running the farm in the primary sector increase total costs as more land, labour and capital resources are required.
- Transport costs increase for the integrated firm as raw materials were previously delivered by external suppliers.

Forward vertical integration occurs when a firm from the primary sector of industry integrates with a firm from the secondary sector, or a firm from the secondary sector integrates with a firm from the tertiary sector. For example, Apple, Levi's and Replay all own shops in which to sell their manufactured products. Shell, the global oil company, owns its entire chain of production: oil mines, oil processing plants and the petrol stations where consumers purchase fuel for their cars.

Apple has shops all over the world dedicated to selling its own goods. Here is its flagship store in London's Regent's Street

> **Activity**
>
> In groups, think of examples of how firms grow globally. What about in your home country or a country of your choice? Can you identify examples of internal growth, external growth and types of integration?

Exam practice

Tyrrells is a UK manufacturer of hand-cooked crisps (chips) which are made from potatoes and other root vegetables. The owner of the business, Will Chase, was originally a potato farmer, who sold his crop to supermarkets. The price of potatoes started to fall and he decided to add value to his potatoes by making them into packaged snacks in 2002. He invested in capital equipment and employed more staff to make the product, and his decision led to an increase in revenue and growth of the business, which is now worth over $28.4 million.

1 Identify the method of growth used by Tyrrells.   [1]
2 Explain two advantages of Tyrrells expanding into manufacturing industry.   [4]
3 Explain two reasons why production costs may have fallen after the expansion. [4]

Conglomerate integration

Conglomerate integration (also known as **lateral integration** or **diversification**) occurs when firms from different sectors of industry, which operate in unrelated areas of business, merge or are taken over by another firm. They may form a single company or be part of a large group of companies. For example, if a clothing manufacturer merges with a chocolate producer, the two firms are in the secondary sector of industry but operate in different areas of manufacturing. They can take advantage of risk-bearing economies of scale (see below), as diversification spreads risk.

An example of a conglomerate is the Tata Group, which has over 100 different companies in its portfolio, ranging from hotels and hospitality enterprises to mining and air conditioning. Another example is the Swire Group, which owns businesses that operate in many different markets, including retailing, beverages, aeronautical operations, property development, mining and car trading.

Diversification spreads risks because the firm has a number of businesses in different sectors of industry and therefore a failing business, which is part of a larger group, may be protected by the successful businesses within the group's larger portfolio.

However, the conglomerate may become too diverse and this may cause problems with the management of capital and human resources. If a segment of the diversified firm is under-performing, it may drain resources from other areas of the business.

Pacific Place, a shopping mall complex in Hong Kong, is one of the core holdings of the Swire Group's property portfolio

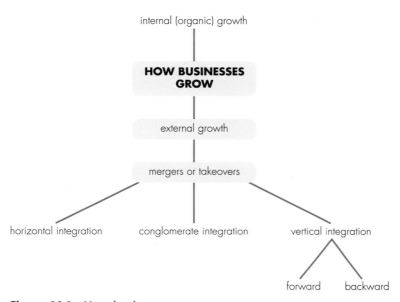

Figure 14.1 How businesses grow

Why do small firms co-exist beside large firms?

Large firms are able to take advantage of **economies of scale** (see below) and therefore their **average costs** of production are lower than those of a small firm. In many economies there are small grocery stores alongside large supermarkets. Supermarkets provide customers with:

- a wide choice of particular products, such as various types of yogurt, cheese or wine
- a wide product range, as in one store you can buy fresh milk, a pair of shoes, a tea pot and a hairdryer.

Modern supermarkets often have other facilities for customers, such as a café, a petrol (gas) station and a cash point (ATM). Supermarkets also have free parking facilities and therefore provide one-stop shopping.

Small grocery stores have to find a way to compete with supermarkets and they do so by providing a range of goods which cannot be bought in a supermarket, such as specialty cheeses and wines.

The small grocery store may be located in a remote area and be the only local seller of provisions. It may provide a personal shopping experience, as compared with the self-service style of a supermarket. Smaller shops can also adapt quickly to changing consumer tastes: for example, a small bakery may make more brown bread to cater for an increase in demand, and a small, independently run, magazine shop will order titles for individual customers.

Examples of products and services provided by small shops are made-to-measure clothing and custom-made furniture. They tend to focus on smaller markets and may cater for specific tastes and for people with higher incomes.

Economies of scale

One meaning of the word 'economy' is reduced expenditure or saving, while the word 'scale' refers to size. Therefore the phrase 'economies of scale' means that average costs of production fall as a firm grows or increases output.

Internal economies of scale

Internal economies of scale are cost savings that arise from within the business.

- Purchasing or bulk-buying economies of scale occur when the cost of raw materials falls as they are bought in large quantities.
- Technical economies of scale occur as large firms can afford to purchase expensive pieces of machinery and automated equipment for the manufacturing process. Large firms also produce in large quantities and therefore the high initial cost of the equipment can be spread across the high quantity of goods produced.
- Financial economies of scale occur as large firms are able to borrow money from banks more easily than small firms because they are perceived to be less risky to financial institutions. A large firm will also have a greater number of assets that can act as security for a loan.

- Managerial economies of scale occur as large firms have the resources to employ specialists to undertake functions within the firm: for example, accountants, engineers and human resources specialists. High salaries paid by large firms will attract experts.
- Risk-bearing economies of scale occur as large firms tend to produce a range of products and operate in many locations. This diversity spreads risks as weak sales in one country can be supported by strong sales in another. Samsung makes a range of products and if one product is experiencing decreasing sales then this loss can be balanced by increased sales of another product.
- Research and development economies of scale occur as large firms may be able to fund research and development, and therefore can be innovative and create products that enable them to be leaders in their area of business. For example, GlaxoSmithKline is a large pharmaceutical company that invests heavily in research and development (R&D), spending around 15 per cent of its sales revenue (or around $6.26 billion) on it.
- Marketing economies of scale occur as big firms tend to have a large advertising budget and therefore can spend large amounts of money on promoting their products. For example, a Nike or IKEA advert exposes all products under the Nike brand and all products sold in IKEA in a cost-effective way.

Activity

1 a) Look for examples of bulk buying economies of scale in your local supermarket. For instance, compare the cost per gram of a large bag of rice with that of a smaller bag of rice.
  b) Study the labels on the supermarket shelves to find three more examples of purchasing economies of scale. Be prepared to share your findings.
2 a) Make a list of the names of businesses that advertise using billboards and on television.
  b) Consider what the firms have in common. Are they large or small firms?
  c) Do the firms tend to be public limited companies (see Chapter 10) or smaller, privately owned firms?

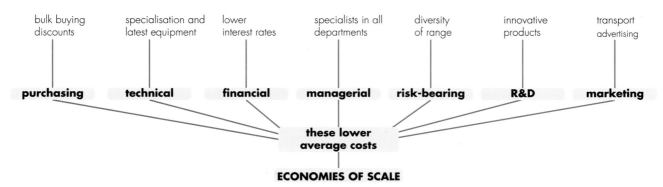

Figure 14.2 Economies of scale

External economies of scale

External economies of scale are economies of scale that arise due to the location of the firm and are therefore external to the business. Examples of external economies of scale are:

- **Proximity to related firms** – Tirupur in India is renowned for textile and garment manufacturing. A garment manufacturer will benefit from having firms that produce zippers, buttons, thread and fabrics located nearby, as this will give it easy access to its suppliers and reduce transport costs.
- **Availability of skilled labour** – In Tirupur there is a pool of skilled machinists and pattern cutters. This should make recruitment of textile workers with the necessary skills relatively easy.
- **The reputation of the geographical area** – This provides a firm with free publicity and exposure. For example, Silicon Valley in California, an area with a worldwide reputation for software creation and the development of information technology systems, has a large number of suitable skilled workers.
- **Access to transport** – Manufacturing firms benefit from being located near to major road networks, ports and cargo facilities. A café or restaurant will benefit from being close to other shops, public transport links and parking facilities. China has invested heavily in developing its infrastructure to facilitate efficient transportation of finished goods to ports and airports. This gives it a competitive advantage over India, where road and rail networks are less developed.

Diseconomies of scale

Diseconomies of scale arise when a firm gets too large and average costs of production start to rise. Therefore, the disadvantages of growth start to outweigh the advantages.

Reasons for increased average costs of production include the following:

Figure 14.3 Diseconomies of scale

- Communication issues may arise when a firm becomes too large. There may be too many branches to control and communicate with effectively, and decision making may be slow due to the number of people in the communication chain. This may lead to increased costs of production.
- A merger between two firms may be unsuccessful due to a clash of cultures, so it may be beneficial to demerge. In 2010 the Fosters Group, which produces beer, sold off its less profitable wine business as the merger had not brought about benefits of economies of scale. The **demerger** allowed Fosters to focus on beer production again.
- It may be necessary to employ more employees for all the branches of the firm, or a new factory may need to be built to accommodate the increased level of production. This will add to total costs of production and average costs of production may rise.

Study tips

In the real world it can be difficult for firms to determine when they have reached their lowest average cost and therefore their ideal level of production. Many factors influence costs, and firms operate in a constantly changing environment. A firm's decision to downsize or demerge from another firm may be based on non-cost reasons, such as difficulties in control and co-ordination, high staff turnover or a loss of focus.

- Workers within a large organisation may find it difficult to feel part of a large firm, so this may lead to a lack of motivation and reduced productivity. Thus average costs will tend to rise.
- The business may become too diverse and start to operate in areas in which it has less expertise. Reduced control and co-ordination may cause costs to increase. Again, this can lead firms to demerge.

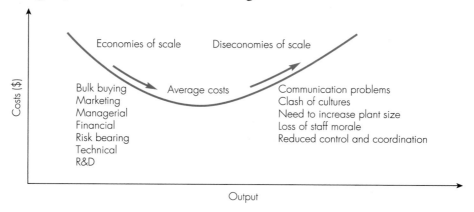

Figure 14.4 Economies and diseconomies of scale and average costs

Exam practice

In 2010 two telecommunications companies, T-Mobile and Orange, merged and became one firm. After the merger, customers of Orange and T-Mobile could switch between networks and the combined firm was able to reduce the number of aerial masts required and have an increased share of the market.

The two brands are owned by a company called Everything Everywhere, which in September 2012 changed its name to EE. EE will provide 4G services to its customers and T-Mobile and Orange will continue to serve their own segments of the market. T-Mobile is considered to be a value-for-money brand and Orange a more premium brand.

1 Identify and explain three types of economies of scale which could be achieved by the merger. [6]

2 Explain two diseconomies of scale which may arise in the future. [4]

3 Discuss the advantages and disadvantages of the merger between the two telecommunication firms. [7]

Chapter review questions

1 What are the two ways in which a firm can grow?
2 How can the size of a firm be determined?
3 Why do small firms co-exist beside large firms in all economies?
4 What are the six main types of internal economies of scale?
5 What is meant by the term 'diseconomies of scale'?
6 Which types of external economies of scale could be experienced by several car manufacturers located in a region of a country?
7 What are the advantages and disadvantages of two supermarket chains merging?
8 What are the advantages and disadvantages of a film production company merging with a chain of cinemas?

Key terms

Average costs are calculated by dividing total costs by the number of units produced.

Backward vertical integration occurs when a firm from the secondary sector of industry merges with a firm from the primary sector, or a firm from the tertiary sector merges with a firm from the secondary sector.

Conglomerate integration occurs when a merger or takeover occurs between two firms from unrelated areas of business.

A demerger occurs when two previously merged firms decide to break up and become two separate firms.

Diseconomies of scale occur when average costs of production start to increase as the size of a firm increases.

Economies of scale occur when average costs of production fall as the size of a firm increases.

External economies of scale are economies of scale that arise from factors outside of the firm, such as the location of the firm, proximity to transport and availability of skilled workers.

Financial economies of scale occur as large firms are able to borrow money from banks more easily than small firms because they are perceived to be less risky to the financial institutions.

Forward vertical integration occurs when a firm from the primary sector of industry merges with a firm from the secondary sector, or a firm from the secondary sector merges with a firm from the tertiary sector.

Horizontal integration occurs when two firms in the same sector of industry and the same industry merge.

Internal economies of scale are economies of scale that arise from the internal organisation of the business – for example, financial, bulk-buying and technological economies of scale.

Managerial economies of scale occur as large firms have the resources to employ specialists to undertake functions within the firm, such as accountants, engineers and human resources specialists.

Marketing economies of scale occur as big firms tend to have a large advertising budget and therefore can spend large amounts of money on promoting their products.

A merger occurs when two firms join together to make one firm.

Purchasing or bulk-buying economies of scale occur when the cost of raw materials falls as they are bought in large quantities thus reducing the average costs.

Research and development economies of scale occur as large firms may be able to fund research and development, and therefore can be innovative and create products that enable them to be leaders in their area of business.

Risk-bearing economies of scale occur as large firms tend to produce a range of products and operate in many locations.

A takeover occurs when a firm is taken over by another firm. A takeover may be hostile or the two firms may have agreed to the takeover.

Technical economies of scale occur as large firms can afford to purchase expensive pieces of machinery and automated equipment for the manufacturing process.

Vertical integration occurs when a takeover or merger takes place between two firms from different sectors of industry.

Role of government in an economy

Chapters

15 Government aims and influences

The role of government in an economy

The government plays a key role as a **producer** of goods and services and as an **employer**.

As a producer, the government supplies goods and services to the general public. For example, it will provide:

● **Public goods** – These products are non-excludable and non-rivalrous in consumption. Examples are national defence, law and order, street lighting, flood control systems, public fireworks displays, lighthouses, online search engines and public roads.

● **Merit goods** – These products are deemed to have social benefits yet are under-consumed without government intervention or provision (see Chapter 5). Examples are education, health care services, work-related training schemes and public libraries.

Services provided by the government

Exam practice

1 Distinguish between public goods and merit goods. [3]

2 Analyse the reasons why a government might choose to provide public goods and merit goods. [6]

- **Public services** – In many countries, the government also directly provides other essential public services, such as postal services, public transport systems, the emergency services (fire, police and ambulance) and immigration services. In some countries, the government goes further to provide public utilities services (such as gas, electricity and telecommunications) and terrestrial television broadcasting services. These services are not run in the same way as they would be if private-sector firms were seeking to maximise profits.
- **Welfare services** – In mixed economic systems (see Chapter 2), the government provides social and welfare services to people in need. These include transfer payments such as unemployment benefits and state pension schemes for the elderly.

  The New Zealand government, for example, spends about NZ$12 billion ($9.88bn) each year on transfer payments.

In order to provide these goods and services, the government must employ factors of production (see Chapter 1), including labour. Thus, the government can have a significant role as an employer – especially those governments that operate a mixed or a planned economic system (see Chapter 2). For example, in countries such as Australia, France, the USA and the UK, the government is a large employer of teachers, health care workers (such as surgeons, doctors and nurses) and urban planners.

Government influence on private producers

Governments influence private producers through the use of regulation, subsidies and taxation policies.

Regulation

Government **regulations** determine the boundaries within which private producers can operate. Examples are the use of employment legislation, consumer protection laws, environmental protection, competition laws and intellectual property rights.

- **Employment legislation** – These regulations protect the interests and safety of employees. For example, private-sector producers should comply with anti-discrimination laws which help to ensure that firms treat their workers fairly, regardless of their age, gender, race or religion.

Activity

Research the employment laws that exist in your country or a country of your choice. How do these laws impact on private-sector producers?

- **Consumer protection laws** – These regulations require private-sector firms to provide truthful descriptions of their goods and services, which must also meet minimal quality standards. Firms that provide demerit goods and services such as gambling, tobacco and alcohol are also heavily regulated to protect consumers. For example, cigarette advertising is banned in countries such as South Africa, Pakistan and Australia. Tobacco advertising has been banned throughout Singapore since 1971. In most countries, cigarette packaging must also carry highly noticeable health risk warnings.

● **Environmental protection** – Laws exist to prevent or reduce the damage to the environment caused by private-sector firms, such as pollution and the depletion of scarce resources. For example, Japan's government has imposed several types of fishing ban to preserve the world's supply of fish and whales. Regulation of carbon emissions also limits the potential damage to the environment caused by private producers.

The European Parliament voted to back fishing policy reform in February 2013, banning the wasteful practice of throwing away healthy fish at sea. Here, Green Party members hold up banners showing fish saying 'thank you'

● **Competition law** – Government regulation is used to prevent anti-competitive practices of private-sector monopolists (see Chapter 13). This helps to protect consumers and smaller firms that are less competitive. For example, in most countries, it is illegal for firms to engage in price fixing to raise prices and thus charge consumers unjustifiably high prices.
● **Intellectual property rights** – To encourage innovation and to safeguard the interest of producers, the government can use copyright, trademark and patent laws to protect the intellectual property of firms. These give private-sector firms legal protection against rival firms copying or imitating their products or inventions.

Recent high-profile cases include Apple versus Samsung smartphone battles (see the Activity below) and Cadbury versus Nestlé on whether you can copyright a colour.

> **Activity**
>
> Use the internet to investigate the legal battle between Apple and Samsung in the smartphone industry, following accusations that they were copying each other's technologies. Why do firms such as Apple and Samsung seek to protect their intellectual property?

Subsidies

A **subsidy** is financial assistance provided by a government to reduce the costs of production for firms. Subsidies are used to encourage output and consumption of certain goods and services. Governments often provide subsidies for educational services, employment purposes, public transport, tourism and agricultural output.

Subsidies are often used for the provision of education

Exam practice

The Mass Transport Railway (MTR) is Hong Kong's railway system and runs both underground and overground services. Founded in 1979, the MTR offers an efficient and affordable public transport system, serving over 4 million passengers on an average weekday. The government provides subsidies for travellers, including young children and the elderly. All retailers that operate at MTR stations pay rent to the MTR Corporation, thus allowing the organisation to keep fares at a low rate for all MTR travellers.

1 What is a subsidy? [2]

2 Explain why the Hong Kong government might want to subsidise public transport systems such as the MTR. [4]

Taxes

A **tax** is a levy or charge imposed by a government to raise costs of production and to reduce consumption of certain goods or services. Governments can use **direct taxes** (imposed on income, wealth or profits) to reduce income inequalities in the economy. They can also use **indirect taxation** (imposed on spending) to affect consumer expenditure. Indirect taxes include sales taxes and excise duties on items such as petroleum, alcohol, tobacco and air passenger travel. The government can also impose **tariffs** (import taxes) to discourage the purchase of foreign goods and services in order to protect domestic businesses and jobs.

The government can then spend its tax revenues to fund items of public-sector expenditure including: social security, national defence, law-and-order systems, transport, infrastructure, health care and education (see Chapter 16). Taxes are covered in more detail in Chapter 17.

Aims of government policies

Government policies tend to be aimed at achieving the five key macroeconomic (economy-wide) objectives: full employment (or reduced unemployment), controlled inflation (price stability), sustainable economic growth, the redistribution of income (lower income inequality) and balance of payments stability.

Full employment (or low unemployment)

Unemployment refers to people who are out of work, but who are of working age, are physically and mentally able to work, and are actively looking for work. Governments strive to reduce the **unemployment rate** – the proportion of a country's workforce who are unemployed. Chapter 19 covers employment in more detail.

Price stability (control of inflation)

Inflation refers to a persistent rise in the general level of prices in the economy. Low and sustainable rates of inflation are vital to achieving economic stability and social wellbeing. For example, inflation reduces the international competitiveness of a country as its prices will be relatively higher. This will lead to lower export sales, thus causing potential job losses. Inflation can be caused by excessive aggregate demand (total demand) in the economy. This is known as **demand-pull inflation**. By contrast, **cost-push inflation** is caused by higher costs of production. Chapter 18 covers price stability in more detail.

Economic growth

Economic growth is the increase in a country's gross domestic product (GDP) over time. Achieving economic growth brings greater prosperity to an economy and therefore tends to raise the standard of living for most people. Economic growth can be achieved by increasing the quantity and/or quality of factors of production, such as through education and training. Discovering resources such as oil will increase the potential output of an economy. Chapter 20 covers economic growth in more detail.

Exam practice

Most countries face the ongoing problem of striving to achieve economic growth and reducing unemployment. For example, Spain and Greece experienced unemployment rates of around 27 per cent in 2013 due to the continuing global financial crisis. In 2008, Zimbabwe's inflation soared to an astronomical 231 million per cent!

1   Define the terms 'economic growth' and 'unemployment'.   [4]

2   Explain why the control of inflation is a key macroeconomic objective.   [4]

Begging has been outlawed in Greece since 2003, but the recent unemployment hike has increased levels of occurrences

Redistribution of income

As an economy grows, the gap between top and bottom income earners tends to widen. For example, huge bonuses are often awarded to executives in the finance industry. This causes greater income inequalities in the economy. The government might therefore intervene by using progressive taxes (see Chapter 17) to redistribute income to low-income households. In some cases, the government could even cut taxes for low-income groups to improve their standard of living.

Exam practice

In 2013, two British banks, Barclays and the Royal Bank of Scotland, awarded a total of 521 employees more than £1 million ($1.5m) each, despite the world still recovering from the global financial crisis. By contrast, US investment bank JP Morgan Chase announced 19 000 job cuts between 2013 and 2014.

1   Explain what is meant by 'income equality'.   [2]
2   Suggest why a government might want to redistribute income within its country.   [4]

Study tips
The five main government objectives can be remembered by using the acronym **GETUP** – **g**rowth, **e**nvironment, **t**rade (balanced), **u**nemployment (low) and **p**rice stability.

Balance of payments stability

The balance of payments is a record of a country's financial transactions with other nations. This includes the money flows into and out of a country from the sale of exports and the purchase of imports. If the money inflows exceed the outflows, then a balance of payments surplus exists. If the outflows exceed the inflows, the country has spent more than it has earned, so a balance of payments deficit occurs. While a deficit drains money from the country, a balance of payments surplus can be inflationary in the long run due to the excess amount of money entering the country. Governments therefore tend to aim to achieve a balance of payments equilibrium. Chapter 24 covers the balance of payments in greater detail.

Conflicts between government aims

As it is not possible simultaneously to achieve all five macroeconomic objectives, there is said to be a trade-off or conflict between these targets. Examples of possible conflicts between a government's macroeconomic goals are considered below.

● **Economic growth versus low inflation** – If an economy grows due to excessive consumer demand, this will force prices to increase, thus creating inflation in the economy. Similarly, the government might choose to deflate the economy to control inflation, but this limits the ability to achieve economic growth. Therefore, it is rather difficult to achieve both macroeconomic objectives at the same time.

● **Low unemployment (or full employment) versus inflation** – In theory, there is an inverse relationship between the level of unemployment and the rate of inflation. For example, an attempt to reduce unemployment via the use of expansionary fiscal policy (see Chapter 16), such as lowering taxes or increasing government spending, can cause demand-pull inflation (see Chapter 18). Similarly, when the government tries to control inflation by using deflationary policies such as higher taxes or higher interest rates (see Chapter 16), the resulting fall in both consumer spending and investment will result in job losses.

- **Economic growth versus a balance of payments equilibrium** – Consumer spending and business investments tend to be high during an economic boom. However, if this is fuelled by a significant rise in spending on imports relative to exports, this leads to a worsening trade deficit on the country's balance of payments.
- **Economic growth versus protection of the environment** – Economic growth often leads to environmental problems such as land degradation, climate change, pollution and the depletion of non-renewable resources.

Case Study: Jakarta's traffic congestion

Jakarta, Indonesia's capital city, is renowned for having one of the world's worst traffic problems. The government tried to build a mass rail transit system in the city in 2004 to deal with the congestion problems, but the lack of funds put the project on hold. The problems of congestion and poor air quality do not seem to be slowing down as Indonesia saw a 27 per cent increase in the demand for new cars between 2012 and 2013.

- **Economic growth versus the redistribution of income and wealth** – As an economy grows, there tends to be a widening income and wealth gap between the rich and the poor (see the Case Study on page 171).

Study tips

It is possible for a government to achieve its macroeconomic objectives without conflicts occurring. For example, it is possible to achieve low inflation along with economic growth through the use of supply-side policies (see Chapter 16). Similarly, if economic growth is export-led (as in the case of China's growth over the past three decades), it will not lead to a deficit on the current account of the balance of payments.

Case Study: The world's richest people

The Forbes Rich List is an annual list of the world's wealthiest billionaires. The top ten wealthiest people on the planet in 2013 had a combined wealth of $451.5 billion – that is more than the combined GDP of the United Arab Emirates, Sri Lanka and Mauritius, and only slightly less than the combined GDP of Nigeria and Pakistan!

Mexican telecoms tycoon, Carlos Slim, is the richest man in the world with a total wealth of $73 billion – or the equivalent of the average annual salary of over 6.94 million people in the country!

Table 15.1 The ten wealthiest people in the world, 2013

Rank	Person	Wealth ($bn)	Company/industry
1	Carlos Slim	73	Telecoms
2	Bill Gates	67	Microsoft
3	Amancio Ortega	57	Zara
4	Warren Buffett	53.5	Berkshire Hathaway
5	Larry Ellison	43	Oracle
6	Charles Koch	34	Diversified
7	David Koch	34	Diversified
8	Li Ka-shing	31	Diversified
9	Liliane Bettencourt	30	L'Oreal
10	Bernard Arnault	29	LVMH

Source: Forbes

Chapter review questions

1 What does it mean by the government being a producer and an employer?
2 How do regulations, subsidies and taxation affect private-sector firms?
3 What are the five major macroeconomic aims?
4 Explain how there might be possible conflicts between the macroeconomic aims.
5 Why might it be possible for a government to achieve its macroeconomic objectives without conflicts occurring?

Key terms

An **employer** is a person or a firm that hires other workers to an organisation.
A **producer** is any firm that deals in the production and/or provision of goods and services.
Regulation refers to the rules and laws that govern business behaviour in the economy, such as employment laws, consumer protection legislation and environmental protection laws.
Subsidies are financial support from the government to reduce the costs of private-sector firms. They are used to encourage output and consumption of certain goods or services, such as public transport.
Taxes are levies or charges imposed by a government to raise the costs of production and reduce the consumption of certain goods or services, such as tobacco, alcohol and petroleum.

16 Government policies

Fiscal policy

Fiscal policy is the use of taxation and government expenditure strategies to influence the level of economic activity and macroeconomic objectives such as employment, economic growth and the control of inflation. For example, taxation (see Chapter 17) can be used to redistribute income and wealth to benefit less wealthy members of society. Government spending can be used to improve standards of living, such as building schools, hospitals and transportation networks.

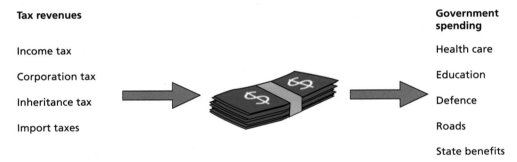

Tax revenues	Government spending
Income tax	Health care
Corporation tax	Education
Inheritance tax	Defence
Import taxes	Roads
	State benefits

Figure 16.1 Tax revenues and government spending

There are other sources of government revenue (such as government borrowing and the proceeds from privatisation, the selling of state assets) but tax revenues are by far the most significant source. If the government manages to balance its revenues and its spending, then a **balanced budget** is said to exist.

However, if the government spends more than it collects from its revenues then a **budget deficit** exists. And if there is more government revenue than is spent, the government has a **budget surplus**.

In the long run, governments strive to balance their budgets. This is partly because increasing government revenues by raising taxes is highly unpopular, while government borrowing to fund a budget deficit is hugely expensive due to the amount of interest owed on such loans.

Activity

Investigate the latest government budget in your country or a country of your choice.
Evaluate its strengths and weaknesses and the impact on various economic agents, such as:
- fixed-income earners
- the elderly
- families
- businesses
- home-owners.

In the UK, a red case is used to represent the budget box and is held up for a photo shoot outside 11 Downing Street, when the Chancellor of the Exchequer announces his annual budget plans

Use of fiscal policy

Fiscal policy can be used either to expand or to contract economic activity in order to achieve macroeconomic objectives and to promote economic stability.

Expansionary fiscal policy is used to stimulate the economy, by increasing government spending and/or lowering taxes. For example, by increasing social security payments (such as unemployment benefits or state pensions), domestic consumption should increase. This type of fiscal policy is used to reduce the effects of an economic recession (see Chapter 20), by boosting gross domestic product and reducing unemployment.

By contrast, **contractionary fiscal policy** is used to reduce the level of economic activity by decreasing government spending and/or raising taxes. For example, countries such as China and the USA have used property taxes to slow down escalating house prices. Contractionary fiscal policies are used to reduce inflationary pressures during an economic boom (see Chapter 20).

Case Study: China's housing bubble

China's phenomenal economic growth rate fuelled the demand for housing, making house prices skyrocket. Low interest rates and increased bank lending were further causes of the so-called 'housing bubble' in China. The government stepped in to slow down the housing market. In 2013, government measures included higher stamp duties (property sales taxes) and the requirement to have a minimum 60 per cent deposit for existing homebuyers wishing to purchase a second property. Mainland Chinese homebuyers wishing to purchase property in

Contractionary fiscal policies have been used in China to slow down the housing market

neighbouring Hong Kong also faced higher barriers, including an additional 15 per cent sales tax for non-permanent residents.

Fiscal policy is also used to **redistribute income and wealth** in the economy. Some countries have quite high rates of income tax to reallocate resources from wealthier individuals to the poorer members of society. Examples include Austria, Belgium, Cuba and Senegal, which all have a top tax rate of 50 per cent. High income tax rates can, however, cause severe distortions to the labour market.

Fiscal policy can also be used in conjunction with **supply-side policies** (see below) to affect the productive capacity of the economy, thus contributing to long-term economic growth. Examples of how fiscal policy can impact the supply side of the economy include:

- **Incentives to work** – Cuts in income tax can be used to create incentives for people to seek employment and to work harder. Some economists argue that reducing social welfare assistance such as unemployment benefits can also create incentives for people to seek employment. Government support for business start-ups can also create incentives for entrepreneurs and business creation.
- **Investment expenditure** – Government capital expenditure on infrastructure (such as railroads, motorways, schools and hospitals) helps to boost investment in the economy. Lower rates of corporation tax can also help to attract foreign direct investment in the country, thereby boosting the economy's potential output.
- **Human capital expenditure** – This refers to government expenditure on the workforce by investing in education and training. Such fiscal policies are designed to boost the productivity of labour (or the human capital of the workforce). Human capital expenditure is often accompanied by government spending on health care and transportation networks, as these help to raise labour productivity (see Chapter 11).

Limitations of fiscal policy

There are three main limitations of using fiscal policy to control the level of economic activity: problems with the timing (time lags), conflicting macroeconomic objectives and political considerations.

There are three problems with the timing of fiscal policy:

- **Recognition lags** – There is a time lag in recognising that government intervention is needed to affect the level of economic activity. This is because governments do not necessarily know if the economy is growing too fast (or declining too quickly).
- **Administrative lags** – There is a time delay between recognising the need for fiscal policy intervention and actually implementings appropriate action, such as approving tax changes or alterations to the government budget.
- **Impact lags** – There is a time lag between implementing fiscal policy and seeing the actual effects on the economy. A cut in income tax, for example, will take time to have a significant impact on the spending habits of households.

A second limitation of fiscal policy is that of conflicting macroeconomic objectives (see Chapter 15). For example, the use of expansionary fiscal policy can certainly help to achieve economic growth, but a combination of tax cuts and increased government spending can fuel domestic inflation. By contrast, contractionary fiscal policy can help to control inflationary pressures but might cause unemployment in the economy.

A final limitation of fiscal policy is its associated political problems. The political cycle (of re-electing political leaders and political parties) can cause artificial shocks to the business cycle (see Chapter 20). For example, expansionary fiscal policy might be used prior to a general election to boost the votes of the governing party, rather than to tackle fundamental economic problems. Such practices can lead to higher government debts due to tax cuts and increased government spending.

Exam practice

1   Explain why expansionary fiscal policy can cause a budget deficit for the government. [4]

2   Examine how fiscal policy can be used to promote long-term economic growth. [6]

Monetary policy

Monetary policy is the manipulation of interest rates, exchange rates and the money supply to control the amount of spending and investment in an economy. Interest rates can refer to the price of borrowing money or the yield from saving money at a financial institution. The money supply refers to the entire quantity of money circulating an economy, including notes and coins, bank loans and bank deposits (see Chapter 6).

Direct control of the **money supply** is relatively difficult, as the definition of money is quite loose and banks can create credit quite easily (see Chapter 6). Manipulation of **exchange rates** (see Chapter 25) is also rather difficult for many countries due to the reliance on international trade and compliance with the regulations of the World Trade Organization (see Chapter 26). Hence, most governments rely on **interest rate policy** to achieve economic stability. In most countries, the central bank or monetary authority (see Chapter 6) is responsible for overseeing exchange rate changes.

Monetary policy is used to control spending and investment in an economy

Use of monetary policy

Like fiscal policy, monetary policy can be used either to expand or to contract economic activity in the economy.

Expansionary monetary policy, also known as **loose monetary policy**, aims to boost economic activity by expanding the money supply. This is done mainly by lowering interest rates. This makes borrowing more attractive to households and firms because they are charged lower interest repayments on their loans. Those with existing loans and mortgages have more disposable income, so they have more money available to spend.

With **contractionary monetary policy**, also known as **tight monetary policy**, an increase in interest rates tends to reduce spending and investment in the economy. Thus, this slows down economic activity. Tight monetary policy is used to control the threat of inflation, although it can harm economic growth and therefore cause job losses in the long run.

Case Study: Quantitative easing

Following the global financial crisis of 2008, the UK and US central banks made significant cuts to interest rates to encourage people to spend money, rather than to save it. However, with interest rates at their lowest levels in history – near 0 per cent – they could not go any lower.

The Bank of England and the Federal Reserve had only one other option – quantitative easing (QE). This form of monetary policy directly injects money into the economy. This is done by the central bank buying bonds (a debt security or a promise to pay a lender at a later date). The institutions selling these bonds, such as commercial banks and insurance companies, then have 'new' money in their accounts, thus helping to boost the money supply and to promote lending (and hence spending).

Activity

Japan's interest rates averaged just 3.26 per cent between 1972 and 2013, and have rarely gone beyond 0 per cent since 1999.

Use the internet to investigate the reasons behind Japan's policy of extremely low interest rates. Here's a starting point: **www.tradingeconomics.com/japan/interest-rate**.

Exam practice

1 Explain how monetary policy can be used to influence the level of economic activity. [4]

2 Explain how the use of interest rate policy can help a country to control its inflation rate. [4]

Limitations of monetary policy

As with fiscal policy, there are time lags to the reaction to interest rate changes in the economy. This can make the effectiveness of monetary policy less certain or even destabilising for the economy.

Furthermore, economic activity is not totally and only dependent on interest rates. Other factors, such as consumer and business confidence levels, have an impact on gross domestic product. The global financial crisis of 2008 proved that, despite interest rates being close to, or equal to, 0 per cent in countries such as Japan, the USA and Hong Kong, the lack of business and consumer confidence led to a prolonged economic recession.

Japan has used a zero interest rate policy. Its interest rates averaged just 3.26 per cent between 1972 and 2013.

Some economists argue that the use of monetary policy can be counterproductive because it restricts economic activity and discourages foreign direct investment in the country. For example, higher interest rates raise the costs of production for firms, as existing and new loans become more expensive. This has negative impacts on profits, job creation, research and development expenditure, and innovation. Hence, higher interest rates (used to combat inflation) can conflict with other macroeconomic objectives, especially with economic growth and employment.

Supply-side policies

Supply-side policies are long-term strategies aimed at increasing the productive capacity of the economy by using policies to improve the quality and/or quantity of factors of production (see Chapter 1). This means that the economy can produce more goods and services at all price levels. This can be shown as an outward shift of the country's **production possibility curve** (see Chapter 1). Examples of supply-side policies are given below.

Privatisation

Privatisation is the policy of selling off state-owned assets (such as property or public-sector businesses) to the private sector, if they can be run more efficiently. This is because private-sector firms are motivated by profit and can, in theory, develop better products and deliver better services. Competition, productivity and efficiency are essential components of the private sector, which help to boost the productive potential of the economy.

For example, during the 1980s and 1990s, the UK government privatised British Steel, British Petroleum, Rolls-Royce and British Airways. In Hong Kong, the government privatised its rail services in October 2000.

Deregulation

Deregulation refers to the removal of barriers to entry, thereby making markets more competitive. For example, labour market reforms can make the labour force more competitive and more productive. Such reforms involve the removal of labour market imperfections, such as decreasing the power of trade unions (see Chapter 8) and reducing the national minimum wage (see Chapter 7).

In the Republic of Ireland, the taxi industry was deregulated to allow for more competition, leading to a dramatic increase in the number of taxis. In New Zealand, postal services and the banking industry have been deregulated, allowing for both domestic and foreign competition.

Capital investment

Some supply-side policies focus on the importance of investment in new technologies, infrastructure and research and development (R&D), thus contributing to the economic development of an economy. In the long run, capital investment helps to increase the productive capacity and productivity of the economy.

Expenditure on new technologies and R&D can help to generate new products for consumption, such as smartphones, tablet computers and environmentally friendly cars. On an international scale, innovation can also be a good source of competitive advantage for a country.

According to the IMF's *World Economic Outlook,* China's capital investment as a proportion of its annual GDP is expected to average 47.25 per cent between 2013 and 2016, whereas the rate for the USA is around 15 per cent. This should, in theory, help China's quest for continual and sustainable economic growth.

Human capital investment

Human capital is the collective knowledge, skills and experiences of a country's workforce. Supply-side policies are used to improve the quantity and/or quality of the workforce in the economy. These policies can be used to create incentives to work. For example, government-funded retraining schemes can help the unemployed to improve their chances of finding paid employment. Increased government spending on education and training are further examples.

Some countries spend a relatively large amount of their GDP on education, such as Finland (6.4 per cent), Sweden (7.7 per cent), Denmark (8.5 per cent) and Brunei Darussalam (9.1 per cent), whereas others, such as Botswana (2.2 per cent) and Bangladesh (2.4 per cent), spend rather less.

Tax reforms

Lower taxes can create incentives for work (see Chapter 17), especially for people on low wage rates. Over time, this can provide a boost to consumption. Tax cuts can also encourage firms to invest in the economy, as they strive to maximise profits.

Enterprise zones

These are areas with relatively high rates of unemployment where the government creates financial incentives for firms to relocate. These incentives include tax rebates and reduced regulations in order to attract private-sector investments. Enterprise zones are common in the UK, USA, China and India.

A newly established enterprise zone in Shenzhen City, China

The main criticism of supply-side policies is the time that it takes to reap the benefits. For example, it might take decades for a nation to enjoy the benefits of an improved education system or better infrastructure in the country.

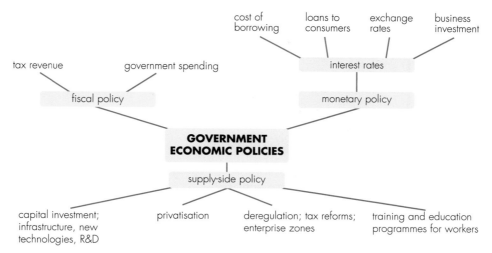

Figure 16.2 Government economic policies

The merits of supply-side policies

The advantages of using supply-side policies to achieve economic stability include:

- **Improved economic growth** – Supply-side policies can be used to achieve sustainable economic growth by increasing the productive capacity of the economy.
- **Lower inflation** – As supply-side policies increase the productive potential of the economy, they help to prevent the general price level from rising beyond control.
- **Lower unemployment** – An increase in the economy's productive capacity will tend to increase national output, thereby creating jobs in the economy in the long term. Also, supply-side policies can help to reduce both frictional and structural unemployment (see Chapter 19).
- **Improved balance of payments** – Since supply-side policies can improve productivity and national output without increasing the general price level, the international competitiveness of the country should improve. For example, firms should become more productive and competitive, which will help to boost the economy's export earnings. Therefore, supply-side policies tend to improve a country's balance of payments (see Chapter 24).

Exam practice

1 Define the term 'supply-side policies'. [2]
2 Examine how supply-side policies can help to achieve any *two* macroeconomic objectives. [6]

Chapter review questions

1 What is fiscal policy?
2 What is the difference between a budget deficit and a budget surplus?
3 What are the differences between expansionary and contractionary fiscal policy?
4 Why might a government choose to use fiscal policy?
5 What is monetary policy?
6 Explain the differences between expansionary and contractionary monetary policy.
7 Why might a government choose to use monetary policy?
8 What are supply-side policies?
9 Why might a government choose to use supply-side policies?
10 What are the limitations of using fiscal, monetary and supply-side policies to control economic activity?

Key terms

Deregulation is a supply-side policy of making markets more competitive by removing barriers to entry and other market imperfections.

Fiscal policy is the use of taxes and government spending to affect macroeconomic objectives such as economic growth and employment.

Monetary policy refers to the use of interest rates, exchange rates and the money supply to control macroeconomic objectives and to affect the level of economic activity.

Privatisation is a supply-side policy of selling off state-owned assets to the private sector.

Supply-side policies are the long-term strategies aimed at increasing the productive capacity of the economy by improving the quality and/or quantity of factors of production.

17 Taxation

By the end of this chapter, you should be able to:
● describe the types of taxation (direct, indirect, progressive, regressive and proportional)
● describe the impact of taxation.

Taken from Cambridge International Examinations Syllabus (IGCSE 0455/O Level 2281)
© Cambridge International Examinations

Taxation

A **tax** is a government levy on income or expenditure. There are various reasons why the government imposes taxes. For example:

● Taxes on salaries and profits raise government revenue and can be used to redistribute income and wealth in the economy.
● Taxes on goods and services raise the costs of production and therefore can limit the output of certain demerit products (see Chapter 5), such as alcohol and tobacco.
● Tariffs imposed on foreign goods and services help to protect domestic firms from overseas rivals (see Chapter 26).

Before the government can spend money on the economy, it must first take the money from taxpayers (both individuals and firms). In addition to other sources of government finance, tax revenues are spent on several key areas, including social security, education, health care, transport, infrastructure and national defence.

 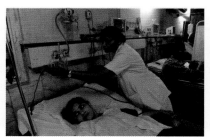 

Taxes are used by governments to pay for infrastructure, health care and national defence

The **tax burden** is the amount of tax that households and firms have to pay. This can be measured in three ways. For a country, the tax burden is measured by calculating total tax revenues as a proportion of gross domestic product (GDP). For individuals and firms, the tax burden can be measured by the absolute value of tax paid or by the amount of tax paid as a proportion of their income or profits.

> **Activity**
>
> At the end of 2012, economists described the situation faced by the US government as a 'fiscal cliff'. Investigate what this means and its potential impact on the economy in the short run and the long run. Be prepared to show the results of your investigation to others in the class.

Types of taxation

There are various classifications of taxes, including the following:

- **Direct taxes** – This type of tax is paid from the income, wealth or profit of individuals and firms. Examples are taxes on salaries, inheritance and company profits.
- **Indirect taxes** – These are taxes imposed on expenditure on goods and services. For example, countries such as Australia and Singapore use a goods and services tax (GST), whereas the European Union uses value added tax (VAT). Other examples are taxes on petrol, alcohol and cigarettes.
- **Progressive taxation** – Under this tax system, those with a higher ability to pay are charged a higher rate of tax. This means that as the income, wealth or profit of the taxpayer rises, a higher rate of tax is imposed (see Figure 17.1). Examples of progressive taxation are income tax, capital gains tax and stamp duty.

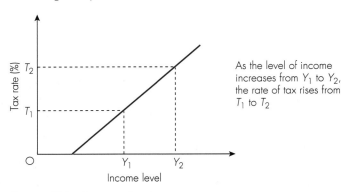

As the level of income increases from Y_1 to Y_2, the rate of tax rises from T_1 to T_2

Figure 17.1   **Progressive taxes**

Exam practice

Suppose in a country the progressive tax rates are 10 per cent (for those earning between $10 001 and $40 000 per year) and 15 per cent (for those earning over $40 000 per year).

1 By copying and completing the table below, calculate the total amount of tax paid by an individual who earns $75 000 per year. [4]

Income level ($)	Tax rate (%)	Amount of tax paid ($)
10 000	0	
10 001–40 000	10	
40 001+	15	
Total tax:		

2 Show how the average rate of income tax paid by the individual is 11 per cent. [2]

- **Regressive taxation** – Under this tax system, those with a higher ability to pay are actually charged a lower rate of tax: that is, the wealthier the individual, the lower the tax paid as a percentage of income (see Figure 17.2). For example, although a high-income earner pays the same amount of airport tax or television licence fee as a less wealthy person, the amount of tax paid is a smaller proportion of the wealthier person's income.

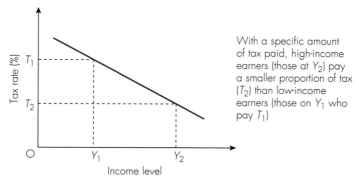

With a specific amount of tax paid, high-income earners (those at Y_2) pay a smaller proportion of tax (T_2) than low-income earners (those on Y_1 who pay T_1)

Figure 17.2 Regressive taxes

- **Proportional taxation** – Under this tax system, the percentage of tax paid stays the same, irrespective of the taxpayer's level of income, wealth or profits (see Figure 17.3). An example would be a flat rate sales tax, such as VAT or GST. Sales taxes vary considerably from country to country: for example, Denmark has a 25 per cent GST, whereas sales taxes in India and Japan are as low as 5 per cent. Another example is an income tax which is 20 per cent for all individuals regardless of level of income. Proportional taxation is generally regarded as regressive.

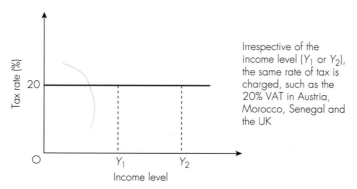

Irrespective of the income level (Y_1 or Y_2), the same rate of tax is charged, such as the 20% VAT in Austria, Morocco, Senegal and the UK

Figure 17.3 Proportional taxes

Activity

Copy the table below. Place ticks in the correct boxes to identify whether the tax is direct or indirect. The first one has been completed as an example.

Tax	Direct	Indirect
Airport tax		✓
Capital gains tax		
Carbon tax		
Corporation tax		
Customs duties		
Excise duties		
Income tax		
Inheritance tax		
Stamp duty		
Tariffs		
VAT or GST		
Windfall tax		

Exam practice

1 Study the data below and answer the questions that follow.

Income ($ per year)	Tax paid per year ($)		
	Tax A	Tax B	Tax C
10 000	1000	1000	1000
15 000	1000	1800	1500
20 000	1000	3000	2000
25 000	1000	4500	2500

a) Identify the tax (A, B or C) that is progressive. [1]

b) Identify the tax (A, B or C) that is proportional. [1]

c) Distinguish between a regressive and a proportional tax. [2]

2 Study the tax system for the three countries below. Calculate the percentage of tax paid on each level of income and identify whether the tax systems are progressive, regressive or proportional. [6]

Tax system A		Tax system B		Tax system C	
Annual income ($)	Amount of tax paid ($)	Annual income ($)	Amount of tax paid ($)	Annual income ($)	Amount of tax paid ($)
4500	900	10 000	1500	8000	800
10 000	1800	20 000	3000	20 000	3000
20 000	2800	30 000	4500	45 000	11 250

Table 17.1 Examples of taxes

Taxes	Definition
Income tax	Levied on personal incomes (wages, interest, rent and dividends). In most countries, this is the main source of tax revenues.
Corporation tax	A direct tax on the profits of businesses.
Sales tax	An indirect tax, such as VAT, charged on an individual's spending.
Excise duties	Indirect inland taxes imposed on certain goods and services, such as alcohol, tobacco, petrol, soft drinks and gambling.
Custom duties	Indirect cross-border taxes on foreign imports.
Capital gains tax	A tax on the earnings made from investments such as buying shares and private property.
Inheritance tax	A tax on the transfer of income and wealth such as property when passed on to another person.
Stamp duty	A progressive tax paid on the sale of commercial or residential property.
Carbon tax	A tax imposed on vehicle manufacturers or firms that produce excessive carbon emissions.
Windfall tax	A tax charged on individuals and firms that gain an unexpected one-off amount of money, such as a person winning the lottery or a firm gaining from a takeover bid.

Passengers shop in the Duty and Tax Free Shop at Cointrin airport in Geneva, Switzerland

Exam practice

Countries such as Saudi Arabia, Gibraltar and Hong Kong do not have a sales tax (a type of indirect tax).

1 What is an indirect tax?　　　　　　　　　　　　　　　　　　　　　　[2]
2 Examine the advantages and disadvantages for countries that do not impose sales taxes.　　　　　　　　　　　　　　　　　　　　　[6]

The impact of taxation

Taxation has varying impacts depending on the type of tax in question. The impact of taxation on economic agents and the economy are considered below.

- **Impact on price and quantity** – The imposition of a sales tax will shift the supply curve of a product to the left (see Chapter 3) due to the higher costs of production. This will increase the price charged to customers and reduce the quantity produced and sold.

- **Impact on economic growth** – Taxation tends to reduce incentives to work and to produce. By contrast, tax cuts can boost domestic spending, thus benefiting businesses and helping to create jobs. Nevertheless, tax revenues are essential to fund government spending (for the construction of schools, hospitals, railways, airports, roads and so on), which fuels economic growth.

- **Impact on inflation** – As taxation tends to reduce the spending ability of individuals and the profits of firms, it helps to lessen the impact of inflation (see Chapter 18). By contrast, a cut in taxes boosts the disposable income of households and firms, thus fuelling inflationary pressures on the economy.

- **Impact on business location** – The rate of corporation tax and income tax will affect where multinational businesses choose to locate. For example, high corporation tax rates in Argentina (35 per cent), Pakistan (35 per cent) and Cameroon (38.5 per cent) can put off some companies thinking of locating in these countries. As a result, foreign direct investment in these countries might be lower than otherwise. By contrast, it might be easier to attract workers in low income tax countries such as Bulgaria (10 per cent), Macedonia (10 per cent), Belarus (12 per cent) and Hong Kong (15 per cent).

- **Impact on social behaviour** – Taxation can be used to alter social behaviour with the intention of reducing the consumption of demerit goods (see Chapter 5). For example, taxing tobacco and alcohol should, in theory, reduce the demand for such products. Taxes are also used to protect the natural environment by charging those who pollute or damage it. For example, countries such as the UK and China tax cars based on the engine size because vehicles with larger engines tend to cause more pollution.

Exam practice

In March 2013, inflation in the Czech Republic slowed to 1.7 per cent, partly due to the reduced spending caused by an increase in the national sales tax.

1 Explain how taxes can be used to reduce the rate of inflation in the Czech Republic. [4]

2 Analyse how an increase in taxation can conflict with any two macroeconomic objectives of the Czech Republic government. [6]

Case Study: Plastic bag levy

Prior to July 2009, Hong Kong used an average of 30 million plastic carrier bags every day! For a relatively small population of 7 million people, this meant the average person in Hong Kong was using more than four plastic carrier bags every day, often on a single-use basis. This staggering figure meant that the country's landfills would be unable to cope with the bags when they were thrown away.

Hong Kong's introduction of a HK$0.5 tax (6.5 US cents) on the use of carrier bags has encouraged people to use recycled shopping bags. In fact, demand for plastic carrier bags fell by 85 per cent within the first 2 days of the tax being introduced.

This follows similar moves made by other countries such as China (in 2009) and Ireland (in 2002).

Source: adapted from *South China Morning Post*

- **Impact on incentives to work** – If taxes are too high, this can create disincentives to work. For example, France tried to introduce a 75 per cent income tax rate in 2012 for individuals earning incomes in excess of €1 million ($1.28 million per year). However, the proposals were overturned, with some economists arguing that the government would actually receive more tax revenues by cutting tax rates. This is because lower rates of tax can create incentives to work and also help to reduce tax avoidance and tax evasion (see below).

- **Impact on tax avoidance and tax evasion** – Some taxes are preventable. Tax avoidance is the legal act of not paying taxes: for example, non-smokers do not pay tobacco tax and non-overseas travellers do not pay air passenger departure taxes.

  However, tax evasion is illegal as it refers to non-payment of taxes due, perhaps by a business under-declaring its level of profits. High levels of taxation will tend to encourage both tax avoidance and tax evasion. By contrast, low rates of taxation create far fewer incentives for households and firms to defraud the government.

- **Impact on the distribution of wealth** – The use of taxes can help to redistribute income and wealth from the relatively rich to the poorer members of society. For example, wealthier individuals will pay more income tax, sales taxes and stamp duty on their private properties. These funds can be used by the government to support education, health care and social benefits for less affluent individuals in the economy.

Exam practice

In November 2008, following the recession caused by the global financial crisis, the UK government reduced the rate of value added tax (VAT) from 17.5 per cent to 15 per cent. However, by January 2011 the government's escalating debt problems forced VAT to increase to 20 per cent.

1 Explain how the reduction in VAT from 17.5 per cent to 15 per cent might help to reduce the effects of a recession. [4]

2 Examine three impacts of the increase in VAT to 20 per cent. [6]

Activity

Some countries, such as Andorra, Brunei Darussalam, Oman and Qatar, have a zero rate of income tax. Other countries, such as Bahamas and Estonia, have a zero rate of corporation tax.

1 Which other countries have a zero rate of income tax?

2 Investigate the reasons behind such government decisions. Be prepared to share your findings with the rest of the class.

Chapter review questions

1 What is the difference between direct and indirect taxes?

2 State two examples of direct taxes and two examples of indirect taxes.

3 What is the difference between progressive, regressive and proportional taxes?

4 How do taxes affect: economic growth, inflation and incentives to work?

5 What is the difference between tax avoidance and tax evasion?

Key terms

Direct taxes are government charges imposed on income and wealth, such as income tax and inheritance tax.

Indirect taxes are taxes imposed on expenditure – for example, value added tax (VAT).

Progressive taxation is a tax system that deducts a greater proportion of tax as a person's income level increases. Progressive taxes include income tax and capital gains tax.

Proportional taxation is a tax system that deducts the same proportion of tax at all income levels.

Regressive taxation is a tax system that deducts a smaller proportion of tax as a person's income increases. Regressive taxes include sales taxes and stamp duties.

Tax avoidance is the legal act of minimising payment of taxes, such as by avoiding spending on items with a large sales tax.

The **tax burden** is the amount of tax that households and firms have to pay.

Taxes are government levies on income and expenditure, used to fund government expenditure and to affect economic activity.

Tax evasion is the illegal act of not paying the correct amount of tax, perhaps due to a firm under-declaring its profits.

Section 6

Economic indicators

Chapters

18 Inflation

Inflation

Inflation is a sustained rise in the general price level in an economy over time. This does not mean that the price of every good and service increases, but that on average the prices are rising.

Governments aim to control inflation because it reduces the value of money and the spending power of households, governments and firms. For example, the inflation rate in the western Asian country of Syria (see Figure 18.1) was around 48 per cent in 2013, meaning that the general price level in Syria increased by an average of 48 per cent in a year. This means that a product priced at 100 Syrian pounds would increase to 148 Syrian pounds by the end of the year. This makes conditions far less economically stable in Syria than in other countries with low and stable rates of inflation, such as Canada, the UK and the USA (see Figure 18.2).

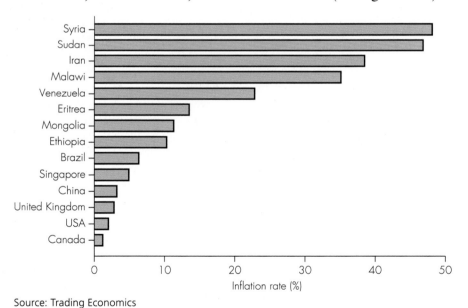

Source: Trading Economics

Figure 18.1　Inflation rates around the world: selected countries, 2013

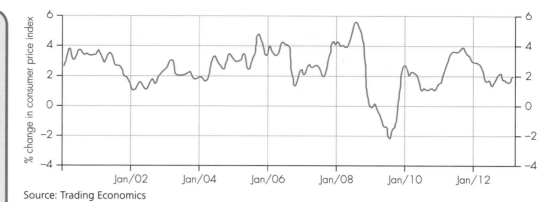

Source: Trading Economics

Figure 18.2 US inflation rates, 2000–13

Case Study: Hyperinflation in Zimbabwe

Major economic problems in Zimbabwe caused the country to suffer from extremely high rates of inflation – known as **hyperinflation** – between 2003 and 2009. In June 2006, the Central Bank introduced a new 100 000 Zimbabwean dollar banknote (less than US$1 back then). However, by July 2008, inflation had reached a whopping 231 000 000 per cent! People carried large bundles of cash to buy their groceries (pictured).

Several months later, in January 2009, the Zimbabwean government launched the 100 trillion Zimbabwean dollar banknote (ZWD100 000 000 000 000)! This meant the currency became worthless, and it was eventually abandoned.

Today, Zimbabwe still does not have its own official currency, with many preferring to use the US dollar. With GDP per capita at $487 (about $1.33 per day), around 80 per cent of the country's 12.6 million people live in extreme poverty.

Exam practice

The hypothetical data below show the inflation rates for a country over three years.

Year	1	2	3
Inflation rate (%)	2.5	1.7	2.3

1 Define the meaning of 'inflation rate'.   [2]
2 Explain why inflation was at its highest in the third year.   [3]

The consumer price index

The **consumer price index** (CPI) is a common method used to calculate the inflation rate. It measures price changes of a representative **basket** of goods and services (those consumed by an average household) in the country. For example, items such as staple food products, clothing, petrol and transportation are likely to be included. However, different weights are applied to reflect the relative importance of each item in the average household's expenditure. For example, a 10 per cent increase in the price of petrol will affect people far more than a 50 per cent increase in the price of light bulbs, batteries or tomatoes. Changes in the CPI therefore represent changes in the cost of living for the average household in the economy.

The statistical weights in the CPI are based on the proportion of the average household's income spent on the items in the representative basket of goods and services. For example, if the typical household in a country spent 15 per cent of its income on food, then 15 per cent of the weights in the index would be assigned to food. Therefore, items of expenditure that take a greater proportion of the typical household's spending are assigned a larger weighting. Changing fashions and trends, such as a hike in household expenditure on smartphones, online apps and tablet computers, require a review (or update) of the weights in the CPI.

In the UK in 2013, ebooks and blueberries were amongst the goods included in the CPI basket

The CPI versus the RPI

Both the consumer price index and the **retail price index** (RPI) can be used to calculate the rate of inflation. Both indices follow a similar pattern (see Figure 18.3). However, there are three key differences to these price indices:

- **The items included in the calculations** – The main difference is that the RPI includes the cost of housing, such as mortgage interest payments and other housing costs. The RPI also includes overseas expenditure by domestic households. The CPI includes costs paid for financial services.
- **The population base** – Both price indices try to measure changes in the cost of living for the average household. However, the RPI excludes low-income pensioner households and very high-income households, as it is argued that these do not represent the 'average' household or the expenditure of the average family.
- **The method of calculation** – The RPI is calculated using the arithmetic mean whereas the CPI uses the geometric mean. What this means is that the RPI tends to be lower than the CPI (unless interest rates for mortgage repayments are extremely low). For example, suppose the price changes for a product in the last three months were 1 per cent, 2 per cent and 3 per cent. The arithmetic mean (RPI) would average these changes to 2 per cent, i.e. $\frac{1+2+3}{3} = 2$. However, the geometric mean (CPI) would average these changes to just 1.8 per cent, i.e. $3\sqrt{1 \times 2 \times 3}$.

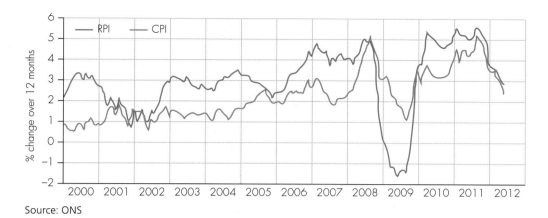

Source: ONS

Figure 18.3   The CPI and RPI for the UK economy, 2000–12

A key political and economic reason for calculating both price indices is that inflation affects the whole economy and can have major impacts on certain stakeholders. For example, payments for state-funded pensions and welfare benefits are linked to inflation, so the use of the CPI will usually save the government money compared with using the RPI. By contrast, the taxes imposed on fuel, alcohol and tobacco are linked to the RPI, thus generating the government more revenue than if it used the CPI. The RPI is also used by trade unions and firms as a starting point for wage negotiations (see Chapter 8).

The CPI is the preferred method for international comparisons of inflation. This is partly because it uses a wider sample of the population when calculating and assigning statistical weights to the index. The CPI, as the key measure of inflation for most countries, is also important as a benchmark when the government sets interest rates (see Chapter 16).

Calculating the CPI or RPI

A price index is used to indicate the average percentage change in prices compared with a starting period called the **base year**. The CPI and RPI compare the price index of buying a representative basket of goods and services with the base year, which is assigned a value of 100. Hence, a price index of 115.2 means that prices have in general increased by 15.2 per cent since the starting period. If prices were to rise by another 5 per cent in the subsequent year, the price index number would become 120.96 (that is, 115.2×1.05), or 20.96 per cent higher since the base year. Price changes in the CPI and RPI are measured on a monthly basis but reported for a 12-month period.

Calculating changes in the CPI or RPI gives the rate of inflation. To do so, two steps are involved:

- collection of the price data on a monthly basis
- assigning the statistical weights, representing different patterns of spending over time.

The simplified example in Table 18.1, with three products in the representative basket of goods and services, shows how the total basket price is calculated. Assume 2012 is the base year, when the total basket price was $20.

Table 18.1 Calculating the total basket price

Product	Price in 2013 ($)	Price in 2014 ($)
Pizza	9	10
Cinema ticket	10	11
Petrol	3	3.5
Total basket price	22.0	24.5

To calculate inflation between 2013 and 2014, first calculate the price indices for the two years in question:

- 2013: $\frac{\$22}{\$20} \times 100 = 110$ (prices in 2013 were 10 per cent higher on average than in 2012).

- 2014: $\frac{\$24.5}{\$20} \times 100 = 122.5$ (prices in 2014 were 22.5 per cent higher on average than in 2012).

The inflation rate between 2013 and 2014 is the percentage change in the price indices during these two periods:

$$\frac{122.5 - 110}{110} \times 100 = \textbf{11.36\%}$$

However, the products measured in the CPI are of different degrees of importance to the typical household, so weights are applied to reflect this. Suppose, for example, in a particular country food consumption accounts for 40 per cent of average household spending whereas entertainment represents 20 per cent, transport represents 25 per cent and all other items represent the remaining 15 per cent. To create a weighted price index, economists multiply the price index for each item (in the representative basket of goods and services) by the statistical weight for each item of expenditure. Applying these weights gives the results shown in Table 18.2.

Table 18.2 Creating a weighted price index

Product	Price index	Weight	Weighted index
Food	110.0	0.40	110 × 0.4 = 44.0
Entertainment	115.0	0.20	115 × 0.2 = 23.0
Transport	116.4	0.25	116.4 × 0.25 = 29.1
Others	123.3	0.15	123.3 × 0.15 = 18.5
Weighted index			**114.6**

Study tips

Although the CPI and RPI are the most widely used price indices for measuring inflation, they only take an average measure. They therefore hide the fact that the prices of some products increase more rapidly than others, while the price of other products might have actually fallen.

While the price of food has increased the least (only 10 per cent) since the base year, spending on food accounts for 40 per cent of the typical household's spending. This has a much larger impact on the cost of living than the 15 per cent increase in the price of entertainment, which accounts for only 20 per cent of the average household expenditure. Without using weights, the average price index would be 116.18: that is, $\frac{110 + 115 + 116.4 + 123.3}{4}$. However, the statistical weights reduce the price index to 114.6 because the relatively higher prices of non-food items account for a smaller proportion of spending by the typical household. This shows that prices have, on average, increased by 14.6 per cent since the base year. Therefore, a weighted price index is more accurate in measuring changes in the cost of living, and hence inflation.

Exam practice

1 **a)** Calculate the inflation rate if the consumer price index changes from 123.0 to 129.15. [2]

   b) Calculate the price index if there is 3.0 per cent inflation during the year and if the index was previously at 130. [2]

   c) Calculate how much a basket of goods and services which is currently priced at $1200 would cost if the CPI increased from 125 to 135. [3]

2 The data below are for a hypothetical country, Jukeland.

Item	Retail prices index	Weight
Clothing	110	10
Food	120	20
Housing	130	30
Others	140	40

   a) Define what is meant by a 'retail price index' (RPI). [2]

   b) 'The typical household in Jukeland spends more money on housing than on food or clothing.' Explain this statement. [3]

   c) Use the data above to calculate the weighted retail price index (RPI) in Jukeland. [4]

The causes of inflation

There are two main causes of inflation. These relate to demand-pull inflation and cost-push inflation.

Cost-push inflation is caused by higher costs of production, which makes firms raise their prices in order to maintain their profit margins. For example, in Figure 18.4, higher raw material costs, increased wages and soaring rents shift the aggregate supply (total supply) curve for the economy to the left from AS_1 to AS_2, forcing up the general price level from P_1 to P_2 and reducing national income from Y_1 to Y_2.

Higher rents in popular locations can cause cost-push inflation

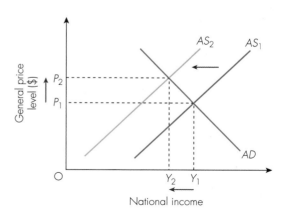

Figure 18.4 Cost-push inflation

Demand-pull inflation is caused by higher levels of aggregate demand (total demand in the economy) driving up the general price level of goods and services. For example, during an economic boom (see Chapter 20), household consumption of goods and services increases due to higher GDP per capita and higher levels of employment. In Figure 18.5, this is shown by a rightward shift of the aggregate demand curve from AD_1 to AD_2, raising national income from Y_1 to Y_2 and forcing up the general price level from P_1 to P_2.

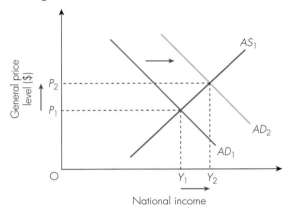

Figure 18.5 Demand-pull inflation

In general, inflation can be controlled by limiting the factors that cause demand-pull inflation and cost-push inflation. For example, the government can raise taxes and interest rates to limit consumption and investment expenditure in the economy. Some countries, such as Iran and France, have used subsidies for food and fuel to reduce prices in the economy. Chapter 16 covers in more detail the various government policies that can be used to control the level of economic activity and hence the rate of inflation.

Other possible causes of inflation are:

● **Monetary causes of inflation** are related to increases in the money supply (see Case Study on Zimbabwe) and easier access to credit, e.g. loans and credit cards.
● **Imported inflation** occurs due to higher import prices, forcing up costs of production and therefore causing domestic inflation.

Exam practice

Study Figure 18.6, which shows the inflation rates in India between 2003 and 2013, and answer the questions that follow.

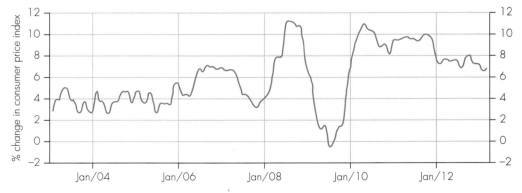

Source: Trading Economics

Figure 18.6 Inflation rates in India, 2003–13

1   Identify when the rate of inflation was at its highest and lowest in India.   [2]

2   Distinguish between cost-push inflation and demand-pull inflation.   [4]

3   Explain why the global financial crisis of late 2008 would have caused a fall in India's rate of inflation.   [4]

Activity

Discuss in small groups of two or three the economic strategies you would use to control demand-pull inflation and cost-push inflation. You may want to refer to Chapter 16 to help with this activity.

The consequences of inflation

Inflation can complicate planning and decision making for households, firms and governments, with many consequences as outlined below.

- **Menu costs** – Inflation impacts on the prices charged by firms. Catalogues, price lists and menus have to be updated regularly and this is costly to businesses. Of course, workers also have to be paid for the time they take to reprice goods and services.
- **Consumers** – The purchasing power of consumers goes down when there is inflation – there is a fall in their real income because money is worth less than before. Therefore, as the cost of living increases, consumers need more money to buy the same amount of goods and services.
- **Shoe leather costs** – Inflation causes fluctuations in price levels, so customers spend more time searching for the best deals. This might be done by physically visiting different firms to find the cheapest supplier or searching online. Shoe leather costs represent an opportunity cost for customers.
- **Savers** – Savers, be they individuals, firms or governments, lose out from inflation, assuming there is no change in interest rates for savings. This is because the money they have saved is worth less than before. For example, if interest rates average 2 per cent for savings accounts in a country but its inflation rate is 3 per cent, then the real interest rate on savings is actually –1 per cent. Hence, inflation can act as a disincentive to save. In turn, this leads to fewer funds being made available for investment in the economy.
- **Lenders** – Lenders, be they individuals, firms or governments, also lose from inflation. This is because the money lent out to borrowers becomes worth less than before due to inflation.
- **Borrowers** – By contrast, borrowers tend to gain from inflation as the money they need to repay is worth less than when they initially borrowed it – in other words, the real value of their debt declines due to inflation. For example, if a borrower takes out a mortgage at 5 per cent interest but inflation is 3.5 per cent, this means the real interest rate is only 1.5 per cent.
- **Fixed income earners** – During periods of inflation, fixed income earners (such as pensioners and salaried workers whose pay do not change with their level of output) see a fall in their real income. Thus, they are worse off than before as the purchasing power of their fixed income declines with higher prices. Even if employees receive a pay rise, the rate of inflation reduces its real value. For example, if workers get a 4 per cent pay rise but inflation is 3 per cent, then the real pay increase is only 1 per cent.

Exam practice

Study the following data and answer the questions that follow.

Year	Inflation rate (%)	Wage increase (%)
1	2.5	3.0
2	3.1	3.5
3	2.9	3.1

1   In which year was there the largest increase in real wages? Explain your answer.   [3]
2   Explain why average wages were higher in Year 3 than Year 2.   [3]

● **Low income earners** – Inflation harms the poorest members of society far more than those on high incomes. Low income earners tend to have a high price elasticity of demand (see Chapter 4) for goods and services. By contrast, those on high incomes and accumulated wealth, such as hip-hop artists (see Table 18.3), are not so affected by higher prices.

Table 18.3   The five wealthiest hip-hop artists

Rank	Artist	Net wealth ($m)
1	Sean 'Diddy' Combs	580
2	Shawn 'Jay-Z' Carter	475
3	Andre 'Dr Dre' Young	350
4	Bryan 'Birdman' Williams	150
5	Curtis '50 Cent' Jackson	125

Source: Forbes Rich List, 2013

● **Exporters** – The international competitiveness of a country tends to fall when there is domestic inflation. In the long run, higher prices make exporters less price competitive, thus causing a drop in profits. This leads to a fall in export earnings, lower economic growth and higher unemployment.
● **Importers** – Imports become more expensive for individuals, firms and the government due to the decline in the purchasing power of money. Essential imports such as petroleum and food products can cause **imported inflation** (higher import prices, forcing up costs of production and thus causing domestic inflation). Hence, inflation can cause problems for countries without many natural resources.
● **Employers** – Workers are likely to demand a pay rise during times of inflation in order to maintain their level of real income. As a result, labour costs of production rise and, other things being equal, profits margins fall. Those in highly skilled professions such as surgeons, doctors, pilots and barristers are in a strong bargaining position because their skills are in short supply and high demand. This can create a **wage–price spiral** whereby demand for higher wages to keep in line with inflation simply causes more inflation.

Inflation also harms employers located in expensive areas. Table 18.4 shows the world's most expensive cities, which means employers in these areas have to pay relatively high wages to attract workers. Tokyo has been the most expensive city in the annual Economics Intelligence Unit (EIU) Worldwide Cost of Living Index a total of 14 times in the past 20 years.

Table 18.4 The world's most expensive cities

Rank	City
1	Tokyo, Japan
2	Osaka, Japan
3	Sydney, Australia
4	Oslo, Norway
5	Melbourne, Australia
6	Singapore
7	Zurich, Switzerland
8	Paris, France
9	Caracas, Venezuela
10	Geneva, Switzerland

Source: EIU Worldwide Cost of Living Index, 2013

- **Business confidence levels –** Inflation also causes business uncertainty. The combination of uncertainty and the lower expected real rates of return on investment (due to higher costs of production) tends to lower the amount of planned investment in the economy.

Tokyo tops the most expensive cities index

Exam practice

Iran's inflation rate climbed above 30 per cent in 2013, reaching 31.5 per cent at the end of the Islamic country's calendar year (Table 18.5). The country, with a population of 74.8 million, had experienced double-digit inflation rates for most of the previous decade. At the end of 2010, the government reduced food and fuel subsidies, thereby fuelling inflation. In addition, international sanctions due to Iran's disputed nuclear programme forced down the value of the Iranian rial, the country's official currency. This added upward pressure on prices in the economy.

Table 18.5 Inflation rate in Iran

Date	Inflation (%)
March 2012	26.4
Dec 2012	27.4
March 2013	31.5

Source: Reuters

1. With reference to the data in Table 18.5, explain why prices in Iran were generally higher in 2013 than in 2012. [4]
2. Explain two reasons why the Iranian government might aim to control the level of inflation in its economy. [4]
3. Examine how some Iranians are likely to have been more affected than others by the double-digit inflation rates. [6]

> **Activity**
>
> Discuss the impact of an increase in oil prices on the rate of inflation in your country or a country of your choice. Which stakeholders are affected the most? Why?

Deflation

While the prices of goods and services tend to rise, the prices of some products actually fall over time. This is perhaps due to technological progress or a fall in consumer demand for the product, both of which can cause prices to fall. **Deflation** is defined as a persistent fall in the general price level of goods and services in the economy – in other words, the inflation rate is negative. The nine countries that experienced deflation during 2013 are listed in Table 18.6.

Table 18.6   Deflation rates around the world, 2013

Country	Deflation rate (%)
Somalia	−15.35
Chad	−4.90
Libya	−3.60
Georgia	−2.12
Ukraine	−0.50
Japan	−0.30
Switzerland	−0.30
Liechtenstein	−0.30
Sweden	−0.20

Source: Trading Economics

Technological advances can cause the prices of many products to fall

The causes of deflation

The causes of deflation can be categorised as either demand or supply factors. Deflation is a concern if it is caused by falling aggregate demand for goods and services (often associated with an economic recession and rising levels of unemployment).

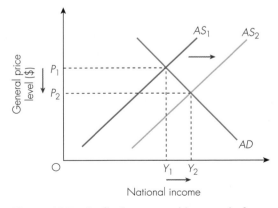

Figure 18.7   Deflation caused by supply factors

Aggregate supply

Deflation can be caused by higher levels of aggregate supply, increasing the productive capacity of the economy (see Chapter 11). This drives down the general price level of goods and services while increasing national income. Such deflation is called **benign deflation** (non-threatening deflation). For example, supply-side policies such as investment in education and infrastructure (see Chapter 16), higher productivity, improved managerial practices, technological advances and government subsidies for major industries all help to raise national income in the long run.

China's high-speed rail

In Figure 18.7, this is shown diagrammatically by a rightward shift of the aggregate supply curve from AS_1 to AS_2, reducing the general price level from P_1 to P_2. This happened in China during the past three decades with the Chinese government pouring huge amounts of investment funds into building new roads and rail networks (the country spent $104 billion on railway investment in 2013).

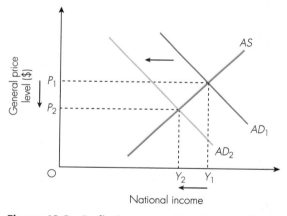

Figure 18.8 Deflation caused by demand factors

Aggregate demand

Deflation can also be caused by lower levels of aggregate demand in the economy, driving down the general price level of goods and services due to excess capacity in the economy. This causes what is known as **malign deflation** (deflation that is harmful to the economy). For example, during an economic recession (see Chapter 20), household consumption of goods and services falls due to lower GDP per capita and higher levels of unemployment. In Figure 18.8, this is shown by a leftward shift of the aggregate demand curve from AD_1 to AD_2, reducing national income from Y_1 to Y_2, and forcing down the general price level from P_1 to P_2. This happened in Japan for much of the past two decades as the Japanese suffered from severe economic recession. This cause of deflation is a concern as it is associated with a decline in national income and standards of living.

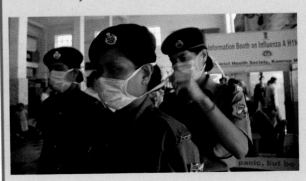

Case Study: Swine flu HINI

Women officials of the Railway Protection Force (RPF) and passengers wearing masks at Guwahati railway station, India, during the height of the outbreak in 2009

In 2009 the world suffered from a pandemic of swine flu, a highly contagious respiratory disease caused by the H1N1 influenza virus, which is found in pigs but has the potential to affect humans.

   The outbreak of the infectious disease in Northern Ireland, the USA, China and India slowed down economic activity to the extent that it caused deflation in all four countries, and falling rates of inflation in other affected nations, such as Australia, the Philippines and Britain.

The consequences of deflation

The consequences of deflation depend on whether we are considering benign deflation or malign deflation. The consequences of benign deflation are positive as the economy is able to produce more, thus boosting national income and employment, without causing an increase in the general price level. This therefore boosts the international competitiveness of the country. However, malign deflation is generally harmful to the economy. The consequences of malign deflation include the following:

● **Unemployment** – As deflation usually occurs due to a fall in aggregate demand in the economy, this causes a fall in the demand for labour – that is, deflation causes job losses in the economy.

● **Bankruptcies** – During periods of deflation, consumers spend less so firms tend to have lower sales revenues and profits. This makes it more difficult for firms to repay their costs and liabilities (money owed to others, such as outstanding loans and mortgages). Thus, deflation can cause a large number of bankruptcies in the economy.

● **Wealth effect** – As the profits of firms fall, so does the value of their shares during times of deflation. This means that dividends and the capital returns on holding shares fall, thus reducing the wealth of shareholders.

● **Debt effect** – The real cost of debts (borrowing) increases when there is deflation. This is because real interest rates rise when the price level falls. For example, if interest rates average 1.0 per cent but the inflation rate is –1.5 per cent, then the real interest rate is 2.5 per cent (imagine the situation of falling house prices while having to pay interest on mortgages taken out when prices were higher). Thus, with deflation and the subsequent rising real value of debts, both consumer and business confidence levels fall, further adding to the economic problems in the country.

- **Government debt** – With more bankruptcies, unemployment and lower levels of economic activity, tax revenues fall while the amount of government spending rises (due to the economic decline associated with malign inflation). This creates a budget deficit for the government, meaning that it needs to borrow money even though the real cost of borrowing rises with deflation.

- **Consumer confidence** – Deflation usually causes a fall in consumer confidence levels, as consumers fear that things will get worse for the economy. Thus, they may postpone their spending, especially on consumer durable goods such as cars and furniture, as they expect prices to fall even further in the future or wait until the economy improves. This clearly does not help the economy to recover, thereby causing a downward deflationary spiral.

It is difficult to break out of a downward deflationary spiral. To do so would require a significant boost to aggregate demand. Business and consumer confidence levels would also need to increase. Interest rates (see Chapter 16) could be cut to encourage consumer spending and increased investment expenditure in the economy.

Exam practice

For much of the past 20 years, Japan has suffered from deflation (see Figure 18.9).

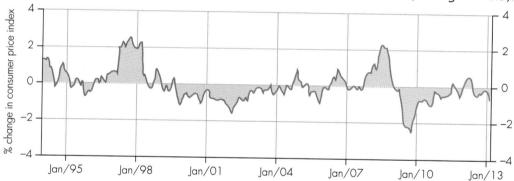

Source: Trading Economics

Figure 18.9 Japan's inflation rate, 1994–2013

1 Define the term 'deflation'. [2]

2 Explain what evidence there is in the chart to suggest that Japan has suffered deflation for most of the past 20 years. [2]

3 Analyse the impact of prolonged deflation on the Japanese economy. [6]

Chapter review questions

1 What is meant by 'inflation'?
2 What is the consumer price index and how does it differ from a retail price index?
3 Why are weights used in the calculation of a CPI or an RPI?
4 What is a base year?
5 What are the two key causes of inflation?
6 Outline the main consequences of inflation.
7 What is deflation?
8 What are the two main causes of deflation?
9 Differentiate between malign deflation and benign deflation.
10 Outline the main consequences of deflation.

Key terms

The **base year** refers to the starting year when calculating a price index.

The **consumer prices index** (CPI) is a weighted index of consumer prices in the economy over time. It is used to measure the cost of living for an average household.

Cost-push inflation is inflation triggered by higher costs of production, forcing up prices.

Deflation is a sustained fall in the general price level in an economy over time – the inflation rate is negative.

Demand-pull inflation is inflation triggered by higher levels of aggregate demand in the economy, driving up the general price level.

Disinflation occurs when the rate of inflation falls, but is above zero – prices are generally still rising, only at a slower rate.

Hyperinflation refers to very high rates of inflation that are out of control, causing average prices in the economy to rise very rapidly.

Imported inflation is triggered by higher import prices, forcing up costs of production and thus causing domestic inflation.

Inflation is a sustained rise in the general level of prices of goods and services over time, as measured by a consumer price index.

The **retail prices index** (RPI) is used to calculate the rate of inflation. Unlike the CPI, the RPI includes the cost of housing, such as mortgage interest payments and other housing costs, but excludes low-income pensioners and high-income households.

A **wage–price spiral** occurs when trade unions negotiate higher wages to keep income in line with inflation but this simply causes more inflation as firms raise prices to maintain their profit margins.

(19) Employment

By the end of this chapter, you should be able to:
- describe the changing patterns and levels of employment
- discuss the causes and consequences of unemployment.

Taken from Cambridge International Examinations Syllabus (IGCSE 0455/O Level 2281)
© Cambridge International Examinations

Changing patterns and levels of employment

Employment refers to the use of factors of production, such as labour, in the economy. For example, people may work in the primary, secondary or tertiary sectors of the economy (see Chapter 1). It also includes those who are self-employed.

Employment patterns change over time with changes in economic trends. For example, there have been large job losses in manufacturing industries in the USA and the UK as many firms have shifted their operations to India and China. On the other hand, other job opportunities in the tertiary sector have been created in the USA and the UK.

Some changing employment patterns in modern economies include:

- **Employment sector** – As a country develops, the number of people employed in the primary industry tends to fall and the majority of workers are employed in the tertiary sector. For example, agricultural output accounts for less than 1.5 per cent of the gross domestic product in Denmark, whereas over 76 per cent comes from the services sector (see Table 19.1).

Table 19.1 Output by sector (%): selected countries, 2012

Country	GDP – composition by sector (%)		
	Primary	Secondary	Tertiary
Denmark	1.3	22.1	76.6
Luxembourg	0.4	13.6	86.0
USA	1.2	19.1	79.7
Ethiopia	46.6	14.6	38.8
Nepal	38.1	15.3	46.6
Somalia	59.3	7.2	33.5

Source: *CIA World Factbook*, 2012

- **Delayed entry to workforce** – As more people study to tertiary education level, the average age of employees entering the workforce rises. Graduates could be aged around 25 by the time they complete their first degree and master's degrees. More females and mature students have also entered tertiary education, again limiting the potential size of the economy's workforce.

● **Ageing population** – This occurs when the average age of the population rises, partly due to lower birth rates and longer life spans in developed economies. The lower labour supply means that firms are more willing to employ older employees and hire people beyond their retirement age. The economic consequences of an ageing population are examined in Chapter 22.

● **Flexible working patterns** – Changes in the world economy have meant that firms need to be far more flexible in order to compete internationally. Examples of flexible working patterns include firms hiring more part-time staff, firms allowing employees to work from home, flexible working hours and outsourcing non-core functions (such as accounting, cleaning, security and ICT) to other service providers.

Governments strive to ensure that everyone who is able and willing to have a job is able to find employment.

Unemployment

Unemployment occurs when people of working age are both willing and able to work but cannot find employment. The United Nation's International Labour Organisation (ILO) states the lower age limit for employment as 15 years old. While there is no official upper limit, many countries use an age limit of between 65 and 70. For example, the official retirement age for females in the UK is 66 years and 5 months, while this figure is 67 years for all workers in Norway, Poland and the USA. Figure 19.1 shows unemployment rates in the USA from 2000 to 2013.

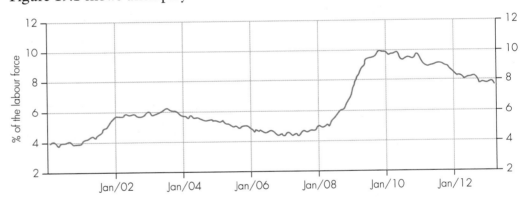

Source: Trading Economics

Figure 19.1 US unemployment, 2000–13

The **unemployment rate** shows the percentage of the country's workforce (those of working age) that is unemployed. It is calculated by the formula:

$$\text{unemployment rate} = \frac{\text{number of unemployed}}{\text{workforce}} \times 100$$

Alternatively, this can be expressed as:

$$\text{unemployment rate} = \frac{\text{number of unemployed}}{\text{number of unemployed} + \text{employed} + \text{self-employed}} \times 100$$

The ILO measures a country's unemployment based on the number of people who are:

- willing to work, but unable to find it
- actively looking for work – that is, they have looked for a job in the last 4 weeks
- able to start work within the next 2 weeks or waiting to start a new job within in the next 2 weeks.

Job-seekers look at employment advertisements at a labour market in China

Activity

Find out the rates of unemployment in your country or a country of your choice for the past 5 years. A good starting point is **www.tradingeconomics.com** or the International Labour Organisation website (**www.ilo.org**). What trends can you identify? Investigate the possible causes of these unemployment trends.

Exam practice

1. Calculate the unemployment rate in a country with a population of 65 million people, of whom 36 million are employed and 4 million are unemployed. [2]
2. Calculate the number of unemployed people in a country with an unemployment rate of 8.5 per cent and the follow ing population data:
   - population = 46 million
   - age 0–14 = 17 million
   - age 15–64 = 20 million
   - age ≥ 65 = 9 million. [2]

Exam practice

With a population of around 163 million, Nigeria is one of the most populated countries in Africa. Over 42 per cent of the population is aged below 15 and Nigeria has a large dependency ratio of almost 86 per cent. Gender inequalities mean the country has one of the lowest female employment rates in the world, with less than 45 per cent of working age females in employment. Most people are employed in primary industries. Nigeria is a large producer of crude oil – about 90 per cent of its export earnings come from the sale of oil. Figure 19.2 shows unemployment rates in Nigeria between 2006 and 2013.

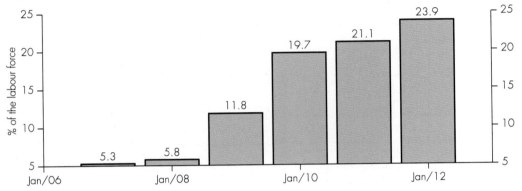

Source: Trading Economics

Figure 19.2 Nigeria's unemployment rate, 2006–13

1   Describe the changing pattern of employment in Nigeria from 2006 to 2013.   [2]

2   Nigeria's **working population** (workforce) is around 87.7 million. With an unemployment rate of 23.9 per cent, calculate the number of unemployed people in the country.   [2]

3   Explain two possible factors contributing to the trend described in the previous question.   [4]

Employment as a macroeconomic objective

High employment, or low unemployment, is a key macroeconomic objective of all governments. There are several reasons for this, as high employment helps to:

● raise standards of living for the average person in the country (see Chapter 21)
● increase economic growth – another key macroeconomic objective (see Chapter 20)
● raise tax revenues (due to higher levels of income and spending in the economy) to finance government spending
● reduce the financial burden and opportunity cost for the government, as spending on welfare benefits falls
● prevent 'brain drain' from the economy – this can occur during periods of high unemployment when highly skilled workers leave the country in search of job opportunities elsewhere
● reduce income and wealth inequalities – poorer people are more affected by unemployment, as they lack savings and wealth.

Exam practice

According to the International Monetary Fund (IMF), Pakistan's annual unemployment rate between 2007 and 2013 was kept steady at between 5 and 6 per cent. This, according to the Central Intelligence Agency (CIA), meant that Pakistan's gross domestic product grew by 3.7 per cent in 2012 and another 5 per cent in 2013. These changes have helped to reduce some of the poverty in the country.

1   Explain why it might be difficult at times to know the exact rate of
    unemployment in a country.   [3]
2   Examine the possible consequences of low unemployment for the Pakistani
    economy.   [6]

Causes of unemployment

There are many potential causes of unemployment. These causes can be explained by examining the various types of unemployment.

- **Frictional unemployment** is transitional unemployment that occurs when people change jobs, due to the time delay between leaving a job and finding or starting a new one. Therefore, frictional unemployment always exists in the economy because it takes time for the labour market to match available jobs with the people looking for jobs.
- **Seasonal unemployment** is caused by regular and periodical changes in demand for certain products. For example, fruit pickers are in high demand during the summer months while retailers tend to hire more temporary workers during the Christmas season (the busiest time of the year for most retailers).

Seasonal workers

- **Technological unemployment** occurs when workers lose their jobs due to firms opting to use capital-intensive technologies (see Chapter 11). This can cause large-scale unemployment in certain industries. For example, supermarkets in Europe introduced self-service checkouts in 2009. Their huge success and cost savings for supermarkets and other retailers mean that fewer workers need to be hired.

- **Youth unemployment** affects members of the working population aged 21 and below. They have relatively fewer skills and less experience, so they are the most likely to be affected during an economic downturn. For example, youth unemployment in Greece hit a record of 58.4 per cent in 2012 (the highest rate ever recorded for an EU nation) and Spain's youth unemployment reached a historic high of 55.7 per cent in 2013.

- **Regional unemployment** occurs when unemployment affects specific geographical areas of a country. While busy central business districts tend to have higher rates of employment, remote rural areas have relatively high rates of unemployment. In the USA, unemployment averaged 7.7 per cent in March 2013. However, the rate was higher in some states such as Mississippi and Nevada (both at 9.6 per cent) and much lower in other districts such as Nebraska (3.8 per cent) and North Dakota (3.3 per cent).

- **Structural unemployment** occurs when the demand for products produced in a particular industry falls continually, often due to foreign competition. There are structural and long-term changes in demand for the products of certain industries. The UK, for example, has suffered from structural unemployment in shipping, textiles, steel production, coal mining and car manufacturing. Those who suffer from structural unemployment usually find it quite difficult to find a new job without retraining.

- **Voluntary unemployment** occurs when workers choose not to work. Voluntary unemployment usually exists in economies with relatively generous welfare benefits for the unemployed as well as high rates of income tax, thus creating disincentives to work at current market (equilibrium) wage rates.

- **Classical (real-wage) unemployment** occurs when real wage rates are set above the market-clearing level, such as in the case of a national minimum wage (see Chapter 7). This leads to excess supply of labour, as the number of job-seekers exceeds the demand for labour. In Figure 19.3, the imposition of a minimum wage raises the cost of labour from W_1 to W_2. At the higher wage rate, demand for labour is N_3 but the supply of labour is N_2; the difference represents unemployment, as firms are unable and/or unwilling to pay workers more than their market (equilibrium) value.

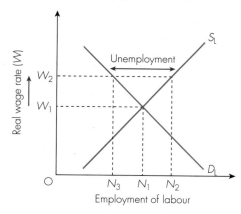

Figure 19.3 Classical unemployment

● **Cyclical unemployment**, also known as **demand-deficient unemployment**, is the most severe type of unemployment because it can affect every industry in the economy. It is caused by a lack of aggregate demand, which causes a fall in national income. In Figure 19.4, the fall in aggregate demand in the economy from AD_1 to AD_2 causes national income to fall from Y_1 to Y_2, creating mass unemployment. Demand-deficient unemployment is experienced during an economic downturn – that is, in recessions and slumps.

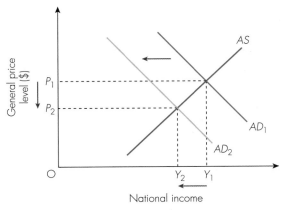

Figure 19.4 Demand-deficient unemployment

While Spain and Greece saw record unemployment rates of 26.6 per cent and 27 per cent respectively in 2012, these are relatively modest compared with the countries with the world's highest unemployment rates (see Figure 19.5).

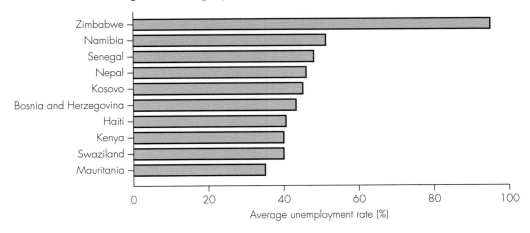

Source: The Heritage Foundation, 2013

Figure 19.5 The world's highest average unemployment rates, 2013

Activity

Find real-world examples of frictional, seasonal, technological and structural unemployment, and use an image or picture to represent each type of unemployment.

Consequences of unemployment

Unemployment affects a range of stakeholders: the unemployed themselves; their families; employers and firms; the government; and society as a whole. The consequences of unemployment include the following:

- The unemployed suffer from stress, low self-esteem, homelessness, depression and other health problems. In extreme cases, unemployment has led to suicide.
- Family and friends may also suffer from lower incomes and this often leads to arguments and even separation or divorce.
- The local community can suffer if there is mass unemployment – for example, there may be poverty, falling house prices (and hence asset values) and increased crime rates in the neighbourhood.
- Firms lose out as there are lower levels of consumer spending, investment and profits. Business failures and bankruptcies are more likely to occur during periods of high unemployment.
- The government may face higher expenditure on welfare benefits and health care for the unemployed. Prolonged periods of high unemployment can lead to increased government debts.
- Taxpayers stand to lose due to the opportunity costs of unemployment – the expenditure projects forgone due to increased spending on unemployment and welfare benefits.
- The economy suffers from being less internationally competitive, due to falling levels of spending and national output.

Policies to deal with unemployment

Governments can try to deal with the problems of unemployment in a number of ways. This partly depends on the causes of unemployment in the economy. As there are many types and causes of unemployment, the government needs to identify the best policies to deal with the problem. There are four general policies for reducing unemployment: fiscal policy, monetary policy, supply-side policy (see Chapter 16) and protectionist measures (see Chapter 26).

- **Fiscal policy** – This is the use of taxation and government spending policies to influence the level of economic activity. It can be used to tackle unemployment caused by demand-side issues, such as cyclical and structural unemployment. The use of expansionary fiscal policy (tax cuts and increased government spending) can boost aggregate demand and real national income, as shown in Figure 19.6. In turn, this will lead to more employment opportunities.

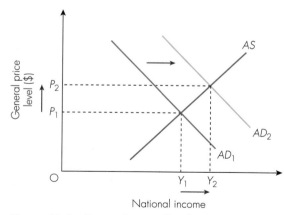

Figure 19.6 Expansionary fiscal policy

- **Monetary policy** – This refers to the use of interest rates to affect the level of economic activity. By lowering interest rates, the cost of borrowing falls, thus encouraging households and firms to spend and invest. In Figure 19.7, higher aggregate demand boosts the demand for labour curve from D_{L1} to D_{L2}. This results in higher levels of employment in the economy, as shown by the move from N_1 to N_2. The resulting rise in real wage rates from W_1 to W_2 also helps to attract more labour, causing an expansion along the supply of labour (S_L) curve. Like fiscal policy, monetary policy tackles demand-side causes of unemployment.

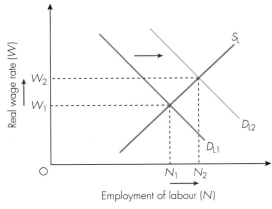

Figure 19.7 Monetary policy and the labour market

- **Protectionist measures** such as tariffs and quotas (see Chapter 26) can be used to safeguard domestic jobs from the threat of international competition. For example, the Japanese government imposes up to 778 per cent import taxes on rice – the highest rate in the world – in order to protect agricultural jobs in the country.
- **Supply-side policies** – These government strategies are used to deal with imperfections in the labour market and to reduce unemployment caused by supply-side factors. Thus, these policies are aimed at addressing frictional, voluntary and classical unemployment, although they can also be used to help reduce structural and cyclical unemployment. Examples of supply-side policies are as follows:
  - ○ **Investment in education and training** helps unemployed people to gain new skills so they can find employment. An example is retraining structurally unemployed manufacturing workers to help them find work in the tertiary sector. Education and training expenditure should also help future generations to become more skilled and employable.
  - ○ **A reduction in trade union powers** means that labour unions are not in such a strong bargaining position to obtain higher wages (see Chapter 8). Strong trade unions have often been able to demand annual pay rises in excess of inflation and the market equilibrium level. Hence, government intervention to reduce the influence and power of trade unions can help to reduce classical (real-wage) unemployment.

○ **Employment incentives** can be offered to firms for training and hiring the long-term unemployed. For example, the government can offer firms tax allowances and/or subsidies to reduce their costs of training and hiring workers. Similarly, **enterprise zones** (see Chapter 16) could be set up in areas of high unemployment to create jobs. However, firms might be reluctant to do so because of the lower productivity and higher risk of hiring the long-term unemployed.

○ A **review of welfare benefits** ensures that there are incentives to seek employment rather than to rely on state welfare benefits. If it is made more difficult for people to claim unemployment benefits, they become more proactive in searching for jobs. This could significantly help to reduce unemployment.

While supply-side policies tend to have more permanent impacts on employment, these effects take longer to accomplish compared with demand-side policies aimed at reducing unemployment in the economy.

Exam practice

In June 2010, Tesco opened Britain's first supermarket without any checkout workers. Instead, one person is hired to supervise the five checkouts, mainly to assist customers who have not used a self-service checkout before. The UK's largest retailer employs around 221 000 workers in the UK, but critics argue that such technological advancement will cause mass job losses.

Source: adapted from *Daily Mail Online*

1   Define the term 'technological unemployment'.   [2]
2   Analyse the ways in which the UK government could reduce technological unemployment.   [6]

Chapter review questions

1   How does the pattern of employment in the three production sectors change as an economy develops?
2   Why has there been a delay in most developed countries for labour to enter the workforce?
3   How have ageing populations in developed economies affected employment patterns?
4   How does the International Labour Organisation measure unemployment?
5   How is the unemployment rate calculated?
6   Why is employment a macroeconomic objective of all governments?
7   Outline the main types (and hence the causes) of unemployment.
8   What are the consequences of high unemployment in the economy?
9   What are the four main government policies that can be used to reduce domestic unemployment?
10 Give three examples of supply-side policies that can be used to reduce unemployment.

Key terms

Employment refers to the use of factors of production in the economy, such as labour.

Unemployment occurs when people of working age are both willing and able to work but cannot find employment.

The **unemployment rate** is a measure of the percentage of a country's workforce that is out of employment.

The **working population** (or labour force) is the number of people in an economy who are of working age and who are willing and able to work.

20 Economic growth

By the end of this chapter, you should be able to:
- define 'gross domestic product' (GDP)
- describe and have a general understanding of the causes and consequences of economic growth
- define the term 'recession'
- describe and evaluate measures and indicators of comparative living standards, such as GDP per head and human development index (HDI).

Taken from Cambridge International Examinations Syllabus (IGCSE 0455/O Level 2281)
© Cambridge International Examinations

Gross domestic product and economic growth

Gross domestic product (GDP) measures the monetary value of goods and services produced within a country for a given period of time, usually one year. The components of GDP are as follows:

- **Consumption expenditure** (C) – This refers to the total spending on goods and services by individuals and households in an economy. Examples of consumer expenditure are the economy's spending on housing, transport, food, clothing and domestic holidays.
- **Investment expenditure** (I) – This refers to the capital expenditure of firms which is used to further production and expand the economy's productive capacity. Examples are the spending on new machinery and the construction of new factories.
- **Government expenditure** (G) – This is the total consumption and investment expenditure of the government. Examples are the spending on infrastructure (such as rail and road networks) and the construction of new schools and hospitals.
- **Export** earnings (X) – This measures the monetary value of all exports sold to foreign buyers. For example, France exports a huge amount of wine, dairy products and fruits, so the earnings from these exports are calculated in the measure of GDP.
- **Import** expenditure (M) – This measures the monetary value of the payments made for all imports. France imports a lot of cars, oil and smartphones. The spending on these items means that money leaves the French economy, so this must be deducted from its calculation of GDP. The difference between the value of a country's exports and imports ($X - M$) is called **net exports**.

Therefore, GDP is calculated using the formula:
$GDP = C + I + G + (X - M)$

Activity

Discuss in pairs the reasons for the following:

1. Why government spending on infrastructure (such as road and rail networks) and training programmes for the unemployed are examples of investment expenditure.
2. Why the spending by foreign tourists in Paris represents export earnings for France.
3. Why investment is important for a country's economic growth.

Economic growth

Economic growth is the increase in the level of national output – that is, the annual percentage change in GDP. Hence, in theory, an increase in any of the components of GDP (consumption, investment, government spending and net exports) can cause economic growth.

An increase in the quantity and/or the quality of factors of production (see Chapter 1) can also create economic growth, such as an increase in the labour supply or improvements in the state of technology.

Economic growth increases the long-term productive capacity of the economy, shown by an outward shift of the production possibility curve (see Chapter 1 and Figure 20.1).

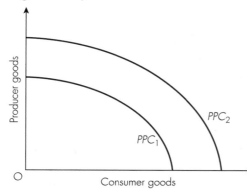

Economic growth can be shown diagrammatically by an outward shift of the production possibility curve for an economy. In this case, a combination of an increase in the quantity and quality of factors of production shifts the PPC outwards from PPC_1 to PPC_2, creating more producer and consumer goods

Figure 20.1 Economic growth

Causes of economic growth

The factors that account for the differences in the economic growth rates of different countries include variations in the following:

- **Factor endowments** – This refers to the quantity and quality of a country's factors of production. For example, Saudi Arabia is well endowed in the supply of oil, France has plenty of arable land for its agricultural output, and Australia has many natural resources such as coal, gold and iron ore. These countries can therefore specialise production on a large scale, thus benefiting from economies of scale

Saudi Arabia is the world's largest supplier of oil

(see Chapter 14), and export their lower-priced products to overseas markets. By contrast, countries that lack natural resources, land and productive labour tend to struggle to achieve economic growth.

- **The labour force** – The size, skills and mobility of the economy's workforce has an impact on the country's economic growth. For example, India's large labour force and Germany's highly skilled workers have contributed to the economic growth of these countries. The mobility of labour refers to the extent to which workers can change between jobs (known as occupational mobility) and the extent to which they are willing and able to move to different locations for employment (known as geographical mobility). Generally, the more occupationally and geographically mobile workers are in a country, the greater its economic growth is likely to be.
- **Labour productivity** – This refers to the amount of goods and services that workers produce in a given time period. It is often referred to as output per worker, expressed as a monetary value (GDP divided by the country's labour force). Labour productivity (the productive use of labour) is a key determinant of economic growth. This is determined by several interrelated factors, such as the qualifications, experience and training, and motivation of the labour force.

  Technological advances, such as the use of internet technology in e-commerce (online trading), can also enhance labour productivity. An increase in the labour productivity of a country helps to improve its international competitiveness and hence its prospects for economic growth.
- **Investment expenditure** – In order to remain competitive in the long run, countries must invest in capital resources. Investment is a component of aggregate demand, so any increase in investment should help to boost the country's GDP. Investment helps to boost the country's productive capacity in the long run. Investment expenditure on physical capital, such as the use of computers in production (see Chapter 11) can also help to improve labour productivity. Policies to encourage foreign direct investment (the investments made by foreign multinational companies in overseas markets) can also help a country's economic growth and development. For example, Japan's Honda, Nissan and Toyota have production plants in the UK, which helps to create jobs in the UK and therefore to boost its GDP.

Japan's Honda, Nissan and Toyota production plants in the UK help to create jobs in the UK and therefore boosts its GDP

Advantages of economic growth

In general, economic growth is desirable due to the advantages that it brings for members of society. These advantages include:

- **Improved standards of living** – Economic growth tends to lead to a higher standard of living for the average person. Higher income levels in a country enable people to spend more money to meet their needs and wants (see Chapter 1). This helps to eliminate absolute poverty in the country.

● **Employment** – Economic growth leads to higher levels of employment in the economy. This helps to raise consumption and encourages further investment in capital, helping to sustain economic growth.

● **Tax revenues** – Economic growth is associated with higher levels of spending in the economy. This generates more tax revenues for the government. For example, the government can collect more from sales taxes (on consumption), corporation tax (on the profits of firms) and import taxes. Hence, there are more funds for the government to use to sustain the growth of the economy.

Exam practice

According to the Economist Intelligence Unit, the economy of Macau grew by 14.3 per cent in 2013 – the highest economic growth rate for any country in the year.

The island nation had enjoyed 9.8 per cent growth in 2012, with gambling revenue increasing by approximately 14 per cent to about $38 billion, making it the world's biggest gambling market – ahead of Las Vegas. In 2011, Macau enjoyed a stunning 20.7 per cent growth rate.

The country is also investing huge amounts of money to attract a wider range of tourists, with casino giants such as Sands and MGM Resort also investing large sums of money in the economy.

1   What is meant by 'economic growth'?   [2]
2   Explain how investment in Macau helps to boost its economic growth.   [4]

Disadvantages of economic growth

Despite the advantages of economic growth, there are also potential drawbacks:

● **Environmental consequences** – High rates of economic growth can create negative externalities such as pollution, congestion, climate change and land erosion (see Chapter 2). Such environmental impacts can damage the wellbeing of people and their quality of life in the long run.

● **The risk of inflation** – If the economy grows due to excessive demand in the economy, there is the danger of demand-pull inflation (see Chapter 18). This can lead to prices of goods and services rising to unstable levels, with negative consequences on the economy such as a decline in the country's international competitiveness.

● **Inequalities in income and wealth** – Although a country might experience economic growth, not everyone will benefit in the same way. Economic growth often creates greater disparities in the distribution of income and wealth – the rich get richer and the poor get relatively poorer, creating a widening gap between rich and poor.

  Forbes magazine reported that in 2012, the top 10 billionaires in the USA had a combined wealth of over $347 billion – the equivalent of 2.3 per cent of the USA's gross domestic product. Put another way, their wealth was 2.5 times larger than Vietnam's GDP or 24 times greater than the GDP of Cambodia!

● **Resource depletion** – Economic growth often involves using up the world's scarce resources at rates that are not sustainable. For example, deforestation and overfishing have led to problems in the ecosystem.

Hence, economic growth does not necessarily resolve a country's socioeconomic problems, such as resource depletion, market failures (see Chapter 5) and income inequality.

Pollution – a negative consequence of rapid economic growth in China

> **Activity**
>
> In small groups, research the economic problems of overfishing. Websites such as **http://overfishing.org** and **http://ocean.nationalgeographic.com** will help. Be prepared to present your findings to the rest of the class.

The business cycle

Economic growth occurs when there is an increase in the level of economic activity in a country over time. The term **business cycle** (also known as the **trade cycle**) describes the fluctuations in economic activity in a country over time. These fluctuations create a long-term trend of growth in the economy, as shown in Figure 20.2.

The various stages in the business cycle are shown in the same diagram.

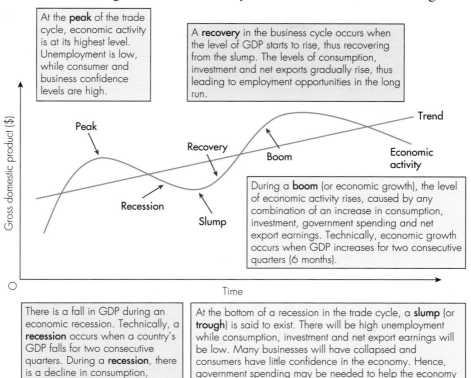

At the **peak** of the trade cycle, economic activity is at its highest level. Unemployment is low, while consumer and business confidence levels are high.

A **recovery** in the business cycle occurs when the level of GDP starts to rise, thus recovering from the slump. The levels of consumption, investment and net exports gradually rise, thus leading to employment opportunities in the long run.

During a **boom** (or economic growth), the level of economic activity rises, caused by any combination of an increase in consumption, investment, government spending and net export earnings. Technically, economic growth occurs when GDP increases for two consecutive quarters (6 months).

There is a fall in GDP during an economic recession. Technically, a **recession** occurs when a country's GDP falls for two consecutive quarters. During a **recession**, there is a decline in consumption, investment and net exports (due to falling export earnings).

At the bottom of a recession in the trade cycle, a **slump** (or **trough**) is said to exist. There will be high unemployment while consumption, investment and net export earnings will be low. Many businesses will have collapsed and consumers have little confidence in the economy. Hence, government spending may be needed to help the economy to recover from the recession.

Figure 20.2 The business cycle

Case Study: Recession in the PIGS economies

Following the global financial crisis of 2008, the economies of Portugal, Ireland, Greece and Spain faced a major economic downturn in their business cycle.

By 2013, both Greece and Spain were experiencing record unemployment rates of 26.8 per cent and 26.6 per cent respectively. Spain's youth unemployment rate (among those aged 21 and below) was 55 per cent – the highest in EU history.

Under such extreme economic circumstances, the government needs to intervene to help the economies to recover. All four PIGS economies received financial bailouts:
- Portugal = $114 billion
- Ireland = $113 billion
- Greece = $159 billion
- Spain = $130 billion

Measures and indicators of living standards

Economists believe that sustained economic growth is an important macroeconomic objective because it is the most practical measure of **standards of living** in a country. For example, China's phenomenal economic growth over the past three decades has led to an increase in the standard of living for the majority of its population. With an average growth of 10 per cent per year, the average Chinese citizen would double their income every seventh year (see Figure 20.3).

The two main measures or indicators of living standards are **GDP per head** (or **GDP per capita**) and the **Human Development Index** (HDI).

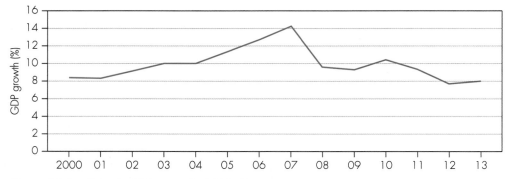

Figure 20.3 China's GDP growth, 2000–13

One problem in using GDP figures to measure standards of living is that the size of the population is ignored. For example, China's GDP is significantly larger than that of Luxembourg or Sweden. However, China's much larger population means that the GDP per head of Sweden and Luxembourg is greater (see Table 20.1). Hence, GDP per capita (per person) is a better measure of standards of living.

Table 20.1 GDP per capita – selected countries

Country	GDP ($bn)	GDP per capita ($)	Population (million)
China	8250.0	6094	1353.82
Sweden	538.3	56956	9.54
Luxembourg	58.42	113533	0.524

Source: adapted from *CIA Factbook*

Another consideration is inflation – a persistent increase in the general level of prices over time (see Chapter 18). Inflation erodes the value of GDP because the value of money falls if there is inflation.

For example, if a country's GDP increases by 5 per cent in a year but inflation also increases by 5 per cent, then the real value of GDP has not changed. Hence, for a more accurate measure of GDP as an indicator of standards of living, the monetary value of GDP must be adjusted for price changes. This adjusted measure is known as **real GDP**. Hence, **real GDP per capita** is a better measure of standards of living.

An alternative measure of standards of living that looks at factors beyond real GDP is called the **Human Development Index** (HDI). This is a composite indicator of living standards in a country, obtained by measuring three dimensions of human development:

- **Health care** – this indicator measures life expectancy at birth. The better the health care in a country, the greater social and economic wellbeing tends to be.
- **Education** – this indicator measures the mean years of schooling and the expected years of schooling in the country.
- **Income levels** – the higher the national income (or GDP) of a country, the greater human development tends to be.

Hence, poor countries such as Mozambique, Afghanistan, Sudan and Rwanda have a low HDI. Wealthy countries such as Norway, New Zealand and Canada have a high HDI.

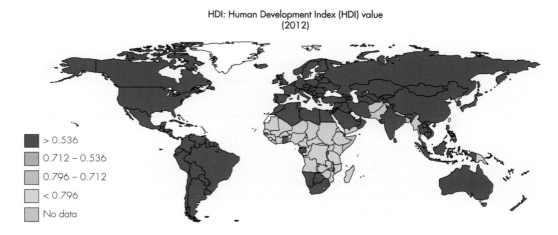

HDI: Human Development Index (HDI) value (2012)

- > 0.536
- 0.712 – 0.536
- 0.796 – 0.712
- < 0.796
- No data

Figure 20.4 Human Development Index rankings

However, there are limitations in using the HDI to measure standards of living:

- **Qualitative factors** – the HDI ignores qualitative measures affecting standards of living, such as gender inequalities and human rights.
- **Income distribution** – the HDI does not take account of inequitable income distribution, thus being less accurate in measuring living standards for the 'average' person.
- **Environmental issues** – the HDI ignores environmental and resource depletion resulting from economic growth.
- **Cultural differences** – although the HDI is a composite indicator, it ignores cultural differences and interpretations of the meaning of standards of living.

Activity

1 Use the internet to research the top ten countries as measured by the HDI.
2 Discuss whether the HDI is a good measure of standards of living in these countries.

Exam practice

The following table gives the HDIs for Australia, Ethiopia, Russia and Vietnam. Determine which country has which HDI. Explain the reasoning behind your answers.

[6]

Country	HDI	Country	HDI
A	0.929	C	0.593
B	0.755	D	0.363

Chapter review questions

1   What is meant by 'gross domestic product' (GDP)?
2   What is economic growth and how is it calculated?
3   What are the causes of economic growth?
4   What are the consequences, both positive and negative, of economic growth?
5   What is meant by 'a recession'?
6   How do calculations of GDP per head help to measure living standards?
7   What are the advantages and disadvantages of using the Human Development Index (HDI) to measure standards of living?

Key terms

Business cycle describes the fluctuations in the economic activity of a country over time, thus creating a long-term trend of economic growth in the economy.

Consumption expenditure is the value of all private household consumption within a country.

Economic growth is the increase in the level of national output – that is, the annual percentage change in GDP.

GDP per head (or GDP per capita) is the gross domestic product of a country divided by the population size. It is a key measure of a country's standards of living.

Government expenditure is the total value of a government's consumption and investment spending and transfer payments, such as unemployment benefits and state pension schemes.

Gross domestic product (GDP) is the monetary value of goods and services produced within a country in a given period of time, usually 1 year.

Human Development Index (HDI) is a composite indicator of living standards in a country, obtained by measuring three dimensions of human development: education, health care and income.

Investment expenditure is the sum of capital spending by all businesses within a country.

Net exports refers to the monetary value of the difference between a nation's exports earnings and its import expenditure.

Real GDP refers to the value of national income (GDP) adjusted for inflation to reflect the true value of goods and services produced in a given year.

Recession occurs in the business cycle when there is a fall in GDP for two consecutive quarters.

Chapters

21 Standards of living

By the end of this chapter, you should be able to:
- describe why some countries are classified as developed and others are not
- discuss differences in standards of living within countries and between countries, both developed and developing
- describe the difference between absolute and relative poverty
- recognise and discuss policies to alleviate poverty.

Taken from Cambridge International Examinations Syllabus (IGCSE 0455/O Level 2281)
© Cambridge International Examinations

Classification of countries

The World Bank classifies economies using the criterion of **gross national income (GNI) per capita**. This calculates the total expenditure in the economy (gross domestic product) plus net income from assets abroad, divided by the population size. Based on a country's GNI per capita, it is classified as a low-income, middle-income (further divided into lower-middle and upper-middle), or high-income country.

Case Study: Examples of World Bank classifications

Examples of the World Bank's classification of countries are shown below:
- **Low-income countries** (GNI of $1025 per capita or less): Afghanistan, Bangladesh, Liberia, Malawi, Nepal and Zimbabwe.
- **Lower-middle income countries** (GNI of $1026 to $4035 per capita): Fiji, Ghana, Indonesia, Pakistan, Sudan and Ukraine.
- **Upper-middle income countries** (GNI of $4036 to $12 475 per capita): Argentina, Brazil, China, Jamaica, Mexico, Peru and Venezuela.
- **High-income countries** (GNI of $12 476 per capita and above): Belgium, Greenland, Hong Kong, Kuwait, Monaco, Switzerland and the United Arab Emirates.

Low- and middle-income countries are often referred to as **developing economies** or **less economically developed countries (LEDCs)**. In these countries, the per capita income is low and standards of living are generally poor. High-income countries are also referred to as **developed economies** or **more economically developed countries (MEDCs)**. In these countries, GDP per capita is high and there is widespread access to goods and services, and thus a high degree of economic prosperity.

Activity

Visit the World Bank website (**http://data.worldbank.org/about/country-classifications/country-and-lending-groups**) to see whether your country is classified as an LIC, LMC, UMC or HIC. What are the advantages and disadvantages of using GNI as the key measure to classify the economic development of countries?

Exam practice

Examine the data for four countries shown in Table 21.1.

Table 21.1 Gross domestic product and population data: selected countries, 2013

Country	Gross domestic product ($bn)	Population (million)
USA	15 094	311.59
China	7 298	1344.13
Japan	5 867	127.82
Germany	3 571	81.73

Source: Trading Economics

1 Define the term 'gross domestic product'.   [2]
2 Explain which of the above countries is most likely to have the highest standard of living.   [4]

However, the classification of countries by income does not necessarily or accurately reflect economic development or standards of living. An alternative to the World Bank classification of countries is the **Human Development Index** (HDI) produced by the United Nations Development Programme (UNDP).

Rather than using only GDP per capita, this method uses several criteria: life expectancy, educational attainment and income per capita. Although HDI is slightly more complicated than GNI per capita to measure, it takes not only income but also life expectancy and literacy rates into consideration when measuring economic development and standards of living in a country.

The index for each country is scored between 0 and 1, with 1 being the most developed. The UNDP classifies countries into four broad human development categories, with 47 countries in each classification of human development: very high (top percentile), high (percentiles 51–75), medium (percentiles 36–50) and low (bottom percentile). Examples are shown in Table 21.2.

Table 21.2 HDI classification of countries (selected countries)

Very high human development			High human development		
Country	UNDP Rank	HDI	Country	UNDP Rank	HDI
Norway	1	0.955	Bahrain	48	0.796
Australia	2	0.938	Bahamas	49	0.794
USA	3	0.937	Belarus	50	0.793
Netherlands	4	0.921	Uruguay	51	0.792
Germany	5	0.920	Montenegro	52	0.791
Medium human development			Low human development		
Country	UNDP Rank	HDI	Country	UNDP Rank	HDI
Tonga	95	0.710	Congo	142	0.534
Belize	96	0.702	Solomon Islands	143	0.530
Dominican Rep.	96	0.702	São Tomé and Príncipe	144	0.525
Fiji	96	0.702	Kenya	145	0.519
Samoa	96	0.702	Bangladesh	146	0.515

Source: UNDP, *HDI Report*, 2013

There are three main criticisms of using the HDI to classify countries. First, the components of the HDI (life expectancy, education and income) are weighted equally, although they do not necessarily contribute to human development in an equal way. Second, the three components are too narrow as an indicator of living standards. For example, the HDI ignores political and economic freedom, which many consider crucial to the standards of living in a country. A third criticism is that the HDI does not take into account inequalities in income and wealth within and between countries, so comparisons of living standards become less meaningful.

Characteristics of developing countries

Less economically developed countries have common characteristics. These are explained below.

- **Low GDP per capita** – For economists, this is probably the key characteristic of developing countries. GDP per capita is calculated by dividing the gross domestic product of a country by its population to find the income level of the average person. The lower the GDP per person, the poorer the country tends to be. According to the World Bank, Luxembourg has the highest GDP per head at $114 508, whereas the Democratic Republic of Congo has the lowest at just $231.

- **Low life expectancy** – Life expectancy measures the number of years that the average person in a country is anticipated to live for, based on statistical trends. The lower the life expectancy, the poorer the country tends to be. Data from the World Bank support this, with the likes of Sierra Leone, Congo, Zambia and Swaziland all having life expectancy of between 48 and 49 years.

- **Low literacy rates** – Literacy rates measure the proportion of the population aged 15 and above who can read and write. Low-income countries have insufficient investment in education and training, so their literacy rates tend to be low. This has major consequence for employment, production and productivity, thus negatively impacting on the GDP of the country. High-income countries have 100 per cent literacy rates whereas low-income countries have very low literacy rates, such as Mali (31 per cent), Chad (34 per cent) and Guinea (41 per cent).

- **High population growth** – Population growth measures the annual percentage change in the population of a country. Poorer countries tend to have high population growth rates for many reasons: a lack of family planning and sex education, poor access to contraception and cultural norms (it is common and widely accepted to have many children in some countries and cultures).

- **Poor infrastructure** – Infrastructure refers to the system of transportation and the communications networks necessary for the efficient functioning of an economy, such as buildings, mass transportation, roads, water systems, ICT systems including the internet, airports and power supplies. According to the World Economic Forum, countries with very poor infrastructure include Bosnia and Herzegovina, Angola, Mongolia, Nepal, Lebanon and Chad. Table 21.3 shows the number of internet users per 100 people in 2012.

Table 21.3 Internet users around the world, 2012

Most connected countries		Least connected countries	
Country	Internet users (per 100 people)	Country	Internet users (per 100 people)
Iceland	96.6	Timor-Leste	0.9
Norway	93.5	Myanmar	1.0
Netherlands	92.1	Ethiopia	1.1
Sweden	90.9	Burundi	1.1
Luxembourg	90.7	Congo, Dem. Rep.	1.2

Source: adapted from the World Bank

- **Low foreign direct investment** – The lack of capital resources also limits the ability of a country to create income and wealth. Foreign direct investment (FDI) refers to cross-border investment made by multinational companies and other investors. Poor countries, with their lack of economic growth and poor infrastructure, do not tend to attract FDI due to the expected high risks and low financial returns.

- **Poor health care** – Insufficient investment in health services hinders the ability of a country to develop. Health care expenditure per capita is low in LEDCs. Their governments are unable to provide preventive and curative health care services for the mass population. According to the World Bank, the United States spends $8362 per person on health care services, whereas this figure is only $21 in Burundi, $18 in Niger, $16 in Ethiopia and just $12 in Eritrea.

- **Low labour productivity** – Labour productivity is a measure of the efficiency of labour in the production process, such as output per worker (see Chapter 11). Due to the combination of low literacy, low capital investment and poor health care, labour productivity in LEDCs also tends to be low.

- **High public debt** – Public debt refers to the money owed by the government (public sector). In general, LEDCs are far more likely to borrow money to finance their public sector expenditure, so the higher the public debt, the lower a country's standard of living tends to be. This is because the government will need to repay its loans, along with interest payments, rather than using the funds for investment in the economy. However, the huge impact of the global financial crisis has harmed MEDCs and not only LEDCs (see Table 21.4 below). Japan tops the chart, largely due to the country's devastating earthquake and tsunami of March 2011, the country's worst natural disaster in history.

Table 21.4 Government debts around the world, 2012

Most indebted countries		Least indebted countries	
Country	**Public debt as % of GDP**	**Country**	**Public debt as % of GDP**
Japan	218.9	Libya	1.9
Zimbabwe	202.7	Oman	3.6
Greece	161.3	Equatorial Guinea	4.3
St Kitts and Nevis	144.4	Liberia	4.4
Antigua and Barbuda	130.0	Azerbaijan	5.4
Lebanon	127.9	Kosovo	5.5
Jamaica	127.3	Kuwait	7.1
Italy	126.1	Gibraltar	7.5
Portugal	119.7	Estonia	8.0
Iceland	118.9	Algeria	8.8

Source: CIA World Factbook

In reality, it is common for LEDCs to pay more for financing their public debts, partly due to the high interest rates imposed and partly due to a fall in the value of their currency. This makes repayment of public debt increasingly unsustainable for LEDCs, leading to further borrowing and ever-increasing debts.

● **Reliance on primary-sector output** – Low-income countries tend to over-rely on the production and export of primary-sector output, such as agricultural products. These tend to have poor terms of trade in comparison with the export of manufactured products or tertiary-sector services. Table 21.5 compares the output from the three sectors of the economy for selected countries.

Table 21.5 Output of the economy by sector: selected countries, 2012

Country	Sector of the economy (%)		
	Primary	**Secondary**	**Tertiary**
Central African Republic	56.4	14.9	28.8
Guinea-Bissau	56.3	13.1	30.7
Chad	51.0	7.0	42.0
Ethiopia	46.6	14.6	38.8
Sierra Leone	43.2	37.4	19.3
Hong Kong	0.0	7.0	93.0
Luxembourg	0.4	13.6	86.0
United Kingdom	0.7	21.1	78.2
Germany	0.8	28.1	71.1
Denmark	1.3	22.1	76.6

Source: adapted from *CIA World Factbook*

● **Corruption** – A final characteristic of LEDCs is their high degree of corruption. There are huge opportunity costs of civil war, dishonest government officials, fraudulent behaviour and the purchase of arms and weapons. Corruption therefore hinders economic development and results in hugely unequal income distribution.

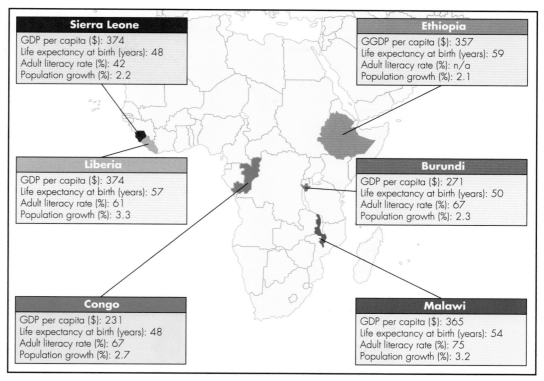

Source: World Bank

Figure 21.1 Selected economic development indicators, 2012

Standards of living

The term standard of living refers to the social and economic wellbeing of individuals in a country at a point in time. Living standards can vary within a country and between countries, whether they are developed or developing countries. There are numerous ways to measure the standard of living in a country, including:

- **GDP per capita** – In general, the higher the level of an individual's income, the better off he or she is. However, this figure is an average of the population and does not reveal anything about inequalities in income and wealth.
- **The cost of living** – While some countries like Japan and Hong Kong have a high GDP per capita, their cost of living is very high, so this tends to adjust the standards of living downwards. In other countries, like Vietnam and Nicaragua, the opposite happens.
- **Material wealth** – This indicator looks at ownership of consumer durable goods by the average person, such as cars, jewellery, televisions, mobile phones (see Table 21.6), washing machines and home computers. This is measured as a percentage of the population. In theory, the higher the percentage of the population with material wealth, the better the standard of living tends to be.

Table 21.6 Number of mobile phones in use – top five and bottom five countries

Rank	Country	Number of mobile phones in use	Population	% of population
1	Hong Kong	13 264 896	7 008 900	187.9
2	Saudi Arabia	46 000 000	27 137 000	169.5
3	Russia	256 117 000	142 905 200	155.5
4	Lithuania	4 960 000	3 341 966	148.4
5	Estonia	1 982 000	1 340 602	147.8
...				
59	Bangladesh	98 470 000	148 090 000	68.0
60	Lebanon	2 720 000	4 224 000	64.4
61	Ethiopia	18 000 000	85 000 020	21.8
62	Cuba	1 300 000	11 200 000	11.6
63	North Korea	1 000 000	24 451 285	4.09

Source: adapted from Wikipedia

Hong Kong ranks top in the table for the percentage of its population who own a mobile phone. Mobile phones can even be used underground on the MTR network

- **Health indicators** – These look at a range of measures related to health care provision, such as life expectancy, infant mortality rates (the number of children who die each year per thousand of the population), the number of patients per doctor and the average food intake per person.
- **Education indicators** – These measures look at educational attainment in terms of literacy rates (the percentage of the population who can read and write) and the proportion of people who graduate from high school and tertiary education.
- **Social and environmental indicators** – These quality of life measures look at the impact that societal norms and the natural environment have on standards of living. Such indicators include the level of stress, the average hours worked in a week, the number of days off from work each year, traffic congestion, pollution levels and crime rates.

Activity

1 In small groups, use the internet to compare and contrast the United Nation's Happiness Index with the New Economics Foundation's Happy Planet Index (HPI).
2 Which indicator of standards of living does your group think is the best measure? Why?

Exam practice

The London-based New Economics Foundation's Happy Planet Index (HPI) is a measure of human well-being and environmental impact. Introduced in July 2006, the index challenges the traditional idea that economic growth leads to better living standards. Instead, the HPI is weighted to give progressively higher scores to countries with lower ecological footprints and thus sustainable economic growth. Supporters of the HPI argue that people ultimately aim to be happy and healthy rather than to be rich and wealthy. Costa Rica, where people beyond 100 years of age commonly live active and happy lives, tops the HPI whereas Botswana is right at the bottom.

1 Outline why GDP per capita is used an indicator of standards of living.   [2]
2 Explain why environmental factors are important in measuring standards of living.   [4]
3 Discuss whether economic growth always results in higher living standards.   [7]

Case Study: The most liveable cities in the world

The world's top ten most liveable cities, according the Economist Intelligence Unit's *Global Liveability Report* are:

1 Melbourne, Australia
2 Vienna, Austria
3 Vancouver, Canada
4 Toronto, Canada
5 Calgary, Canada
5 Adelaide, Australia
7 Sydney, Australia
8 Helsinki, Finland
9 Perth, Australia
10 Auckland, New Zealand

At the bottom, ranked 140th, Dhaka in Bangladesh is rated the least liveable city.

The rankings are based on a wide range of factors that affect standards of living, such as the widespread availability of goods and services, personal safety and effective infrastructure.

Melbourne and Sydney feature in the top ten most liveable cities
Source: adapted from EIU, *The Global Liveability Report*

Absolute and relative poverty

Poverty is a condition that exists when people lack adequate income and wealth to sustain a basic standard of living. The eradication of poverty is a fundamental macroeconomic objective for many governments around the world. This is because poverty creates many social and economic problems. For example, there are costs of poor health (such as malnutrition and famine), deaths, crime, high unemployment, welfare provision and lost national output.

The United Nations defines overall poverty as 'a lack of income and productive resources to ensure sustainable livelihoods'. This includes:

● hunger and malnutrition
● ill health and mortality from illness
● limited or lack of access to education and other basic services
● homelessness and inadequate housing
● unsafe environments
● social discrimination and exclusion.

Table 21.7 shows the countries with the highest and the lowest GDP per capita for 2012. According to the *CIA World Factbook*, Qatar in the Middle East had the highest GDP per capita (around $281 per day) while the Republic of Congo had the lowest (at just $1.09 per day).

Table 21.7 The world's richest and poorest, 2012

The world's richest countries			The world's poorest countries		
Rank	Country	GDP per capita ($)	Rank	Country	GDP per capita ($)
1	Qatar	102 800	1	Congo	400
2	Liechtenstein	89 400	2	Zimbabwe	500
3	Luxembourg	80 700	3	Somalia	600
4	Macau	74 900	4	Burundi	600
5	Bermuda	69 900	5	Liberia	700
6	Singapore	60 900	6	Eritrea	800
7	Jersey	57 000	7	Central African Republic	800
8	Falkland Islands	55 400	8	Malawi	900
9	Norway	55 300	9	Niger	900
10	Hong Kong	50 700	10	South Sudan	900

Source: *CIA World Factbook*

Study tips

Poverty exists in all countries, although it is more visible in poorer countries with mass poverty. Even in wealthy nations, economic recession or natural disasters can cause widespread poverty. It is therefore incorrect to assume that only low-income countries suffer from poverty.

Exam practice

According to the US Census Bureau, 15 per cent of individuals in the United States live below the poverty line. The aftershock of the global financial crisis meant rising unemployment and related economic problems. This resulted in over 46 million people living in poverty in America, more than at any point in the nation's history.

1 Define the term 'poverty'. [2]
2 Explain why poverty is a concern for the American government. [4]
3 Discuss whether the standard of living is always higher in developed than in developing countries. [7]

There are two categories of poverty: absolute poverty and relative poverty.

Absolute poverty

Absolute poverty exists when there is extreme, outright poverty. People in absolute poverty are undeniably poor. Their income, if any, is spent entirely on minimal amounts of food, clothing and shelter – that is, the basic human needs necessary for survival. For many, absolute poverty can mean being unable to eat and drink, and have clothing and shelter.

There is more than one way to measure absolute poverty. The most common method is to calculate the number of individuals living below a certain level of income (called the **income threshold** or the **poverty line**). A common threshold for poverty is $1.25 a day – many people around the world still live below this amount, which means they are unable to buy enough food to survive.

Since 1995, the United Nations has adopted the definition of absolute poverty as follows:

A condition characterised by severe deprivation of basic human needs, including food, safe drinking water, sanitation facilities, health, shelter, education and information. It depends not only on income but also on access to services.

Case Study: Sierra Leone

Sierra Leone is one of the poorest countries on the planet, with around 70 per cent of its population of 5.6 million people living below the poverty line. GDP per capita in the West African country is a meagre $374 (or $1.02 per day), with 58.5 per cent of its GDP coming from agriculture. Sierra Leone has a staggering infant mortality rate of 76.64 deaths per 1000 live births; one of the highest rates in the world. The median age is only 19.1 years and life expectancy is just 56.55 years.

Source: adapted from *CIA World Factbook*

Study tips

It is possible for people to be relatively well-off but still to live in absolute poverty. This is because these people can earn more than the average person yet still face financial difficulties in meeting their basic human needs.

Relative poverty

Relative poverty is a comparative measure, rather than an absolute measure, of poverty. People in absolute poverty are undeniably impoverished, whereas those in relative poverty have a lower standard of living in comparison with the average member of society. For example, it is rather pointless to compare what is meant by poverty for someone living in Singapore or Luxembourg with someone living in poverty in Sierra Leone or Niger.

Relative poverty measures the extent to which a person's financial resources fall below that of the average income for the population. Although real national income (see Chapter 20) and standards of living have grown over time, these gains are not evenly distributed across the population.

Policies to alleviate poverty

In theory, all governments have a range of policies to alleviate poverty, although achieving this in practice is far more difficult. Such policies can be categorised as fiscal, monetary and supply-side policies (see Chapter 16).

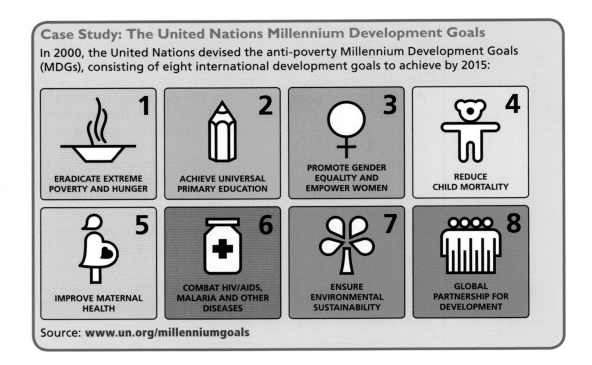

Case Study: The United Nations Millennium Development Goals

In 2000, the United Nations devised the anti-poverty Millennium Development Goals (MDGs), consisting of eight international development goals to achieve by 2015:

1 ERADICATE EXTREME POVERTY AND HUNGER

2 ACHIEVE UNIVERSAL PRIMARY EDUCATION

3 PROMOTE GENDER EQUALITY AND EMPOWER WOMEN

4 REDUCE CHILD MORTALITY

5 IMPROVE MATERNAL HEALTH

6 COMBAT HIV/AIDS, MALARIA AND OTHER DISEASES

7 ENSURE ENVIRONMENTAL SUSTAINABILITY

8 GLOBAL PARTNERSHIP FOR DEVELOPMENT

Source: **www.un.org/millenniumgoals**

Fiscal policies

These policies are used to redistribute income and wealth by using a combination of taxation and government spending policies. For example:

- Progressive tax systems (see Chapter 17) to reduce the wide gap between the rich and poor members of the country. Higher-income groups pay a higher percentage of their incomes in tax, with the tax proceeds being used by the government to support the lower-income groups or those without any income.
- Government transfer payments (see Chapter 15) give the unemployed and disadvantaged financial assistance to meet their basic needs. Examples of transfer payments are unemployment benefit, state pension funds for the elderly and child benefit (to reduce child poverty). This helps to provide a social safety net to ensure that every citizen has access to basic necessities.
- Government provision of basic services such as health care services, education and housing. This helps to improve access to such basic services for everyone and narrows the gap between the rich and the poor.

Monetary policies

These policies are used to control the money supply by manipulating interest rates and exchange rates:

- Low interest rates can encourage borrowing and investment to increase spending in the economy. In the long run, this can help to create more jobs and alleviate the problems of poverty.
- Low exchange rates (see Chapter 25) can encourage export sales as the price for foreign buyers is lower. As higher export earnings help to boost GDP, this can also help to create more jobs and wealth in the economy over time.

Supply-side policies

These policies are used to boost the long-run productive capacity of an economy (see Chapter 16). For example:

- Policies to reduce unemployment (see Chapter 19), because unemployment is a major cause of poverty and inequality. Examples include government incentives to attract foreign direct investment and government-funded job creation and retraining schemes.
- Policies to increase the quantity and quality of education in the economy. Over time, this will help to improve the human capital and productive capacity of the country.
- Sustained economic growth, which helps to create more income and wealth for the country (see Chapter 20). This can then be redistributed to the deprived and underprivileged members of society.
- Labour market reforms to improve the efficiency and productivity of the workforce (see Chapter 11). The introduction of a national minimum wage, or imposing a higher minimum wage rate, can improve the standards of living for low-income households.

Foreign aid

A fourth and final policy that can be used to alleviate poverty is **foreign aid**. Fiscal, monetary and supply-side policies tend to be internal methods: that is, they are within the control of the domestic government. However, with foreign aid there is a huge reliance on the donor – something that cannot be controlled by the government. Foreign aid can be a stimulus for reducing poverty, inequalities and unemployment in the economy. Successful foreign aid programs help to increase the country's productive capacity, thus shifting out its production possibility curve (see Chapter 1). There are various forms of foreign aid that can be used to tackle the problems of poverty:

- **Bilateral foreign aid** – This is official financial assistance from one government to another, usually due to political and economic interests. It provides immediate access to aid.
- **Multilateral foreign aid** – This is official financial assistance from more than one source, such as foreign governments, international organisations such as the World Bank, and non-governmental organisations such as Oxfam and Unicef.
- **Development aid** – This is official financial assistance from governments and agencies such as the World Bank to fund the economic development of a country, thus helping to alleviate poverty in the long run.
- **Humanitarian aid** – This is philanthropic (charitable) financial assistance for saving lives and maintaining human dignity. It is often used in response to major crises such as natural disasters and outbreaks of infectious diseases. Examples include medical aid, food aid and emergency relief assistance.

Activity

In pairs, research the roles of the World Bank and the International Monetary Fund (IMF) in promoting economic development. What are the terms and conditions of the loans that they make to countries? How does the World Bank differ from the IMF? Be prepared to present your findings to the class.

Chapter review questions

1 How does the World Bank classify countries in terms of economic development?
2 Distinguish between more economically developed and less economically developed countries.
3 What is the Human Development Index?
4 What are the criticisms of using the HDI as a measure of standards of living?
5 What are the main characteristics of less economically developed countries?
6 Define the term 'standards of living'.
7 Why do standards of living vary within and between countries?
8 Distinguish between absolute poverty and relative poverty.
9 What is the poverty line?
10 What are the main policies that can be used to alleviate poverty?

Key terms

Absolute poverty is an extreme form of poverty indicating the number of people who cannot afford minimal standards of basic human needs (food, clothing, health care and shelter).

Foreign aid is a form of financial assistance for economic development from other countries or non-government organisations such as Oxfam and Unicef.

The **Human Development Index** (HDI) is the UN's measure of wellbeing, obtained by using three criteria: life expectancy, educational attainment and income per capita.

Less economically developed countries (LEDCs) are developing countries with low GDP per capita, so their standards of living are generally poor.

More economically developed countries (MEDCs) are developed countries with high GDP per capita, so their standards of living are generally good.

Poverty is a condition that exists when people lack adequate income and wealth to sustain basic standards of living.

Relative poverty is a comparative measure of poverty. Those in relative poverty have a lower standard of living in comparison with the average member of society.

Standards of living refer to the social and economic wellbeing of individuals in a country at a point in time.

Population

> **By the end of this chapter, you should be able to:**
> - describe the factors that affect population growth (birth rate, death rate, fertility rate, net migration)
> - discuss reasons for the different rates of growth in different countries
> - analyse the problems and consequences of these population changes for countries at different stages of development
> - describe the effects of changing size and structure of population on an economy.
>
> Taken from Cambridge International Examinations Syllabus (IGCSE 0455/O Level 2281)
> © Cambridge International Examinations

Factors that affect population growth

Population refers to the total number of inhabitants of a particular country. Economists are interested in population size because people are essential for the economic prosperity of a country and also responsible for the depletion of the Earth's scarce resources. **Population growth** refers to the rate of change in the size of a country's population. Change in population size can have huge and long-lasting effects on the world's economy and the natural environment.

The higher a country's birth rate, the greater its population growth tends to be

Changes in four key factors affect the rate of population growth.

Birth rate

The **birth rate** measures the number of live births per thousand of the population in a year. It is measured by dividing the total number of births in a country by the population size, expressed per thousand of the population. For example, in 2012 Swaziland had a population of around 1386 915 and about 36 280 live births. Thus, its birth rate was equal to 26.16 per thousand of the population. The higher a country's birth rate, the greater its population growth will tend to be. According to the *CIA World Factbook*, Niger, Mali and Uganda have the highest birth rates (of 47.6, 46.6 and 45.8 respectively) whereas Monaco, Hong Kong and Japan have the lowest birth rates (of 6.85, 7.54 and 7.72 respectively).

Death rate

The **death rate** measures the number of deaths per thousand of the population in a year. It is measured by dividing the total number of deaths in a country by the population size, expressed per thousand of the population. For example, in 2012 Canada had a population of around 34 300 085 and about 277 490 deaths, meaning that its death rate was 8.09 per thousand of the population. The lower a country's death rate, the greater its population growth will tend to be. According to the *CIA World Factbook*, South Africa, Ukraine and Lesotho have the highest death rates (of 17.23, 15.76 and 15.18 respectively) whereas Qatar, the United Arab Emirates and Kuwait have the lowest death rates (of 1.55, 2.04 and 2.13 respectively). The death rate is dependent on factors that affect the quality of life, such as income levels, health technologies, nutrition and housing.

Fertility rate

The **fertility rate** measures the average number of children born per woman, thus indicating the potential for population change in a country. Economists consider a fertility rate of two children per woman to be the minimum **replacement fertility rate** for a stable population (the number of children that the average women must have to replace the existing population). Fertility rates above two children indicate a growing population, with a declining median age for the population. By contrast, lower fertility rates indicate a falling population, with the average age of the population increasing. Fertility rates tend to fall as an economy develops, due to the higher opportunity costs of raising children. According to the *CIA World Factbook*, Niger, Mali and Somalia have the highest fertility rates (of 7.16, 6.35 and 6.26 respectively) whereas Singapore, Macau and Hong Kong have the lowest fertility rates (of 0.78, 0.92 and 1.09 respectively).

Net migration rate

Study tips

The net migration rate measures the overall level of population change resulting from the movement of migrants. It does not distinguish between worker migrants, refugees and undocumented migrants.

The size of a population can also change due to the physical movement of people in and out of a country. **Immigration** occurs when people enter a country to live and to work. **Emigration** occurs when people leave a country to work and live abroad. The **net migration rate** measures the difference between the number of people entering and leaving a country per thousand of the population in a year. It is calculated using the formula:

Net migration rate = immigration – emigration

If more people enter a country than leave in the year, there is said to be **net immigration**. For example, in 2012 Qatar, Zimbabwe and the British Virgin Islands had net immigration rates of 40.62, 23.77 and 18.56 respectively. By contrast, if more people leave a country than enter the country, there is said to be **net emigration**. For example, in 2012 Jordan, Syria and Micronesia had net emigration rates of –33.42, –27.82 and –20.97 respectively.

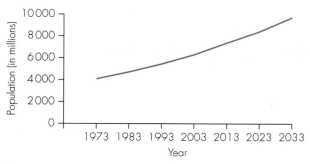

Source: adapted from **www.ibiblio.org**

Figure 22.1   The world's population, 1973–2033 (projected)

Activity

What do you think is the exact size of the world's population? Take a look here to see how accurate or imprecise you were: **www.ibiblio.org/lunarbin/worldpop**

Other factors that affect the size of a population, and hence the potential growth of the population, include the following:

- **Life expectancy** – This measures the number of years an average person in the country is expected to live. The longer the life expectancy, the greater the population size tends to be. Monaco, Macau and Japan have the world's longest life expectancy (at 89.68, 84.43 and 83.91 respectively). By contrast, Chad, Guinea-Bissau and South Africa have the lowest life expectancy (at 48.69, 49.11 and 49.41 respectively).

- **Social changes** – In economically developed countries, women are choosing to have children at a later age, partly due to the high cost of raising children but also because more women opt to have a professional career. In China, the one-child policy has significantly reduced the population growth of the world's most populous country.

- **Natural disasters, diseases and war** – These unpredictable events can cause a significant change in population size. For example, in 2003 the outbreak of severe acute respiratory syndrome (SARS) in Hong Kong spread to 37 countries and caused 775 deaths worldwide. On a much larger scale, the Tōhoku earthquake and tsunami in Japan in March 2011 proved to be the country's worst natural disaster, claiming 15 881 lives.

Study tips

Changes in any combination of the factors that affect the size of a population will also have an impact on population growth.

Japan has an ageing population in which around 30 per cent of the population are aged over 60

Table 22.1 The world's most populous countries, 2013

Rank	Country	Population (millions)
1	China	1344.13
2	India	1241.49
3	USA	311.59
4	Indonesia	242.30
5	Brazil	196.65

Source: Trading Economics

Table 22.2 The world's least populous countries, 2013

Rank	Country	Population (millions)
1	Monaco	0.04
2	Liechtenstein	0.04
3	Cayman Islands	0.06
4	Seychelles	0.09
5	São Tomé and Príncipe	0.17

Source: Trading Economics

Activity

Investigate the costs of raising a child up to the age of 18 in your country or a country of your choice. Try to be as accurate as possible by including and itemising the costs of food, clothing, education, health care, recreation and holidays. Compare results with others in your class. Why might such findings be of interest to economists?

Population distribution

Apart from the population size and population growth rates, economists also look at **demographics** – the study of population distribution and trends. Such demographics include differences in the composition of gender, age distribution and the dependency ratio.

Gender

This refers to the number of males compared with the number of females in the population. For the vast majority of countries, the gender split is quite even. Data from the *CIA World Factbook* for Denmark, for example, show the following gender ratios:

- at birth: 1.06 male(s) per female
- under 15 years: 1.05 male(s) per female
- 15–64 years: 1.01 male(s) per female
- 65 years and over: 0.8 male(s) per female
- total population: 0.97 male(s) per female.

Age distribution

This refers to the number of people within different age groups in the population. Low-income countries tend to have a relatively larger proportion of their population in the younger age groups. For example, around 39 per cent of the population in Ghana are aged 14 and below, with only about 4 per cent of the population aged 65 and over. By contrast, wealthier countries tend to have an ageing population with a growing number of elderly people. For example, only 13.5 per cent of people in Japan are aged 14 and below, while 38.8 per cent are aged 55 and above. **Population pyramids** are a graphical representation of the age and gender distribution of a country's population (see Figures 22.2 and 22.3).

Study tips

Population pyramids can provide insights into the social, political and economic stability of a country. The population distribution is shown along the x-axis, with males shown on the left and females on the right, and the population is broken down into 5-year age groups, with the youngest age group at the bottom.

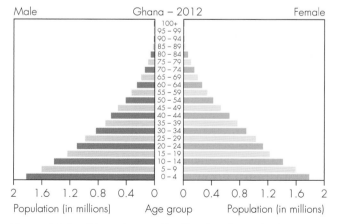

Figure 22.2 Ghana's age distribution (population pyramid)

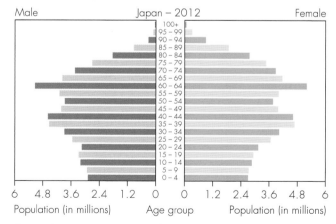

Figure 22.3 Japan's age distribution (population pyramid)

Dependency ratio

The **dependency ratio** is a comparison of the number of people who are not in the labour force with the number of people in active paid employment. For economists, the dependent population will typically include all those aged between 0 and 14 (those below the school leaving age) and those aged 65 and above (those above the retirement age). However, it also includes full-time students and the unemployed. The dependency ratio measures the dependent population as a proportion of the **working population**: that is, the total active labour force (those aged between 15 and 65). It is therefore calculated using the formula:

Dependency ratio = dependent population ÷ working population

The higher the dependency ratio, the greater the tax burden on the working population to support those who are not economically active (not in active paid employment). The dependency ratio can rise due to several reasons, such as:

- high birth rates, mainly in less economically developed countries
- a higher compulsory school leaving age, thus keeping school students as part of the dependent population for longer
- social changes such as workers entering the labour force at a later stage due to the demand for higher education, or more people choosing early retirement (thus reducing the size of the working population).

Exam practice

Study the data below from the CIA World Factbook for the gender ratios in China, and answer the questions that follow.
- at birth: 1.13 male(s) per female
- under 15 years: 1.17 male(s) per female
- 15–64 years: 1.06 male(s) per female
- 65 years and over: 0.92 male(s) per female
- total population: 1.06 male(s) per female

1   Briefly explain how China's one-child policy might have influenced the gender ratios in China.   [2]

2   Outline two economic implications for a country that has an uneven gender ratio.   [4]

The optimum population

While there are reasons for different population sizes and different rates of population growth in different countries, economists argue that there is an optimal (best or ideal) population for each country. The **optimum population** exists when the output of goods and services per head of the population is maximised (see Figure 22.4).

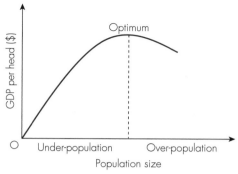

Figure 22.4 The optimum population

A country is **under-populated** if it does not have sufficient labour to make the best use of its resources. In this situation, GDP per head of the population could be further increased if there were more human resources. Fertility rates below the replacement level can lead to under-population, causing potential economic decline. In this case, to reach the optimum population, the government could introduce measures to increase the population size, such as encouraging immigration.

A country is **over-populated** if the population is too large, given the available resources of the country. Fertility rates above the replacement level can lead to potential over-population, with negative economic consequences such as famine, housing shortages, energy shortages and diseases. This causes a fall in GDP per capita as there are insufficient resources to sustain the population. In this case, to reach the optimum population, the government could either introduce measures to reduce the population size or introduce measures to boost investment and productivity in the economy.

Over-population in Brazilian cities has resulted in vast slums due to housing shortages

Table 22.3 Countries with the highest and lowest population growth rates (%)

Highest population growth			Lowest population growth		
Rank	Country	Growth	Rank	Country	Growth
1	Qatar	4.93	1	Cook Islands	−3.14
2	Zimbabwe	4.36	2	Moldova	−1.01
3	Niger	3.36	3	Saint Pierre and Miquelon	−0.98
4	Uganda	3.30	4	Jordan	−0.97
5	Turks and Caicos Islands	3.17	5	Northern Mariana Islands	−0.96

Source: adapted from *CIA World Factbook*

Consequences of population changes

The world's population reached 1 billion people around 1804. This doubled to 2 billion people by 1927 and reached 5 billion in 1987. The United Nations claims that the world's population exceeded 7 billion people in October 2011 and will reach 9 billion by 2050. This phenomenal and unprecedented population growth offers both opportunities and challenges for economists.

The economic consequences of population growth were first presented by Reverend Thomas R. Malthus (1766–1834). His **Malthusian growth theory** suggested that uncontrolled population growth would put pressures on the resources of the country, thus negatively impacting living standards. This is because, according to Malthus, population growth occurs at a geometric rate: that is, it grows at a common ratio of 2 (1, 2, 4, 8, 16, 32 and so forth) whereas food production only grows at an arithmetic rate (1, 2, 3, 4, 5). If the theory materialised, this would mean that population growth would eventually exceed food output for the population. This has not happened in reality for two main reasons:

● There have been slower population growth rates than expected, especially in more economically developed countries, due to social changes such as the high opportunity costs of raising children.
● There has been a geometric progression in food production due to advances in food technology, such as improved farm machinery, irrigation systems, genetics, pesticides and fertilisers.

Economists have found that the core concern about the continuing depletion of the planet's finite resources by rising populations can be met by improved efficiency in the production of food and the development of alternative renewable energy sources.

There are, nevertheless, varying consequences of these population changes for countries at different stages of economic development. In particular, employment patterns are likely to change. There are three basic sectors of employment in the economy: the primary, secondary and tertiary sectors.

● **Primary-sector** output is concerned with the extraction of raw materials and other natural resources. Employment in this sector includes work in agriculture, fishing, mining and oil exploration. The primary sector tends to dominate in less economically developed countries.
● **Secondary-sector** output involves manufacturing – that is, the use of natural resources to produce man-made resources such as machinery, vehicles, buildings and other capital resources. Examples of employment in this sector are jobs

in car manufacturing, textile production, chemical engineering and textbook publishing. This is the dominant sector in most industrialising and developing countries.

- **Tertiary sector** output refers to the provision of services. Examples of jobs in this sector are accountants, teachers, doctors, lawyers, financial advisers and retailers. The tertiary sector tends to be the most important in high-income economies.

As an economy develops, there tends to be a shift away from reliance on primary- and secondary-sector production towards tertiary output (see Table 22.4). In general, countries with a low level of GDP per capita are at their early stages of economic development, so most people work in the primary sector. As these countries advance, the majority of their gross domestic product is generated from the secondary sector. Finally, in economically developed countries with a high income per capita, the tertiary sector accounts for the largest share of employment and of the country's GDP.

Table 22.4 Comparison of employment by sector: selected countries, 2013

Country	Primary (%)	Secondary (%)	Tertiary (%)
Kenya	24.2	14.8	61.0
China	9.7	46.6	43.7
Luxembourg	0.4	13.6	86.0

Source: adapted from *CIA World Factbook*

The changing size and structure of the population also has effects on an economy. It has an impact on the following:

- **Consumers** – The demand for goods and services changes with variations in population trends. Customers have different demands based on their age, gender, religion, ethnic group and family size. For example, elderly people in a country with an ageing population might spend proportionately more of their money on health care and related products. By contrast, parents of young children might spend more of their income on housing, education, clothing, family vacations and toys. Firms will seek to exploit these changes in demand for different goods and services.
- **Firms** – The demand for, and supply of, labour will change following long-term changes in population trends. For example, rapid population growth should increase the future supply of labour. By contrast, the combination of low birth rates and net emigration will reduce the future supply of workers in the country. According to the World Health Organization, a staggering 2 billion people will be aged 60 years and over by 2050 – more than triple the number in 2000. By the end of 2012, only Japan had more than 30 per cent of its population aged at least 60, but some 64 countries are expected to have reached this figure by 2050. The ageing population of these nations, especially in the case of high-income countries, will have profound impacts on the future supply of labour.
- **Government** – A growing population can bring about benefits if it means the government is able to collect more tax revenues from a larger workforce. However, it can also mean added pressure for the government to provide more public services, welfare benefits and state pensions. As a result, many governments have introduced compulsory pension savings schemes and have raised official retirement ages. For example, France increased the retirement age from 60 to 62 years in 2011, with plans to increase this gradually to 68 years of age.

- **The economy** – Continual population growth puts more pressure on an economy's scarce resources. This can lead to inflationary pressures or an increase in the demand for imports if the country cannot produce enough to meet the needs and wants of the population. For example, land in prime locations is scarce, so a larger population in these areas is likely to force land prices to soar. Inflation can create problems for the economy (see Chapter 18) and cause economic growth to slow.
- **The natural environment** – An increase in the size of a population also puts strain on the environment. Non-renewable resources are depleted in the production process and the increased level of production also puts strain on the natural environment. For example, pollution and traffic congestion are by-products of overpopulated regions of the world.

Activity

1 Use the internet to investigate the effects of the changing size and structure of population on a country of your choice. Consider the impact of these changes on households, firms and the government in the country.
2 Investigate China's one-child policy and answer the following questions:
   a) Why was the one-child policy introduced?
   b) What are the exemptions to the policy?
   c) What are the positive and negative consequences of the policy for future generations?
   A good starting point is to watch this video clip on YouTube:
   www.youtube.com/watch?v=LVEx5ifxtro

China's army of 'little emperors' is seen as a consequence of the one-child policy

Exam practice

1   According to World Bank statistics, the population of Nigeria has increased from around 45 million back in 1960 to over 163 million in 2013, an increase of over 262 per cent. Figure 22.5 illustrates the growth in Nigeria's population.

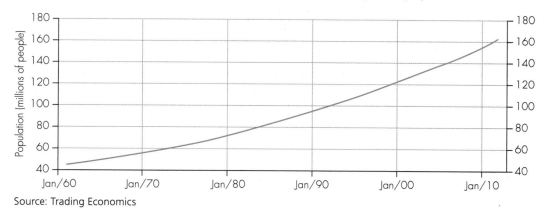

Source: Trading Economics

Figure 22.5   Nigeria's population, 1960–2013

   a) Explain two possible causes of the rise in the size of Nigeria's population.   [4]
   b) Identify and briefly explain two economic problems that could be associated with the rise in the size of Nigeria's population.   [4]
   c) Discuss two measures that the Nigerian government could use to overcome the problems of population growth in its country.   [8]

2   The median age of the UK population back in 1985 was 35.4 years, but it had climbed to 39.7 by 2010. It is projected that the median age will reach 42.2 by the year 2035. The percentage of people aged 65 and above also increased in the same time period, from 15 per cent of the population to 17 per cent (an increase of 1.7 million people). By 2035 the percentage of the UK population aged 65 and over is expected to reach 23 per cent.

Source: adapted from ONS

   a) What is meant by an 'ageing population'?   [2]
   b) Explain three causes of the increase in the percentage of people aged 65 and above in the UK.   [6]
   c) Examine the effects of an ageing population on:
       i   government expenditure and revenue   [6]
       ii economic growth.   [6]

Chapter review questions

1 What are the four key factors affecting the rate of population growth?
2 How is the net migration rate calculated?
3 How do social changes impact on the population size and potential population growth?
4 How might economists use population pyramids?
5 What are the economic consequences of an ageing population?
6 What is the dependency ratio and why is it important?
7 What is the optimum population and why do governments strive to reach this?
8 What is the Malthusian growth theory?
9 How does employment in the three sectors of the economy change as an economy develops?
10 What are the economic consequences of rapid population growth for the economy and the natural environment?

Key terms

The **birth rate** measures the number of live births per thousand of the population in a year.

The **death rate** measures the number of deaths per thousand of the population in a year.

Demographics is the study of population distribution and trends.

The **dependency ratio** is a comparison of the number of people who are not in the labour force with the number of people in active paid employment.

The **fertility rate** measures the average number of births per woman. It is used as a component in the measurement of population growth.

Life expectancy measures the number of years an average person in the country is expected to live.

The **net migration rate** measures the difference between immigration and emigration rates for a country, thus indicating the physical movement of people into and out of the country.

Optimum population exists when the output of goods and services per head of the population is maximised.

Population refers to the total number of inhabitants of a particular country.

Population growth refers to the rate of change in the size of a country's population.

Population pyramids are a graphical representation of the age and gender distribution of a country's population.

The **replacement fertility rate** is the number of children whom the average women must have to replace the existing population and maintain a stable population size.

Working population refers to the active labour force aged 15–65, i.e. those who are willing and able to work. This consists of those in paid employment, the self-employed and the unemployed.

Section 8

International aspects

Chapters

23 Specialisation

By the end of this chapter, you should be able to:
- describe the benefits and disadvantages of specialisation at regional and national levels.

Taken from Cambridge International Examinations Syllabus (IGCSE 0455/O Level 2281)
© Cambridge International Examinations

Specialisation

Specialisation occurs when individuals, firms, regions or countries concentrate on the production of a particular good or service. For example:

- **Individuals** – People might specialise, for example, as accountants, bankers, construction workers, dentists or engineers. Specialisation allows workers to become more skilled and efficient at their jobs, thus increasing the quantity and quality of the goods or services being provided. Chapter 7 examines the advantages and disadvantages of specialisation for individuals.

Activity

Discuss why primary school teachers are less specialised than secondary school teachers, who are less specialised than university lecturers.

- **Firms** – McDonald's, Burger King, KFC and Pizza Hut specialise in the output of fast food, whereas DHL, FedEx and TNT specialise in the provision of courier services. Further examples appear in Table 23.1.

Table 23.1 The world's three largest producers in selected industries

Industry	Rank		
	1st	2nd	3rd
Accountancy	PwC	Deloitte	Ernst & Young
Airline (freight)	FedEx Express	UPS Airlines	Cathay Pacific
Airline (passenger)	American Airlines	Delta Air Lines	United Airlines
Car manufacturers	Toyota	General Motors	Volkswagen
e-Commerce	Alibaba.com	eBay	Amazon.com
LCD TVs	Samsung	LG	Sony
Mobile network operators	China Mobile	Vodafone	Airtel
Mobile phones	Samsung	Nokia	Apple
Personal computers	Lenovo	HP	Dell
Restaurant chains (sales)	McDonald's	Subway	Burger King
Social network websites	Facebook	Twitter	LinkedIn

- **Regions** – Silicon Valley in northern California, USA, specialises in the provision of high-tech information communication technologies; London, Tokyo and Shanghai are financial districts; Paris and Milan are major world cities for fashion and design. These are examples of **regional specialisation**.
- **Countries** – Bangladesh and India are major producers and exporters of textiles; Scotland is famous for its whisky; Thailand and Vietnam specialise in the production of rice; and Caribbean countries such as Jamaica and Tobago specialise in tourism. Other examples are outlined in Table 23.2.

International specialisation occurs when certain countries concentrate on the production of certain goods or services due to cost advantages – perhaps arising from an abundance of resources.

Table 23.2 The world's three largest producers of selected products

Product	Rank		
	1st	**2nd**	**3rd**
Aluminium	China	Russia	Canada
Coal	China	USA	Australia
Coffee	Brazil	Vietnam	Indonesia
Copper	Chile	USA	Peru
Cotton	China	India	USA
Fruit	China	India	Brazil
Meat	China	USA	Brazil
Oil	Saudi Arabia	Venezuela	Iran
Rubber	Thailand	China	Indonesia
Sugar	Brazil	India	China
Tea	China	India	Kenya
Vegetables	China	India	USA

Source: *The Economist Pocket Book*

> **Study tips**
>
> While this chapter examines the advantages and disadvantages of specialisation at regional and national levels, remember that specialisation can also be applied to individuals, firms, machinery and technology (capital equipment).

> **Activity**
>
> Discuss how specialisation might work in schools, restaurants and supermarkets. What are the advantages and disadvantages of specialisation to the employees and firms in these markets?

Benefits of specialisation

The benefits of specialisation at regional and national level include the following:

- **Efficiency gains** – Specialisation makes better use of scarce resources. As a result, productivity increases, thereby increasing the country's gross domestic product. Taiwan and South Korea, for example, have been able to raise their standards of living by specialising in the production of manufactured consumer electronic devices. Taiwan's Foxconn is the world's largest manufacturer of smartphones and tablet computers. South Korea's Samsung is the world's largest maker of LCD televisions.

- **Labour productivity** – Workers become more skilled in the jobs they do because they are able to concentrate on what they do best. Therefore, it improves labour productivity (see Chapter 11) and enables better-quality products to be produced. Thus specialisation can benefit firms, regions and the country.
- **Increased productive capacity** – International specialisation can help to shift the production possibility curve of a country outwards due to its increased productive capacity, as shown in Figure 23.1. Thus, specialisation leads to increased national output.

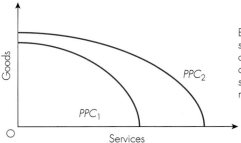

By specialising, the country's *PPC* will shift outwards. In this case, as the country chooses to specialise in the output of services, there is a larger shift along the *x*-axis as the economy moves from *PPC*₁ to *PPC*₂.

Figure 23.1 Specialisation and the *PPC*

- **Economies of scale** – Specialisation increases national output and global trade. Therefore, firms are able to enjoy cost-saving benefits from large-scale operations, known as economies of scale (see Chapter 14). This can help to keep prices down and therefore helps to keep inflation under control (see Chapter 18).
- **Improved competitiveness** – Specialisation helps to enhance international trade and exchange. Competitive prices also improve the international competitiveness of a country, thereby boosting its economic growth. After all, specialisation and trade are essential for improving a country's standard of living (see Chapter 21).

Activity

Investigate the economic reasons behind China's rising dominance in one of the following industries (or another one of your choice): coal mining, oil, steel, automobiles, commercial banking, insurance, e-commerce, tourism or telecommunications. Be prepared to share your findings with the rest of the class.

Exam practice

1 Explain how the concept of specialisation can explain why nations trade with each other. [4]

2 'Specialisation in international trade always benefits nations.' Discuss this statement. [6]

Disadvantages of specialisation

The benefits and disadvantages of specialisation for the individual are covered in Chapter 7. Despite the potential benefits of regional and national specialisation, there are several drawbacks.

- **Overspecialisation** in a region can cause structural and regional unemployment (see Chapter 19). *The Full Monty*, the highest grossing British movie, which cost only $3.5 million to produce but made over $250 million at the box office, was about six unemployed men in Sheffield, UK, which used to be a major producer of steel. Although the film was produced as a comedy, it featured some key consequences of the collapse of steel production in the UK, such as regional unemployment, stress, depression and suicide.

   Countries that overspecialise also suffer the most during an economic downturn, as they do not have a variety of goods and services that they can rely on to survive. For example, Liberia is highly dependent on its agricultural output, which accounts for around 61 per cent of its GDP. Adverse weather conditions could wipe out much of its agricultural production, thus severely harming the economy.

- **High labour turnover** occurs if lots of workers choose to leave their jobs in search of more challenging and less boring ones. In a country that has a labour turnover rate of 12.5 per cent, one worker in every eight changes jobs each year. The higher this rate, the more expensive it is for the economy, as firms have to continually hire and train workers. Industries that suffer from high labour turnover tend to pay low wages to low-skilled workers, such as those working in call centres, retailing, catering (including fast-food restaurants), supermarkets and hotels.

- **Low labour mobility** – Low-skilled and poorly paid workers tend to receive little training, so they may not develop the necessary skills to find alternative jobs. Again, this can lead to structural unemployment.

   Highly skilled workers, such as pilots, dentists, software developers, financial advisors and attorneys can also find it extremely difficult to change to alternative professions and careers.

   Job specialisation also makes cross-functional training difficult – in other words, workers only have a narrow understanding of the overall business. By contrast, cross-functional training would help to make workers more versatile and expand their skills. This lack of labour market flexibility can reduce the economic efficiency and international competitiveness of the country.

Staffordshire used to have a thriving pottery industry (another example of overspecialisation) – now the area is full of derelict factories

● **Lack of variety for consumers** – Specialisation often leads to standardised, mass-produced goods. An example is Foxconn, which manufactures the iPhone and iPad for Apple. These devices lack variety and only come in one of two colours. Domestic customers may look at alternative imported products from foreign suppliers, thereby reducing the competitiveness of domestic firms that overspecialise.

● **Cost** – Firms that employ workers with highly specialised skills tend to face very high salary demands. For example, *Forbes* magazine estimates that the earnings of the world's top ten highest-paid supermodels exceeded $100 million, with Gisele Bündchen earning about $45 million. Wayne Rooney was reported to be paid a stunning $300 192 ($456 292) per week at Manchester United Football Club! This can have a negative impact on the profits of firms and potentially reduce their competitiveness.

In 2013, David Beckham topped the list of the best-paid footballers in the world (€36 million), €1 million ahead of Lionel Messi in second place and a further €5 million more than Ronaldo in third. Wayne Rooney made a respectable seventh place, earning €18 million (Source: *France Football*)

Exam practice

1 Define the term 'specialisation'.   [2]
2 Explain why, during a recession, highly specialised firms are less likely to survive than diversified firms.   [4]

Chapter review questions

1 What is meant by 'specialisation' at regional and national levels?
2 Give two examples of regional specialisation.
3 Give two examples of national specialisation.
4 What are the advantages of regional and national specialisation?
5 What are the disadvantages of regional and national specialisation?

Key terms

International specialisation occurs when certain countries concentrate on the production of certain goods or services due to cost advantages, perhaps due to their abundant resources.

Overspecialisation occurs when an individual, firm, region or country concentrates too much on producing a very limited number of goods and services. This exposes the economic agent to a far higher degree of risk.

Regional specialisation occurs when certain areas concentrate on the production of certain goods or services. For example, Hollywood, in Los Angeles, is famous for its motion pictures industry.

Specialisation occurs when individuals, firms, regions or countries concentrate on the production of a particular good or service.

(24) Balance of payments

The balance of payments

The **balance of payments** is a financial record of a country's transactions with the rest of the world for a given time period, usually over 1 year. This includes the country's trade in goods and services with other countries.

In theory, the balance of payments must always balance over time. This is because a country, like an individual, can only spend (on imports, for example) what it earns (from export earnings, for example).

The current account

One of the components of the balance of payments is the **current account**, which is a record of all exports and imports of goods and services and net income flows and transfers with other countries between a country and the rest of the world. The current account is structured in three parts.

Visible trade balance

The **visible trade balance** is a record of the export and import of physical goods. It is also known as the **balance of trade in goods**. It is the trade in goods, such as raw materials, semi-manufactured products and manufactured goods. **Visible exports** are goods that are sold to foreign customers, with money flowing into the domestic economy. For example, the export of Toyota cars results in an inward flow of money to Japan's visible balance. **Visible imports** are goods bought by domestic customers from foreign sellers, such as Japanese residents buying German-made cars. This results in money flowing out of the Japanese economy.

Toyota cars are an example of visible exports

Invisible trade balance

The **invisible trade balance** is a record of the export and import of services (intangible products), such as banking, insurance, shipping and tourism. It is sometimes called the **balance of trade in services**. For example, American tourists in France would represent export earnings (or an **invisible export**) for the French economy. By contrast, French customers who fly on American Airlines represent an **invisible import** for the country.

Net income flows and transfers

Net income flows and transfers are a record of a country's net income earned from capital flows. Examples include:

● interest, profits and dividends paid to foreigners who own assets in the country
● income earned on foreign assets owned by domestic residents and firms

Examples of transfers include:

● money spent on foreign aid
● money sent home by people working abroad
● taxes received by the government from foreign residents and firms
● bank deposits held in overseas banks.

The sum of the visible and invisible trade balances gives what is known as the **balance of trade** or simply the **trade balance** – the difference between a country's total export earnings and its total import expenditure. The trade balance is the largest component of the current account. It is often referred to as **net exports**. Therefore, the current account is calculated as follows:

$$\text{Current account} = \text{visible trade balance} + \text{invisible trade balance} + \text{net income flows and transfers}$$

$$\text{Net income flows and transfers} = \text{income flows and transfers earned overseas} - \text{income flows and transfers sent overseas}$$

Study tips

The easiest way to distinguish between invisible exports and imports is to consider flows of money (where the money comes from or goes to) rather than the flows of services.

Table 24.1 The current account balance, selected countries (top and bottom five ranks)

Rank	Country	$bn
1	China	213.8
2	Germany	208.1
3	Saudi Arabia	150.0
4	Japan	84.7
5	Russia	81.3

Rank	Country	$bn
1	USA	−487.2
2	India	−80.15
3	Brazil	−65.13
4	Canada	−59.92
5	Turkey	−59.74

Source: *CIA Factbook*, 2012

Activity

Investigate the main exports and imports for your country, or a country of your choice. Does your chosen country currently have a positive or negative trade balance?

Exam practice

1 Classify the following transactions by using a tick (✓) in the correct column, from the perspective of the UK economy.

	Transaction	Visible		Invisible	
		Export	Import	Export	Import
a)	The purchase of UK-produced chemical products by a German company				
b)	American tourists flying to the UK on British Airways				
c)	UK supermarkets purchase of French wine and cheese				
d)	UK government maintaining foreign embassies overseas				
e)	German tourists buy theatre tickets to see *Les Misérables* in London				
f)	A British firm buys a fleet of lorries (trucks) from Japan				
g)	Global sales of *Harry Potter* books by British author J. K. Rowling				

[8]

2 Study the data below and answer the questions that follow.

Trade balance for Country B ($bn), 2013

Exports	85
Goods	57
Services	28
Imports	_____
Goods	88
Services	15
Visible balance	_____
Invisible balance	_____
Trade balance	_____

a) Define the term 'trade balance'. [2]

b) Calculate the missing figures in the data above. [4]

Current account deficits

A country is said to have a **current account deficit** if its financial outflows are greater than its financial inflows. Hence, the current account has a negative balance. By contrast, a **current account surplus** exists if the financial inflows are greater than its financial outflows. This means the country will have a positive balance on its current account.

Causes of current account deficits

A deficit on the current account can occur due to a combination of two factors:

- **Lower demand for exports** – This could be caused by a decline in manufacturing competitiveness, perhaps due to higher labour costs in the domestic economy. Another factor is declining incomes in foreign markets, perhaps due to an economic recession. This means households and firms have less money available to spend on another country's exports. A third cause of lower demand for exports is a higher exchange rate (see Chapter 25). This makes exports more expensive for foreign buyers, so it reduces the volume and value of exports.
- **Increased demand for imports** – Domestic buyers tend to buy more imports if they are cheaper or of better quality. For example, a higher exchange rate means the domestic currency can buy more foreign currency, so this makes it cheaper to buy imports. Alternatively, domestic inflation means that imports are relatively cheaper, so more domestic residents and firms will tend to buy foreign goods and services.

Exam practice

Examine Figure 24.1, which shows the balance of trade for Sri Lanka, and answer the questions that follow.

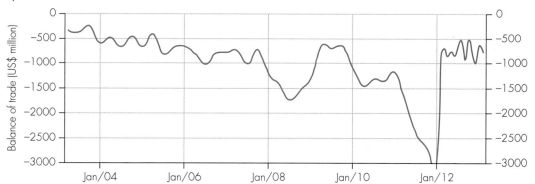

Figure 24.1 The balance of trade for Sri Lanka, 2004–13

1 Define the term 'balance of trade'. [2]
2 Explain two possible causes of the trend in Sri Lanka's balance of trade. [4]

Consequences of current account deficits

There are consequences of current account deficits for the domestic economy. Like an individual, a country cannot spend more (on imported goods, services and capital flows) than it earns (from the export of goods, services and capital).

The severity of these consequences depends on the size and duration of the deficit. Nevertheless, a current account deficit is generally considered to be unfavourable for the economy for the reasons outlined below:

- **Reduced aggregate demand** – A trade deficit means the economy is spending more money on imports than it receives from the export of goods and services. This can cause aggregate demand in the economy to fall, thus triggering a recession (see Chapter 20). The USA's trade deficit with China (see the Exam Practice question below) has been blamed for much of the country's recent economic problems.

● **Unemployment** – As the demand for labour is a derived demand (see Chapter 7), a fall in aggregate demand is likely to cause unemployment in the economy. Workers may also have to take a pay cut in order to correct the deficit. For example, the UK has experienced a decline in manufacturing jobs as there has been a fall in the demand for British exports of coal, steel, textiles and motor vehicles.

● **Lower standards of living** – If the current account deficit is caused by a negative balance on net income flows and transfers, this means monetary outflows exceed monetary inflows for the country. An economy with less income is likely to suffer from lower standards of living. In addition, to cut the current account deficit, households and firms may need to reduce their spending.

● **Increased borrowing** – Just like an individual cannot spend more than he or she earns in the long run, countries need to borrow money or attract foreign investment in order to rectify their current account deficits. In addition, there is an opportunity cost of debt repayment, as the government cannot use this money to stimulate economic growth.

● **Lower exchange rate** – A fall in demand for exports and/or a rise in the demand for imports (causing the current account deficit) reduces the exchange rate. While a lower exchange rate can mean exports become more price competitive, it also means that essential imports (such as oil and foodstuffs) will become more expensive. This can lead to imported inflation (see Chapter 18). The consequences of fluctuating exchange rates are covered in more detail in Chapter 25.

In general, large and persistent current account deficits are a sign that the country is internationally uncompetitive, which has more severe consequences for the domestic economy. These deficits will have a negative impact on economic growth and standards of living.

> **Study tips**
>
> A manageable deficit on the current account is not necessarily a bad thing. For example, the deficit might be the result of strong economic growth, with residents purchasing more foreign goods and services. This allows the country's residents to enjoy a higher standard of living, as they are able to benefit from access to a range of good-quality imports.

Exam practice

Despite the USA exporting more to China than ever before, the USA's trade deficit with China is at its highest level (Table 24.2). The imports include consumer electronics, clothing and machinery (such as power generation), toys, sports equipment, furniture and footwear.

Table 24.2   Trade between the USA and China, 2011–12

	2012 ($bn)	2011 ($bn)
US exports to China	110.6	103.9
US imports from China	425.6	399.3

Source: adapted from US Census

1   Explain how it is possible that 'the USA's trade deficit with China is at its highest level' even though the USA reported record export sales to China.   [2]

2   Calculate the trade balance for the USA with China for 2011 and 2012.   [2]

Dealing with current account deficits

There are four main policies that can be used to improve a country's current account balance: fiscal and monetary policies (which tackle demand-side issues), supply-side policies and protectionist measures. These macroeconomic policies are covered in more detail in Chapter 16.

- **Fiscal policies** – These measures use a combination of higher taxes and reduced government spending in order to reduce the amount of money available to spend on imports. In theory, this helps to reduce the current account deficit.
- **Monetary policies** – Higher interest rates make new and existing loans more expensive for households and firms. Therefore, this reduces their demand for imports. Alternatively, the central monetary authority of a country (see Chapter 6) might decide to devalue the exchange rate to improve the nation's competitiveness. This also has the effect of reducing the price of exports and making imports more expensive.
- **Supply-side policies** – These policies strive to raise the productive capacity of the economy. Examples are:
  - investment in education and health care to improve the economy's human capital, productivity and international competitiveness
  - investment in infrastructure to support businesses and industries, especially those engaged in export markets
  - measures to encourage export-driven business start-ups and industries, such as government subsidies and tax incentives.
- **Protectionist measures** – These measures reduce the competiveness of imports, thereby making domestic consumption more attractive. For example, tariffs (import taxes) raise the price of imports while quotas (see Chapter 26) limit the amount of imports available.

Exam practice

'A current account deficit on the balance of payments is undesirable during a recession but is not really a problem during periods of economic growth.'

1   Define the term 'current account deficit'.   [2]
2   Explain the validity of the above statement.   [4]

Current account surpluses

Causes of current account surpluses

A surplus on the current account can occur due to a combination of two factors:

- **Higher demand for exports** – This could be caused by an improvement in manufacturing competitiveness, perhaps due to higher labour productivity in the domestic economy. Another factor is higher incomes in overseas markets, meaning that foreign households and firms have more money to spend on the country's exports. A third cause of higher demand for exports is a lower exchange rate (see Chapter 25), which makes exports less expensive for foreign buyers.

- **Reduced demand for imports** – Domestic buyers tend to buy fewer imports if they are more expensive or of lower quality than those provided by domestic firms. For example, a lower exchange rate means the domestic currency can buy less foreign currency, so this makes it more expensive to buy imports. Another reason is that inflation in overseas countries causes imports to be more expensive, so individuals and firms buy more home-produced goods and services.

Consequences of current account surpluses

The consequences of a country having a current account surplus include the following:

- **Employment** – A sustained current account surplus can be desirable, as higher export sales help to create jobs. However, a consequence of this is that job losses are created in other countries. For example, the USA has blamed China's large current account for causing large-scale unemployment in America.
- **Standards of living** – A favourable current account balance means the country receives a higher income because domestic firms have a competitive advantage in the products they export. This can lead to a higher standard of living (see Chapter 21).

Oil exporting countries such as Saudi Arabia, Kuwait, Qatar and the United Arab Emirates have consistently enjoyed current account surpluses, thus boosting their GDP and standards of living

- **Inflationary** – Higher demand for exports can lead to demand-pull inflation (see Chapter 18). Therefore, the current account surplus can diminish the international competitiveness of the country over time as the price of exports rises due to inflation.
- **Higher exchange rate** – The higher demand for exports can cause the currency to appreciate in value (see Chapter 25). Subsequently, foreign buyers will find it more expensive to import goods into their countries.

Study tips

A surplus on the current account is not necessarily a good thing. For example, former communist nation Romania had a trade surplus by using trade protectionism (see Chapter 26). This limited access to foreign goods and services, thus causing living standards to be lower.

Exam practice

Examine Figure 24.2, which shows the current account balance for Kuwait, and answer the questions that follow.

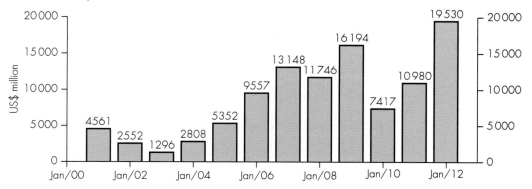

Source: Trading Economics **www.tradingeconomics.com/kuwait/current-account-to-gdp**

Figure 24.2 Current account balance for Kuwait, 2001–12

1 Define the term 'current account surplus'. [2]

2 Explain three consequences of Kuwait's continual current account surplus during the twenty-first century. [6]

Chapter review questions

1 What is the balance of payments?
2 What is the difference between the visible trade balance and the invisible trade balance?
3 What does the 'net income flows and transfers' component of the current account record?
4 How does a current account deficit differ from a current account surplus?
5 What are the two main causes of a current account deficit?
6 How might a government deal with a current account deficit?
7 How might a current account surplus be detrimental to the country?

Key terms

The **balance of payments** is a financial record of a country's transactions with the rest of the world for a given time period, per time period.

The **balance of trade** (or simply the **trade balance**) is the difference between a country's total export earnings and its total import expenditure.

The **current account** is a component of the balance of payments that records all exports and imports of goods and services and net income flows and transfers with other countries between a country and the rest of the world.

A **current account deficit** occurs when a country's financial outflows are greater than its financial inflows.

A **current account surplus** occurs when a country's financial inflows are greater than its financial outflows.

Invisible exports refer to the earnings from selling services to foreign customers.

Invisible imports refer to the spending on services provided by firms in overseas countries.

The **invisible trade balance** is a record of the trade in services, such as transportation and financial services.

Net income flows are a record of a country's net income earned from monetary flows.

Transfers are money flows from one country to another, e.g. income sent by a foreign worker to their home country, or a gift of money from one government to another.

Visible exports are goods that are sold to foreign customers.

Visible imports are goods bought by domestic customers from foreign sellers.

The **visible trade balance** is a record of the export and import of physical goods.

25 Exchange rates

Exchange rates

An **exchange rate** is the price of one currency measured in terms of other currencies. For example, the exchange rate of the US dollar in terms of the pound sterling might be $1.5 = £1 (or $1 = £0.67). This means that a British tourist spending $600 on hotel accommodation in the USA would have spent the equivalent of £400 ($600 ÷ 1.5).

Exchange rates can change over time, so if the US dollar fell against the pound sterling to $1.60 = £1, then the tourist would pay £375 ($600 ÷ 1.6) for staying at the hotel in the USA. The British tourist would pay the same price in US dollars but this equates to fewer pounds sterling.

Activity

1 Use **www.oanda.com** (or another relevant internet website) to find out which countries use the following currencies:
   - a) ringgit
   - b) dong
   - c) lek
   - d) won
   - e) kwacha
   - f) rufiyaa

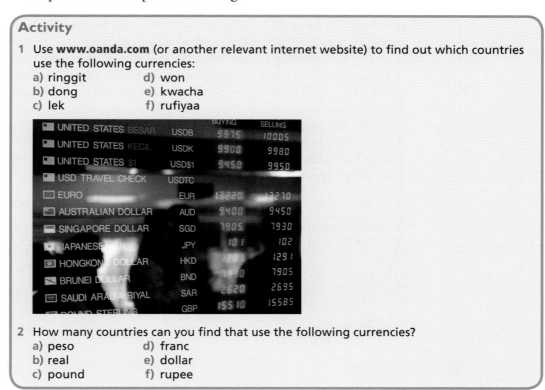

2 How many countries can you find that use the following currencies?
   - a) peso
   - b) real
   - c) pound
   - d) franc
   - e) dollar
   - f) rupee

Exam practice

1 Suppose the exchange rate between the Australian dollar (AUD) and the Chinese yuan renminbi (CNY) is AUD1 = CNY6.5. Calculate the price for customers in China of buying textbooks priced at AUD65 from Australia.　　[2]

2 Suppose that the exchange rate between the Canadian dollar (CAD) and the British pound (GBP) is CAD1 = GBP0.65 and the exchange rate between the Canadian dollar and the euro (EUR) is CAD1 = EUR0.75. Calculate the exchange rate of the British pound against the euro.　　[2]

The importance of exchange rates

Since different countries use different forms of money, exchange rates are fundamental in facilitating international trade (see Chapter 25). In theory, the demand for exports of goods and services increases if exports become cheaper. Likewise, the demand for imports falls if the price of imports becomes more expensive.

Consider Table 25.1 as an example. The table shows that the price of a 64 GB iPad in Hong Kong is HKD6000 (Hong Kong dollars). Study the impact that fluctuations in the exchange rate of the pound sterling have on the price of the iPad for British tourists in Hong Kong.

As the price of the pound sterling increases from $10.5 to $13.5, the price of the iPad falls from £571.43 to £444.44 for the British tourist in Hong Kong. This means that as the value of a country's currency rises, its demand for imports tends to increase. Hong Kong's exports to the UK should therefore increase.

Looking at this from the perspective of Hong Kong, the fall in its exchange rate (from $10.5 = £1 to $13.5 = £1) means that imports will become more expensive. To illustrate this, suppose that a Hong Kong supermarket imports supplies from the UK. An order valued at £50 000 used to cost the Hong Kong firm $525 000 (i.e. £50 000 × $10.5), but will now cost $675 000 (i.e. £5000 × $13.5). This means that as the value of a country's currency falls, its demand for imports tends to fall. The UK's exports to Hong Kong should therefore fall.

Table 25.1 The price of an iPad at different exchange rates (GBP:HKD)

Exchange rate (GBP:HKD)	HKD price	GBP price
£1 = $10.5	$6000	£571.43
£1 = $11.5	$6000	£521.74
£1 = $12.5	$6000	£480.00
£1 = $13.5	$6000	£444.44

However, the demand for some imports is price inelastic because they are not readily available in the domestic economy yet are essential for production (such as oil and other vital raw materials). Therefore, domestic firms have to spend more on these important imports when the exchange rate falls in value. For example, if the Mexican peso (MXN) falls against the Canadian dollar (CAD) from 12.5:1 to 14:1, then Mexican firms buying Canadian oil at a price of CAD100 per barrel pay a higher price of MXN1400 per barrel instead of the previous price of MXN1250 per barrel. This means Mexican firms may need to reduce their price by around 12 per cent to remain competitive, despite their higher costs of production due to the fall in the value of the Mexican peso.

In the same way that changes in the exchange rate can affect the demand for exports and imports, they can also affect the amount of tourism revenue and the profitability of businesses, and can therefore impact upon unemployment and economic growth.

Floating exchange rate systems

There are two broad types of exchange rate system: floating and fixed.

In the **floating exchange rate system**, the value of a currency is determined by the market forces of demand for the currency and supply of the currency. For example, overseas tourists buy (demand) the foreign currency by selling their domestic currency. Countries that adopt this system allow the value of their currency to be determined by the market. Examples are Belgium, Chile, Luxembourg, Spain, Japan, New Zealand, Sweden and the United Kingdom.

If banks in New Zealand offer investors higher interest rates than those in the UK, this can cause investors to take advantage by buying the NZD. This will increase the demand for the NZD, thus shifting its demand from D_1 to D_2 in Figure 25.1. This raises the price (or exchange rate) of the NZD from £0.55 to £0.65. By contrast, a fall in interest rates is likely to drive investors away as they search for investments that generate a better financial return.

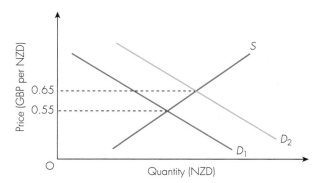

Figure 25.1 Changes in interest rates and the impact on exchange rates

In a floating exchange rate system, there is an **appreciation** in the exchange rate if the exchange rate is rising against other currencies. By contrast, there is a **depreciation** of the exchange rate if its value falls against other currencies.

Fixed exchange rate systems

Under the **fixed exchange rate system**, the government intervenes in **foreign exchange markets** to maintain its exchange rate at a predetermined level. For example, the Hong Kong dollar has been pegged (fixed) against the US dollar since 1972. Since 1983 the HKD has been pegged to both the USD (at a rate of HKD7.8 = USD1) and the Macanese pataca (at a rate of HKD1 = MOP1.03).

The main advantage of fixing exchange rates is that it reduces uncertainties for international trade. This allows firms, both foreign and domestic, to be certain about future costs and prices, thereby encouraging international trade and exchange.

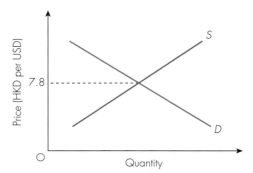

Figure 25.2 The fixed exchange system

In Figure 25.2, the exchange rate between the USD and the HKD is pegged at HK$7.8 = US$1 (although it is allowed to fluctuate within a small range of HK$7.75 to HK$7.85). This is achieved by the respective governments buying and selling foreign currencies to maintain this 'peg'.

For example, if the HKD declines against the pegged USD, the Hong Kong Monetary Authority (HKMA) can raise the value by increasing the demand for its currency. To prevent the HKD falling from 7.8 to 7.7, perhaps due to speculators selling the HKD, the HKMA intervenes in the foreign exchange market by buying enough HKD (thus raising its price) to maintain the exchange rate at the fixed rate of 7.8. Similarly, the HKMA would sell HKD if the exchange rate were to approach 7.9 (increasing the supply of HKD in order to reduce its price). This function of central banks (see Chapter 6) requires careful management and plenty of currency reserves.

There are two main criticisms of a fixed exchange rate system. First, it reduces the country's ability to use monetary policy changes in order to affect the economy (which is particularly useful during an economic recession). Second, there is a huge opportunity cost in using large amounts of foreign exchange reserves to maintain the fixed rate.

It is possible to change the pegged rate over time. For example, the HKD was originally fixed at HK$5.65 = USD1 back in 1972. As the USA's economy developed, it currency was revalued to HK$7.8. In a fixed exchange rate system, there is a **revaluation** of the exchange rate if it is rising against other currencies. By contrast, the exchange rate is **devalued** under a fixed exchange rate system if the value of the currency falls against other currencies.

> **Activity**
> Prepare a presentation on why a government might want to have lower exchange rates. Consider whether this is a sustainable economic policy.

Causes of exchange rate fluctuations

Any factor that influences the demand for a currency or its supply will have an impact on the exchange rate. These factors include the following:

- **Changes in demand for exports** – An increase in the demand for exports, perhaps due to improved quality or successful advertising, will also increase the demand for the country's currency. Therefore this increases the exchange rate.
- **Changes in demand for imports** – An increase in the demand for imports, perhaps due to an increase in the competitiveness of foreign firms, will raise the value of the foreign currency in order to facilitate the purchase of foreign goods and services.
- **Prices and inflation** – An increase in the price of goods and services caused by domestic inflation will tend to decrease the demand for exports. This will therefore tend to cause the exchange rate to fall in value.
- **Foreign direct investment** (FDI) – Globalisation and the economic activity of multinational companies mean that investment in overseas production plants requires the use of foreign currencies. For example, Nissan's car manufacturing plant in India requires the Japanese car-maker to buy Indian rupees to pay for the materials, labour and other production costs. Thus, inward FDI will boost the demand for a currency. By contrast, outward FDI will increase the supply of a currency.

A Nissan car plant in Chennai, India

- **Speculation** – Foreign exchange traders and investment companies move money around the world to take advantage of higher interest rates (see Figure 25.1) and variations in exchange rates to earn a profit. As huge sums of money are involved (known as 'hot money'), this can cause exchange rate fluctuations, at least in the short run. Speculators might also lack confidence in certain economies and therefore withdraw their investments, thereby depreciating the currency (see the Case Study below).
- **Government intervention** – All the above factors can affect the exchange rate under a freely floating exchange rate system. In addition, government intervention in the foreign exchange market can affect the exchange rate. For example, if greater

demand for American goods causes an appreciation of the dollar, the US Federal Reserve can sell its dollar reserves (thereby increasing the supply of dollars), leading to a fall in the value of its currency.

The Chinese government limits currency flows by only allowing individuals to change up to 20000 yuan (around $3185) each day.

Case Study: The collapse of Landsbanki and Kaupthing

The global financial crisis of 2008 saw the collapse of Iceland's major banks, including Landsbanki (founded in 1886) and Kaupthing (founded in 1930). Investors across Europe feared the Icelandic banks would default on their debts. This resulted in a selling frenzy which caused a rapid fall in the value of the krona (Iceland's currency).

Exam practice

The value of a currency will change if the demand for and/or supply of the currency changes. Explain, with the use of a demand and supply diagram, the effects of the following events from the perspective of the USA:

1   The USA buys more imports from Brazil.   [4]
2   Millions of American tourists visit France.   [4]
3   There is an increase in American exports to Russia.   [4]
4   The Federal Reserve (the USA's central bank) raises the rate of interest.   [4]
5   Speculators feel that the US dollar will rise in value against other major currencies. [4]

Consequences of exchange rate fluctuations

Exchange rate fluctuations affect different stakeholders in different ways, depending on whether the consequences are seen from the perspective of customers or producers (importers and exporters).

The following is an analysis of a strong US dollar, due to either a currency appreciation or a currency revaluation. The opposite results would apply in the case of a currency depreciation or devaluation.

- **Customers** have greater purchasing power when the exchange rate increases. For example, if the exchange rate changes from $1.6 = £1 to $1.4 = £1, then Americans would require fewer dollars to buy British goods and services. Thus, American firms and individuals are likely to buy more British goods and services.
- **Exporters** face more difficult trading conditions when the exchange rate increases. This is because the price of their goods and services will become more expensive for foreign customers. For example, if the exchange rate changes from $1.5 = €1 to $1.3 = €1 then customers from the European Union will need to spend more money to buy American goods and services. Therefore, demand for US exports is likely to drop.
- **Importers** potentially gain from a strong dollar because this makes it cheaper for US firms to import raw materials, components and finished goods from abroad. For example, if the exchange rate appreciates from $1.5 = €1 to $1.3 = €1, the American importers only need to spend $1300 on each €1000 order of goods and services from Europe, rather than $1500. While this is bad for US firms trying to compete with American imports, it can help to reduce cost-push inflation (see Chapter 18).

Exchange rate fluctuations also have consequences for macroeconomic objectives. An increase in the exchange rate will have the following effects on the balance of payments, employment, inflation and economic growth:

- **Balance of payments** – If a currency appreciation has a larger impact on exports than imports (that is, there is a net fall in the value of exports), then the balance of payments will worsen. This is because a strong currency will make it more difficult for exporters to sell their goods and services in overseas markets.
- **Employment** – A fall in net exports and deteriorating profits will, in the long run, cause job losses in export-oriented businesses. This will therefore cause unemployment in the economy.

   Greece and Spain suffered from high unemployment in 2012–13 due to the strength of the euro, with unemployment reaching record levels of 26.8 per cent and 26.1 per cent respectively. In Spain, youth unemployment (among those aged 21 and below) reached a historic high of 55 per cent.
- **Inflation** – Lower levels of spending in the economy, caused by higher unemployment, will tend to reduce the rate of inflation. In addition, if the country relies heavily on certain imports, such as oil or food supplies, then the higher exchange rate will help to reduce the general price level even further.
- **Economic growth** – In the long run, economic growth is likely to fall due to the combination of lower export sales and higher unemployment caused by the higher exchange rate.

People queuing outside a job centre in Spain

Exam practice

Since China's admission to the World Trade Organization in November 2001, the USA has complained that the Chinese government has deliberately kept its exchange rate artificially low. The low value of the yuan compared with the dollar has contributed to the economic problems of the US economy.

1   Define the term 'exchange rate'.   [2]

2   Explain two advantages of a weak yuan for the Chinese economy.   [4]

Coping with a strong exchange rate

Firms can deal with a higher or strong exchange rate in a number of ways, such as:

- cutting export prices to maintain their price competitiveness against foreign rivals, which means the domestic firms will have to accept lower profit margins
- seeking alternative overseas suppliers of cheaper raw materials and components
- improving productivity (efficiency) gains to keep average labour costs under control
- focusing on supplying more price inelastic and income inelastic products because customers become less sensitive to exchange rate fluctuations
- focusing on non-price factors that are important to overseas customers, such as brand awareness and social responsibility
- relocating production processes overseas, where costs of production are relatively low and where operations are less exposed to exchange rate fluctuations.

> **Study tips**
>
> It is possible for some firms to gain from a stronger currency while others lose out. Review the main points in this chapter to make your own judgement on this.

Exam practice

1   Explain, with the aid of a numerical example, what is meant by an 'appreciation' in the value of a currency.   [3]

2   Examine the likely effects of a country's currency appreciation on its exports and imports.   [6]

> **Chapter review questions**
>
> 1   What is an exchange rate?
> 2   What is the likely impact on a country's exchange rate following an increase in the demand for its exports?
> 3   What is the likely impact on a country's exchange rate following a decrease in the rate of interest?
> 4   What are the causes of exchange rate fluctuations?
> 5   What are the consequences of exchange rate fluctuations for importers, exporters and customers?
> 6   How does a strong currency impact upon a country's macroeconomic objectives?

Key terms

Appreciation of a currency occurs when there is an increase in the value of the exchange rate relative to another currency operating in a floating exchange rate system.

Depreciation of a currency occurs when there is a fall in the value of the exchange rate relative to another currency operating in a floating exchange rate system.

Devaluation occurs when the price of a currency operating in a fixed exchange rate system is officially and deliberately lowered.

The **exchange rate** is the price of one currency measured in terms of other currencies.

A **fixed exchange rate system** exists when the central bank (or monetary authority) buys and sells foreign currencies to ensure the value of its currency stays at the pegged value.

A **floating exchange rate system** means that the currency is allowed to fluctuate against other currencies according to market forces without any government intervention.

A **foreign exchange market** is the marketplace where foreign currencies can be bought and sold.

Revaluation occurs when the price of a currency operating in a fixed exchange rate system is officially and deliberately increased.

Trade and trade protectionism

Free trade

International trade is the exchange of goods and services beyond national borders. It entails the sale of **exports** (goods and services sold to overseas buyers) and **imports** (foreign goods and services bought by domestic households and firms).

Free trade means that international trade can take place without any forms of protection (**barriers to trade**), such as quantitative limits or taxes being imposed on exports.

The merits of international trade (that is, the reasons why countries trade with one another) include the following:

● **Access to resources** – International trade enables firms and consumers to gain access to goods and services that they cannot produce themselves. For example, countries without a manufacturing industry, like the Maldives, can purchase laptop computers, motor vehicles and Hollywood movies produced around the world.

These laptops are made in China but can be purchased by people in countries that do not have a manufacturing industry, thanks to international trade

Study tips

Make sure you can distinguish between the merits of **international trade** and the merits of **free trade** – they are not quite the same, as not all international trade entails free trade. Thus, the merits of free trade (without any trade barriers) are greater than the benefits of international trade (which may entail some trade barriers).

- **Lower prices** – Free trade reduces the costs of trading, whereas protectionism increases the costs of trading. For example, it is cheaper for Germans to purchase foreign-produced smartphones made in China and Taiwan because of the high labour costs in Germany. Unfavourable weather conditions in Sweden mean it is better off importing tropical fruits from Jamaica. By contrast, the imposition of trade barriers would mean that both domestic firms and consumers have to pay more for imported goods and services.

- **Economies of scale** – By operating on a larger scale in global markets, firms can benefit from economies of scale (see Chapter 14). These cost savings can be passed on to consumers in the form of lower prices and/or kept by the firms in the form of higher profits.

- **Greater choice** – Free trade enables consumers and firms to access a larger variety of goods and services from different producers around the world. For example, while Germans can choose from domestic motor vehicles such as Audi, BMW or Mercedes-Benz, they are also able to choose from foreign suppliers such as Lexus (Japan), Jaguar (India) and Cadillac (USA).

- **Increased market size** – International trade enables firms to earn more revenues and profits. For example, US firms can sell products to a domestic market of 300 million people, whereas they can sell to a larger market of more than 2.4 billion potential customers by selling their products to China and India.

- **Efficiency gains** – Free trade forces domestic firms to focus on improving the quality of their output due to foreign competition. For example, Japanese car-makers and South Korean electronics firms have forced US producers such as General Motors and Apple to create better-quality products. By contrast, protectionist measures give domestic firms a false sense of security, which can make them inefficient.

- **Improved international relations** – The absence of trade barriers encourages international trade and cooperation between countries. By contrast, if a country uses international trade barriers, other nations are likely to retaliate by doing the same.

Activity

1 Have a look at the products you have at home, such as your family's computer, television, watch, car and clothes. How many have these products have been imported? Why might this be?

2 Use the internet to investigate the types of goods and services that are exported and imported from one high-income country and one low-income country of your choice. Find out the main trading partners of these countries. As a starting point, you may want to use *The Economist's* country briefs (**www.economist.com**) and/or the CIA website (**www.cia.gov/library/publications/the-world-factbook/**).

Exam practice

Bangladesh is one of the world's largest producers of rice and tropical fruits. In Brunei Darussalam, crude oil and natural gas account for around 90 per cent of the country's gross domestic product. This makes Brunei Darussalam one of the leading producers of oil in Southeast Asia.

1   Explain two reasons why countries such as Bangladesh and Brunei Darussalam trade with each other. [4]

2   Outline one problem for Brunei Darussalam in relying on oil exports. [2]

3   Explain how Bangladesh's export of rice and tropical fruits helps its farmers to achieve economies of scale. [4]

Trade protection

Despite the benefits of international trade, there are drawbacks that mean there could be a need for trade protection. **Trade protection** refers to the use of trade barriers to restrain foreign trade, thereby limiting overseas competition. There are a variety of restrictive government measures designed to discourage imports and to prevent competition in domestic markets.

Reasons for trade protection

● Protectionist measures help to protect **infant industries** (new, unestablished businesses) from foreign competition. The Chinese government, for example, only allows 20 Hollywood movies to enter the country's cinemas each year, thus allowing the Chinese movie industry to develop.

Lost in Thailand is China's highest-grossing homegrown film. Trade protection enables the Chinese movie industry to develop

- Protection from free trade can also help to protect **domestic jobs**. French car-maker Renault announced that it would have to make 7500 workers unemployed between 2013 and 2016, partly due to the higher sales of Japan's Toyota across Europe as a result of free trade. In extreme cases, fierce competition from foreign rivals can even force domestic firms out of business.
- It prevents foreign countries from **dumping** their goods in the domestic economy. Dumping occurs when foreign firms sell their products in large quantities at prices deliberately below those charged by domestic firms, often even below the cost of production. This clearly gives the foreign firms an unfair price advantage, so protectionist measures may be needed. The European Union has recently accused China of dumping its glass solar panels and the USA has accused Vietnam of dumping its shrimps.
- Protection can also be a source of **government revenue**. For example, India imposes a $535 per 10 gram tariff on the import of gold, thus helping to raise tax revenue for the government.
- Protection might also be required to overcome a **balance of payments deficit** (see Chapter 24). If a country's expenditure on imports exceeds the revenue earned from its exports, the country will experience problems as it spends more than it earns. Protectionist measures to restrict imports would help to deal with this imbalance.
- In terms of **strategic arguments**, the government might use protectionism to safeguard the country against being too dependent on goods and services from other countries. For instance, if a war were to break out then protectionist measures give the country the ability and capacity to produce all the goods and services that it needs, rather than having to rely on foreign countries. A country such as Canada or the UK might want to have more oil production in order to be less reliant on imports from oil-rich nations that have the ability to distort world oil prices and oil supplies.

Arguments against protectionism

Despite the merits of protectionism, there are potential drawbacks:

- Government intervention **distorts market signals** and therefore can lead to a global misallocation of resources. For example, domestic consumers may not be able to purchase lower-priced imports which are of higher quality than those produced domestically. Protected firms and industries can become too reliant on the government and thus become inefficient.
- Protection can lead to **increased costs of production** due to the lack of competition and of incentives to be efficient or innovative. Domestic producers may need to pay higher prices for vital imported raw materials and components, so this could lead to imported inflation (see Chapter 18), thus leading to higher domestic prices.

● Other countries are likely to react by **retaliating** and imposing their own trade barriers. For example, in October 2012 the US International Trade Commission imposed tariffs on imports of solar cells from China, and by January 2013 Beijing had imposed a 5-year anti-dumping tariff on two chemicals (ethylene glycol and diethylene glycol) from the USA. Such actions may hinder global economic growth and prosperity.

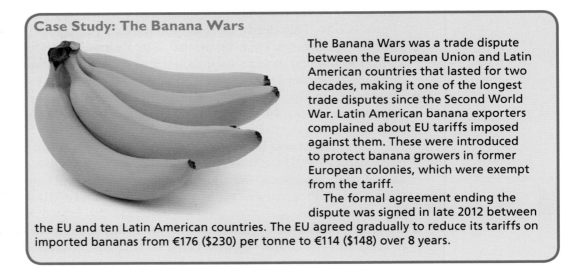

Case Study: The Banana Wars

The Banana Wars was a trade dispute between the European Union and Latin American countries that lasted for two decades, making it one of the longest trade disputes since the Second World War. Latin American banana exporters complained about EU tariffs imposed against them. These were introduced to protect banana growers in former European colonies, which were exempt from the tariff.

The formal agreement ending the dispute was signed in late 2012 between the EU and ten Latin American countries. The EU agreed gradually to reduce its tariffs on imported bananas from €176 ($230) per tonne to €114 ($148) over 8 years.

Types of trade protection

The most common form of trade protection is the use of **tariffs**. The other types of trade protection are collectively known as **non-tariff barriers**. These are explained below.

● Tariffs – A tariff is a tax on imports. For example, the USA has recently placed a 35 per cent tariff on all tyres imported from China. Tariffs increase the costs of production to importers, thus raising the price of foreign goods in the domestic market and lowering the amount of products imported (see Figure 26.1).

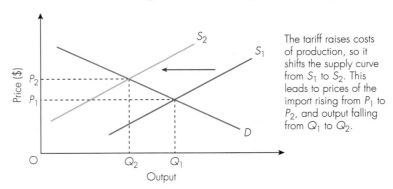

The tariff raises costs of production, so it shifts the supply curve from S_1 to S_2. This leads to prices of the import rising from P_1 to P_2, and output falling from Q_1 to Q_2.

Figure 26.1 The impact of tariffs

- **Quotas** – An import quota sets a quantitative limit on the sale of a foreign good into a country. For example, the Indonesian government imposes import quotas on fruits and vegetables from Thailand. The quota limits the quantity imported and thus raises the market price of foreign goods (see Figure 26.2).

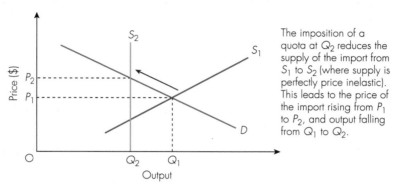

The imposition of a quota at Q_2 reduces the supply of the import from S_1 to S_2 (where supply is perfectly price inelastic). This leads to the price of the import rising from P_1 to P_2, and output falling from Q_1 to Q_2.

Figure 26.2   The impact of quotas

- **Subsidies** – Governments can provide subsidies (lump-sum payments or cheap loans to domestic producers) to help local firms to compete against foreign imports. Subsidies lower the costs of production for home firms, thereby helping to protect local jobs (see Chapter 15). For example, the European Union subsidises its farmers to encourage agricultural output (see Figure 26.3).

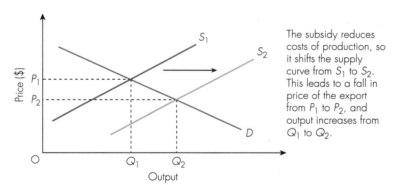

The subsidy reduces costs of production, so it shifts the supply curve from S_1 to S_2. This leads to a fall in price of the export from P_1 to P_2, and output increases from Q_1 to Q_2.

Figure 26.3   The impact of subsidies

- **Administrative barriers** – Countries often use bureaucratic rules and regulations as a form of protection. Examples include strict rules regarding food safety, environmental standards and product quality. Complying with these rules and regulations consumes a lot of time, and increases the costs for overseas firms.
- **Embargo** – An embargo is a ban on trade with a certain country, often due to a trade dispute. An embargo rarely benefits local consumers, who suffer from a lack of choice and higher prices (due to the lack of supply). For example, Malaysia has imposed trade embargoes on the Philippines while the USA has trade embargoes with Cuba.

Exam practice

1   British beef is sold throughout the world. Using an appropriate demand and supply diagram, explain the consequences for the following if an import tariff is imposed on British beef:

   a) the price of British beef   [4]

       the quantity demanded of British beef   [4]

   b) producers and consumers of British beef   [8]

2   China accounts for over 25 per cent of the world's output of car tyres. Since 2009, China has been the world's largest producer, consumer and exporter of tyres. The China Passenger Car Association reported that over 20 million new cars were sold in China in 2012, with annual sales growth of over 10 per cent over the next few years. According to the USA's Bureau of Labor Statistics, the average US employer had to pay about $35 per hour (salary and benefits) to hire a production line worker whereas an employer in China could do the same for just $1.36 per hour. The USA simply could not compete, thus prompting the need for protectionist measures.

   a) With reference to the above information, explain two reasons why countries use protectionism.   [4]

   b) Discuss which method of trade protection would be best for the USA to impose. Justify your answer.   [8]

Activity

Use the internet to investigate the following:

1   What is the World Trade Organization?
2   What are the main functions of the WTO?
3   How effective has the WTO been in encouraging free international trade?

Chapter review questions

1   What is meant by 'free trade'?
2   Outline the merits of free trade.
3   What is trade protectionism?
4   Outline the merits of protection.
5   Distinguish between tariff and non-tariff trade barriers.

Key terms

Barriers to trade are obstructions to free trade, imposed by a government to safeguard national interests by reducing the competitiveness of foreign firms.

Dumping is the act of selling exports at artificially low prices, below those charged by domestic firms, and often less than the costs of production.

An **embargo** is a type of protection that involves placing a ban on the trade of a certain good or with a particular country.

Exports are goods and services sold to overseas buyers.

Free trade is international trade without any protectionist barriers between countries.

Imports are foreign goods and services bought by domestic households and firms.

International trade refers to the exchange of goods and services beyond national borders.

A **quota** is a type of protection that sets a numerical limit on the number of imports allowed into a country over a specified time period.

Subsidies are a form of financial support from the government to lower the production costs of domestic firms, thereby raising their competitiveness.

Tariffs are import taxes that are imposed on foreign goods.

Trade protection is the use of trade barriers to safeguard a country against excessive international trade and foreign competition.

Glossary

Absolute poverty is an extreme form of poverty; it indicates the number of people who cannot afford minimal standards of basic human needs (food, clothing, health care and shelter).

Appreciation of a currency occurs when there is an increase in its value relative to another currency operating in a floating exchange rate system.

Average costs are calculated by dividing total costs by the number of units produced.

Backward vertical integration occurs when a firm from the secondary sector of industry merges with a firm from the primary sector of industry or a firm from the tertiary sector of industry merges with a firm from the secondary sector of industry.

Bad debts occur when people or businesses cannot repay a loan.

Balance of payments is a financial record of a country's transactions with the rest of the world for a given time period, per time period.

Balance of trade (or simply the **trade balance**) is the difference between a country's total export earnings and its total import expenditure.

Barriers to entry are the obstacles that prevent other firms from effectively entering the market. Examples include the existence of intellectual property rights, large advertising budgets of existing firms and legal constraints to prevent wasteful competition.

Barriers to trade are obstructions to free trade, imposed by a government to safeguard national interests by reducing the competitiveness of foreign firms.

Bartering is the act of swapping items in exchange for other items through a process of bargaining and negotiation.

Base year refers to the starting year when calculating a price index.

Basic economic problem is how to allocate scarce resources to satisfy unlimited needs and wants.

Birth rate measures the number of live births per thousand of the population in a year.

Borrowing occurs when an individual, firm or the government takes out a loan from a financial institution, paying back the debt with interest over a period of time.

Business is an organisation that sells goods and/or services.

Business cycle describes the fluctuations in the economic activity of a country over time, thus creating a long-term trend of economic growth in the economy.

Capital refers to manufactured resources used to further the production process, e.g. tools, machinery and buildings.

Capital-intensive production happens when a firm spends proportionately more money on capital costs than any other factor of production.

Central bank is the term used to describe the monetary authority that oversees and manages the supply of money and the banking system of the nation.

Chain of production describes how businesses from the primary, secondary and tertiary sectors work interdependently to make a product and sell it to the final customer.

Collateral means security for a loan, e.g. property in the case of a mortgage, or the car purchased in the case of a car loan.

Collective bargaining occurs when a trade union representative negotiates on behalf of its members with the employer to reach an agreement which both sides find acceptable.

Commercial banks are retail banks that provide financial services to their customers, such as accepting savings account deposits and approving bank loans.

Complements are products that are demanded (for their use) together with other products. For example, tea and milk or the cinema and popcorn are jointly demanded.

Conglomerate integration/lateral integration/ diversification occurs when a merger or takeover occurs between two firms from unrelated areas of business.

Conspicuous consumption occurs when people purchase highly expensive goods and services due to status or a desired image.

Consumer prices index (CPI) is a weighted index of consumer prices in the economy over time. It is used to measure the cost of living for an average household.

Consumer spending refers to the amount of household expenditure per time period.

Consumption is the value of all private household consumption within a country.

Co-operatives are business organisations set up, owned and run by their members, who may be employees and/or customers.

Cost-push inflation is a cause of inflation, triggered by higher costs of production, which force up prices.

Costs are the payments made by firms during the production process, e.g. the cost of land, labour, capital and enterprise.

Current account is a component of the balance of payments that records all exports and imports of goods and services and net income flows and transfers with other countries between a country and the rest of the world.

Current account deficit occurs when a country's financial outflows are greater than its financial inflows.

Current account surplus exists if a country's financial inflows are greater than its financial outflows.

Death rate measures the number of deaths per thousand of the population in a year.

Deflation is the sustained fall in the general price level in an economy over time, i.e. the inflation rate is negative.

Demand refers to the willingness *and* the ability of customers to pay a given price to buy a good or service. The higher the price of a product, the lower its demand tends to be.

Demand for labour is the number of workers firms are willing and able to employ at a given wage rate.

Demand-pull inflation is a cause of inflation, triggered by higher levels of aggregate demand in the economy, which drive up the general price level.

Demerger occurs when two previously merged firms decide to break up and become two separate firms.

Demerit goods are goods or services which when consumed cause negative spillover effects in an economy, e.g. cigarettes, alcohol and gambling. Demerit goods are over-consumed due to imperfect consumer information about such goods.

Demographics is the study of population distribution and trends.

Dependency ratio is a comparison of the number of people who are not in the labour force with the number of people in active paid employment.

Depreciation of a currency occurs when there is a fall in its value relative to another currency operating in a floating exchange rate system.

Deregulation is a supply-side policy of making markets more competitive by removing barriers to entry and other market imperfections.

Derived demand means that the demand for factors of production occurs not for their own sake but for the goods and services that they are used to produce.

Devaluation occurs when the price of a currency operating in a fixed exchange rate system is officially and deliberately lowered.

Direct taxes are government charges imposed on income and wealth, such as income tax and inheritance tax.

Diseconomies of scale occur when average costs of production start to increase as the size of a firm increases.

Disinflation occurs when the rate of inflation falls, but is above zero, i.e. prices are generally still rising, only at a slower rate.

Disposable income refers to the earnings of an individual after income tax and other charges have been deducted.

Dissaving occurs when people spend their savings.

Diversification is when a merger or takeover occurs between firms from different sectors of industry that operate in unrelated areas of business.

Division of labour is the specialisation of labour by getting workers to focus on one aspect of the production process.

Dumping is the act of selling exports at artificially low prices, below those charged by domestic firms, and often less than the costs of production.

Economic agents are households (private individuals in society), firms that operate in the private sector of an economy and the government (the public sector of an economy).

Economic goods are those which are limited in supply.

Economic growth is the increase in the level of national output, i.e. the annual percentage change in GDP.

Economic system describes the way in which an economy is organised and run, including how to best allocate society's scarce resources.

Economies of scale occur when average costs of production fall as the size of a firm increases.

Embargo is a type of protection by placing a ban on the trade of a certain good or with a particular country.

Employer refers to a person or a firm that hires other workers to an organisation.

Employment refers to the use of factors of production in the economy, such as labour.

Equilibrium occurs when the quantity demanded for a product is equal to the quantity supplied of the product, i.e. there are no shortages or surpluses.

Equilibrium wage rate is determined when the wage rate workers are willing to work for equals the wage rate that firms are prepared to pay.

Excess demand occurs when the demand for a product exceeds the supply of the product at certain price levels. This happens when the price is set below the equilibrium price, resulting in shortages.

Excess supply occurs when the supply of a product exceeds the demand at certain price levels. This results in a surplus because the price is too high, i.e. above the market equilibrium price.

Exchange rate refers to the price of one currency measured in terms of other currencies.

Exports are goods and services sold to overseas buyers.

External benefits are the positive side effects of production or consumption incurred by third parties for which no money is paid by the beneficiary.

External costs are the negative side effects of production or consumption incurred by third parties for which no compensation is paid.

External economies of scale are economies of scale that arise from factors outside of the firm, for example, the location of the firm, proximity to transport, availability of skilled workers.

Externalities (or spillover effects) occur where the actions of firms and individuals have either a positive or negative effect on third parties.

Fertility rate measures the average number of births per woman. It is used as a component to measure population growth.

Financial economies of scale occur as large firms are able to borrow money from banks more easily than small firms because they are perceived to be less risky to the financial institutions.

Fiscal policy is the use of taxes and government spending to affect macroeconomic objectives such as economic growth and employment.

Fixed exchange rate system exists when the central bank (or monetary authority) buys and sells foreign currencies to ensure the value of its currency stays at the pegged value.

Floating exchange rate system means that the currency is allowed to fluctuate against other currencies according to the market forces without any government intervention.

Foreign aid is a form of financial assistance for economic development from other countries or non-government organisations such as Oxfam and Unicef.

Foreign exchange market is the marketplace where foreign currencies can be bought and sold.

Forward vertical integration occurs when a firm from the primary sector of industry merges with a firm from the secondary sector of industry or a firm from the secondary sector of industry merges with a firm from the tertiary sector of industry.

Free goods are goods which are unlimited in supply, such as air or seawater.

Free riders are people who take advantage of the goods or services provided by the government but have not contributed to government revenue through taxation.

Free trade refers to international trade without any protectionist barriers between countries.

Functions of money describe the role that money plays in the economy: money is a medium of exchange, a store of value and a measure of value (or unit of account).

Fundamental economic questions are the key questions that all economic systems strive to answer: what, how and for whom production should take place.

GDP per head (or GDP per capita) measures the gross domestic product of a country divided by the population size. It is a key measure of a country's standards of living.

Geographical mobility occurs when a person is prepared to relocate to another area for a job.

Go-slow occurs when workers decide to complete their work leisurely and therefore productivity falls.

Goods are physical items such as tables, cars, toothpaste and pencils.

Government expenditure is the total value of a government's consumption and investment spending and transfer payments, such as unemployment benefits and state pension schemes.

Gross domestic product (GDP) measures the monetary value of goods and services produced within a country for a given period of time, usually one year.

Horizontal integration occurs when two firms in the same sector of industry and same industry merge together.

Human Development Index (HDI) is the UN's measure of wellbeing which uses three criteria: life expectancy, educational attainment and income per capita.

Hyperinflation refers to very high rates of inflation that are out of control, causing average prices in the economy to rise very rapidly.

Imported inflation is a cause of inflation triggered by higher import prices, forcing up costs of production and thus causing domestic inflation.

Imports are foreign goods and services bought by domestic households and firms.

Income is the total amount of earnings an individual receives in a period of time. It may consist of wages, interest, dividends, profits and rental income.

Indirect taxes are taxes imposed on expenditure, i.e. sales taxes such as value added tax (VAT).

Industrial action is any deliberate act to disrupt the operations of a firm in order to force the management to negotiate better terms and conditions of employment, e.g. strike action.

Inflation is the sustained rise in the general level of prices of goods and services over time, as measured by a consumer price index.

Innovation is the commercialisation of new ideas and products. It is a vital source of productivity.

Interdependence means that the three sectors of industry are dependent upon each other and cannot operate independently to produce goods and services.

Internal economies of scale are economies of scale that arise from the internal organisation of the business, for example, financial, bulk-buying and technological economies of scale.

International specialisation occurs when certain countries concentrate on the production of certain goods or services due to cost advantages, perhaps due to their abundant resources.

International trade refers to the exchange of goods and services beyond national borders.

Investment expenditure is the sum of capital spending by all businesses within a country.

Investments are goods that are purchased not to be consumed but to create wealth.

Invisible exports refer to the earnings from selling services to foreign customers.

Invisible imports refer to the spending on services provided by firms in overseas countries.

Invisible trade balance is a record of the trade in services, such as transportation and financial services.

Labour force participation rate is the percentage of the working-age population that is working.

Labour-intensive production occurs when labour costs account for proportionately more of a firm's costs than any other cost of production.

Labour supply consists of people who are of working age and are willing and able to work at prevailing wage rates.

Less economically developed countries (LEDCs) are developing countries, with low GDP per capita, so standards of living are generally poor.

Life expectancy measures the number of years an average person in the country is expected to live.

Limited company is a company owned by shareholders who have limited liability.

Limited liability means that in the event of a company going bankrupt, the owners would not lose more than the amount they invested in the company.

Managerial economies of scale occur as large firms have the resources to employ specialists to undertake functions within the firm, e.g. accountants, engineers, human resources specialists.

Managers are responsible for controlling all or part of a company.

Market economy is a type of economic system that relies on the market forces of demand and supply to allocate resources with minimal government intervention.

Market failure occurs when the market forces of demand and supply fail to allocate resources efficiently and cause external costs or external benefits.

Market structure refers to the key characteristics of a particular market, such as the number and size of firms in the market, the degree and intensity of price and non-price competition, and the nature of barriers to entry.

Marketing economies of scale occur as big firms tend to have a large advertising budget and therefore can spend large amounts of money on promoting their products.

Merger occurs when two firms join together to make one firm.

Merit goods are goods or services which when consumed create positive spillover effects in an economy, e.g. education, training and health care. Merit goods are under-consumed so government intervention is often needed.

Mixed economy is a type of economic system that combines elements of both the planned and market economic systems, with some resources being owned and controlled by private individuals and firms whilst others are owned and controlled by the government.

Monetary policy refers to the use of interest rates, exchange rates and the money supply to control macroeconomic objectives and to affect the level of economic activity.

Money is anything that is widely accepted as a means of exchange (and acts as a measure and store of value).

Money supply refers to the amount of money in the economy at a particular point in time.

Monopoly is a market structure where there is only one supplier of a good or service, with the power to affect market supply or prices.

More economically developed countries (MEDCs) are developed countries, with high GDP per capita, so standards of living are generally good.

Mortgage is a secured loan for the purchase of property.

Multinational corporations are businesses that operate in two or more countries. Examples include Apple, BMW, HSBC, Marks & Spencer, Nike and Sony.

National minimum wage is the lowest amount a firm can pay its workers and is set by the government.

Nationalisation is the process of taking assets into state ownership. A nationalised organisation is also known as a public-sector organisation.

Needs are goods that are essential for survival.

Net exports refers to the monetary value of the difference between a nation's export earnings and its import expenditure.

Net income flows are a record of a country's net income earned from capital flows.

Net migration rate measures the difference between immigration and emigration rates for a country, and thus indicates the physical movement of people in and out of a country.

Occupational mobility is when a person can easily move from one type of job to another.

Opportunity cost is the cost of the next best opportunity foregone when making a decision.

Optimum population exists when the output of goods and services per head of the population is maximised.

Overspecialisation occurs when an individual, firm, region or country concentrates too much on producing a very limited number of goods and services. This exposes the economic agent to a far higher degree of risk.

Owners have a legal right to the possession of something.

Partnerships are businesses owned by between two and twenty owners, who pool funds and take risks together, but have to share profits between themselves.

Perfect competition describes a market where there is immense competition due to the absence of barriers to entry. This means there are many small firms competing in the market, none of which have any power to influence market supply or price.

Planned economy is a type of economic system that relies on the government allocating scarce resources. It is often associated with a communist political system that strives for social equality. Also referred to as the socialist or command system.

Population refers to the total number of inhabitants of a particular country.

Population growth refers to the rate of change in the size of a country's population.

Population pyramids are a graphical representation of the age and gender distribution of a country's population.

Poverty is a condition that exists when people lack adequate income and wealth to sustain a basic standard of living.

Price is the amount of money expected or given in payment for something.

Price discrimination is the practice of charging different prices to different customers for essentially the same product. It occurs because of the customers' differences in PED.

Price elastic demand describes demand for a product that is relatively responsive to changes in price, usually due to substitutes being available.

Price elasticity of demand (PED) measures the extent to which demand for a product changes due to a change in its price.

Price elasticity of supply (PES) measures the degree of responsiveness of quantity supplied of a product following a change in its price.

Price inelastic demand describes demand for a product that is relatively unresponsive to changes in price, mainly because of the lack of substitutes for the product.

Price maker (or setter) describes a firm with significant market power so it can control enough of the market supply in order to affect the price level.

Price stability means that inflation is under control so that price movements are predictable.

Price takers are firms that set their price according to the market forces of demand and supply, rather than determining their own prices.

Private benefits are the benefits of production and consumption enjoyed by a firm, individual or government.

Private costs of production and consumption are the actual costs of a firm, individual or government such as wages and raw material costs.

Private limited company has limited liability and can sell shares to raise finance but not to the general public.

Privatisation is a supply-side policy of selling off state-owned assets to the private sector.

Producer refers to any firm that deals in the production and/or provision of goods and services.

Production refers to the total output of goods and services in the production process.

Production possibility curve (PPC) represents the maximum amount of goods and services which can be produced in an economy, i.e. the productive capacity of the economy.

Productivity is a measure of efficiency arrived at by calculating the amount of output per unit of a factor input (such as output per worker or output per machine hour).

Profit is the positive numerical difference between revenues and costs. It is the reward for risk-taking in business.

Progressive taxation is a tax system that deducts a greater proportion of tax as a person's income level increases, e.g. income tax and capital gains tax.

Proportional taxation is a tax system that deducts the same proportion of tax at all income levels.

Protection is the use of trade barriers to safeguard a country from excessive international trade and foreign competition.

Public limited company is a firm that can sell its shares on a stock exchange, e.g. Microsoft, HSBC and Samsung.

Public corporations (public sector organisations) are organisations that are wholly owned and funded by a government, such as the postal office.

Purchasing or bulk buying economies of scale occur when the cost of raw materials falls when bought in large quantities thus reducing the average costs.

Quota is a type of protection that sets a numerical limit on the number of imports allowed into a country over a specified time period.

Real GDP refers to the value of national income (GDP) adjusted for inflation to reflect the true value of goods and services produced in a given year.

Recession occurs in the business cycle when there is a fall in GDP for two consecutive quarters.

Regional specialisation occurs when certain areas concentrate on the production of certain goods or services, e.g. Hollywood, in Los Angeles, is famous for its motion pictures industry.

Regressive taxation is a tax system that deducts a smaller proportion of tax as a person's income increases, e.g. sales taxes and stamp duties.

Regulation refers to the rules and laws that govern business behaviour in the economy, e.g. employment laws, consumer protection legislation and environmental protection laws.

Relative poverty is a comparative measure of poverty. Those in relative poverty have a lower standard of living in comparison with the average member of society.

Replacement fertility rate is the number of children that the average woman must have to replace the existing population in order to maintain a stable population size.

Research and development economies of scale occur as large firms may be able to fund research and development and therefore can be innovative and create products that enable them to be leaders in their area of business.

Retail prices index (RPI) is used to calculate the rate of inflation. Unlike the CPI, the RPI includes the cost of housing, including mortgage interest payments and other housing costs but excludes low-income pensioners and high-income households.

Revaluation occurs when the price of a currency operating in a fixed exchange rate system is officially and deliberately increased.

Risk-bearing economies of scale occur as large firms tend to produce a range of products and operate in many locations.

Salary is a fixed monthly payment in return for labour services.

Sales revenue refers to the money a firm earns from its sales, before deducting costs of production.

Saving occurs when a person puts aside some of their current income for future spending.

Savings ratio refers to the proportion of household income which is saved instead of consumed in an economy.

Services are non-physical items such as haircuts, bus journeys, telephone calls and internet access.

Shareholders are the part-owners of a limited liability company.

Sit-in is when union members go to their place of work, occupy the premises but do not undertake their normal work.

Social benefits are the true (or full) benefits of consumption or production, i.e. the sum of private benefits and external benefits.

Social costs are the true (or full) costs of consumption or production, i.e. the sum of private costs and external costs.

Sole trader is a person who owns and runs a business as single proprietor. S/he takes all the risks but keeps any profit made by the business.

Specialisation occurs when individuals, firms, regions or countries concentrate on the production of a particular good or service.

Specialisation of labour occurs when a worker becomes an expert in a particular profession or in a part of a production process.

Stakeholders are any economic agents with a vested interest in the operations of a business, e.g. shareholders, employees and customers.

Standards of living refer to the social and economic wellbeing of individuals in a country at a point in time.

Stock exchange is the term used to describe an institutional marketplace for trading the shares of public limited companies.

Stocks (or inventories) are the raw materials, components and finished goods (ready for sale) used in the production process.

Strike occurs when union members withdraw their labour services by refusing to work.

Subsidies are a form of financial support from the government to lower the production costs of domestic firms, thereby raising their competitiveness.

Subsidy is a sum of money given by the government to a producer to reduce the costs of production or to a consumer to reduce the price of consumption.

Substitutes are products that are in competitive demand as they can be used in place of each other. For example, tea and coffee or McDonald's and Burger King meals are substitute products.

Supply is the willingness *and* the ability of firms to provide a good or service at given prices. The higher the price of a product, the higher its supply tends to be.

Supply-side policies are the long-term strategies aimed at increasing the productive capacity of the economy by improving the quality and/or quantity of factors of production.

Takeover occurs when a firm is taken over by another firm. A takeover may be hostile or the two firms may have agreed to the takeover.

Tariffs are import taxes that are imposed on foreign goods.

Tax avoidance is the legal act of minimising payment of taxes, such as by avoiding spending on items with a large sales tax.

Tax burden is the amount of tax that households and firms have to pay.

Tax evasion is the illegal act of not paying the correct amount of tax, perhaps due to a firm under-declaring its profits.

Taxes are government levies on income and expenditure, used to fund government expenditure to affect economic activity.

Technical economies of scale occur as large firms can afford to purchase expensive pieces of machinery and automated equipment for the manufacturing process.

Trade protection is the use of trade barriers to safeguard a country against excessive international trade and foreign competition.

Trade union is an organisation which aims to protect the interests of its members, namely the terms of pay and conditions of employment.

Transfers are money flows from one country to another, e.g. income sent by a foreign worker to their home country, or a gift of money from one government to another.

Unemployment occurs when people of working age who are both willing and able to work cannot find employment.

Unemployment rate is a measure of the percentage of a country's workforce that is out of employment.

Unitary price elasticity occurs when the percentage change in the quantity demanded (or supplied) is proportional to the change in the price, so there is no change in the sales revenue.

Unlimited liability means that if a business goes bankrupt, the owner(s) is/are personally liable for the debts, even if it means personal belongings have to be sold.

Vertical integration occurs when a takeover or merger takes place between two firms from a different sector of industry.

Visible exports are goods which are sold to foreign customers.

Visible imports are goods bought by domestic customers from foreign sellers.

Visible trade balance is a record of the export and import of physical goods.

Wage-price spiral occurs when trade unions negotiate higher wages to keep income in line with inflation but this simply causes more inflation as firms raise prices to maintain their profit margins.

Wage is the return for labour services, paid hourly or weekly. Payment depends on the amount of time worked.

Wants are goods and services that are not necessary for survival but are demanded by economic agents.

Wealth is measured by the value of assets a person owns minus their liabilities (the amount they owe to others).

Work-to-rule means that workers literally work to fulfil the minimum requirements of their job and do nothing outside what is written in their contract of employment.

Working population (or labour force) is the number of people in an economy who are of working age and are willing and able to work.

Index